DJ Alan White with Kevin "Notepad" Stanley,
Alan's good friend, running buddy,
and his 20+ year Event Manager.
(in 2018)

Selected stories about these and more from the Forrest Gump-like meanderings of America's Original Nightclub DJ, artist representative, music business entrepreneur, and Internet radio pioneer.

1910 Fruitgum Company • Len Barry
Chuck Berry • Diane Birch • The Brooklyn Bridge
Alicia Bridges • The British Walkers • Roy Buchanan
The Champs • The Chartbusters • The Chiffons
Petula Clark • The Coasters • Turk Coury
The Crystals • The Five Stairsteps & Cubie
Gene & Debbe • Joey Dee • The Fifth Dimension
Ronnie Dove • José Feliciano • Brute Force
The Classics IV • Daryl Hall
Little Willie & The Hand Jives • George Harrison
Bobby Hebb • Jimi Hendrix • The Electric Indian
Jimmy Jones • Janis Joplin • The Kalin Twins
• The Kasenetz-Katz Singing Orchestral Circus •
Kemp Muhl & Sean Lennon • The Lemon Pipers
Jerry Lee Lewis • Bobby Lewis • Mark Lindsay
Johnny Maestro • Steve Martin • Eddie Money
Napoleon XIV • John Oates • The Peppermint Rainbow
Gary Puckett • Mickey Rooney
David Lee Roth • The Shangri-Las • Dee Dee Sharp
Blaze Starr • BJ Thomas • Ted Turner
Frankie Valli • Virginia Wicks • J. Frank Wilson
Weird Al Yankovic • Dennis Yost

ROCK AROUND THE BLOCK

Copyright © 2019 Alan Ray White
All Rights Reserved

ROCK AROUND THE BLOCK
Imprint: Blue Room Books
ISBN-13: 9780985462390
© 2019 Alan Ray White
All Rights Reserved

ROCK AROUND THE BLOCK
BLUE ROOM BOOKS
DECATUR, GA 30033

9 780985 462390

Senior Editor:
Angela K. Durden | angeladurden.com

Editor:
Tom Whitfield

Cover art "The Baltimore Block - circa 1959" by:
Leanna Sherfy Myrick | **instagram.com/leannamyrick/**

Back cover and interior current photography
of Kevin Stanley and Alan Ray White:
David Hobbs | **davidhobbsphotography.com/**

Alan Ray White hairstyle by:
Shearious Salon | **shearious.com**

ROCK
AROUND
THE
BLOCK

ALAN RAY WHITE

Jim —
Thanks so much!

[signature]

Alan Ray White [signature]

Is this the exact way every single thing went down? Probably not. Out of necessity, I re-created and/or paraphrased some of the dialogue. This is, however, the way I remember it. If you were there and remember it differently, I'll be interested to read your book.

This one is mine.

Alan Ray White
Atlanta, Georgia
March 2019

This book is dedicated to

The greatest adventure of them all,
my two sons:
Alan Ray White, Jr.
and Zachary Karl White

**To my beloved foster son
who left us way too soon:**
Peter "P.R." Grim (1967-2018)

And to my pals:
Thomas "Turk" Coury (1941-2010)
Roger "The Lodger" Kunzig
Peter "The Flying Dutchman" Berry
Leonard "Len Barry" Borisoff
Joan "Jenny Fields" Meltzer (1938-2010)
Edward "Eddy" Rahn (1951-2014)
Nancy Rahn
Melody Hester-Tall (1954-1990)
Kevin "Notepad" Stanley

They always had my back.

Halleluiah Anyway

With your eyes as wide as circles,
you ask me for the answers
and I don't know what to tell you.
As we listen to the thunder
of the distant drums of hatred
and I wonder, yes I wonder,
why in spite of all the madness,
I think we ought to sing instead of cry.
For singing is a kind of loving
and morning comes up every day.
So even though we live
in troubled times,
Halleluiah Anyway,
Halleluiah Anyway.

Still you ask about the sorrows
you stare at in the mirror
and read of in the headlines.
Is it just some crazy printer
writing lies to sell
his papers in the winter?
Will this winter never end?
And I don't what to tell you,
but if it helps at all,
I am your friend.

And friendship is a kind of loving
and morning comes up every day.
So even though we live in troubled times,
Halleluiah Anyway,
Halleluiah Anyway.

So you see I have no answers.
I don't even know the questions.
I'm a frightened Pollyanna
holding on to things like singing.
As if singing songs of friendship could
really help this world survive
or shut a final door
on poverty and war.
But at least we're not alone,
at least we are alive.
And living is a kind of loving
and morning comes up every day.
So even though we live in troubled times,
Halleluiah Anyway,
Halleluiah Anyway.
I said *Halleluiah Anyway.*

Joan Meltzer
(Copyright 1972. Lyrics reprinted with permission.)

Table Of Contents

FOREWORD

The Baltimore Block, infamous around the world, was roughly six square blocks filled with strip joints, burlesque houses, pizza-by-the-slice hole in the walls, quickie-loan storefronts, and cheap steakhouses. One famous club, The Flamingo, featured strippers who did the bump-and-grind to all-black Jazz trios. When the strippers weren't dancing, the house bands let me sit in with them and play drums.

> The Block.
> It was the dawn of Rock & Roll.
> And that is where I began
> Rockin' Around The Block.

The Outlaw Country singer/songwriter David Allen Coe *(left)* once said in an interview that people who grow up in institutions are different people. He couldn't say exactly how, just "we're different from other folks."

For Coe it was reform school, jail, and finally prison from the time he was 10 until age 29.

For me it was boarding school from 8 until about 17. First military school, followed by a couple of isolated preparatory boarding schools and an endless array of annual summer camps. Boarding school and summer camps aren't jail. The food is better and there's more of it. Still, you're somewhere you don't necessarily want to be and being told what to do by people not related to you.

You are in charge of you but must watch your back. Adults will lie to you and the system will control you. There is often abuse, physical as well as sexual.

Grownups cannot be completely trusted.

Coe has a point. In many ways those of us who grew up in institutions, jails, prisons, boarding schools, orphanages, etc. are a different breed. Not better, nor worse.

Just different. I know I was.

I didn't know any more about what I wanted to do with my life than any other kid, but I thoroughly understand Coe's outlaw persona. You have to take charge of yourself at such an early age.

I put all of that behind me and went out on my own. I was 17. Music was for sure, but my path would prove to be random.

Around 1960, when I was 19, there was the big hit TV show *Route 66* (*right*). It was a one-hour drama about Tod and Buz who traveled along U.S. Route 66 — the Mother Road as it was called since it was one of the first highways in the U.S. In a hot Corvette, going  from one place to another, the guys met new and interesting people, and had great adventures each week. At the end of the show they'd drive out of town and over the coming horizon looking for the next great experience.

Another show around the same time was *Adventures In Paradise* about a cool guy with a big sailboat who did essentially the same thing in the South Pacific.

In a general sense it was the kind of thing which appealed to me more than any other.

Let life happen.

Keep it moving.

Adventures in adventure.

And so, with little forethought, that's pretty much what I did. No Corvette, though. Just a series of cool convertibles, a fading horizon in my rearview, and an approaching horizon just ahead.

Every time I left a place I'd worry about how much I might miss it and all the people I'd met. But when I got on the road, I found myself focused entirely on what was ahead. Every town. Every time. To my astonishment — at least until I got used to it — I'd stop thinking about where I'd been and become totally engaged in thinking about wherever it was I was headed.

This book is about some of the people I met along the way. Many of them celebrities at the time, on their way up, on their way down, but mostly in and around the world of the business of music. *(Bill Haley and the Comets, below. "Rock Around The Clock" inspired the title of* **Rock Around The Block**.*)*

This is not a book about drugs, booze, trashing hotel rooms, or what we did with the girls we met along the way.

Back in the day gentlemen didn't talk about what went on with the girls they met. I still don't.

1 Chuck Berry, Part 2

Sometime in the summer of 1972 I stopped into The Gentlemen II on Charles Street on a rainy night in Baltimore to see my old friend Mike O'Harro.

Chuck Berry was just coming off stage after closing his first show with a rousing rendition of the classic risqué ditty "My Ding-A-Ling".

I rounded up a glass of Chivas and ice. Walking back to the front of the club, I noticed Berry sitting all by himself in a corner booth, back up against the wall, drinking coffee.

I walked over and introduced myself. "Hi Chuck, I'm Alan White, Len Barry's manager."

He smiled. "Ah, Len Barry. Loved '1-2-3'. Great record. Sit down. Join me."

So I did.

He was sharp-eyed and intense, looking like he was completely prepared should you try to put your hand in his pocket. We talked about how funny it was that he and Len had the same last name, albeit with different spelling, and that they shared a reverse racial stereotype.

Chuck Berry's early hits ("Johnny B. Goode" and "Maybelline" as well as "Too Much Monkey Business" and "Memphis") were all Country songs. Promoters and club owners all thought Chuck was white.

Len Barry's early hits as lead singer of The Dovells ("The Bristol Stomp", "Bristol Twistin' Annie", "You Can't Sit

Down", and "Hully Gully Baby") were R&B Doo Wop songs. Promoter and club owners thought The Dovells were black.

When The Dovells showed up at the Apollo, the theater's managers were shocked they were a white group. So that was a fun discussion and then we chatted some more and he drank his coffee and I worked on my double Chivas and then, as I remember it, the following conversation occurred pretty much word for word.

Me: You ought to put "My Ding-A-Ling" out as a single. I guarantee it would be a number one record, a million-seller, and probably your biggest hit.

Chuck: Nah, radio would never play it.

Me: I'm gonna take a wild guess that you haven't been listening to radio much lately.

Chuck: You're right. I hate that hippie shit. I listen to Country music.

Me: Well trust me, radio's changed. Today, they'd play it.

Chuck: The Chess Brothers would never put it out anyway.

Then there was silence. I quietly worked on my Chivas.

Me: Would you mind if I made a little suggestion?

Chuck: [Increasingly suspicious, eyebrows go up.]

Me: [Waiting, hoping I hadn't overstepped my bounds.]

Chuck: Go ahead. What's your big suggestion?

Me: Why don't you call up the Chess Brothers and say, "Hi, I'm Chuck Fucking Berry. I'm carrying your whole stupid record company, so put the goddamned record out."

Chuck: [Spitting coffee all over the table. Laughing so loudly it scared me.] Hahaha! Chuck Fucking Berry! Haha! Haha! Funniest thing I've ever heard. The Chess Brothers. Chuck Fucking Berry. Ha ha, ha, ha!

I never saw Chuck Berry again after that night but only a few months later "My Ding-A-Ling" came out as a single and

I'm pretty sure I know how that conversation with the Chess Brothers must have gone.

The record did exactly as I had predicted: It was a number one record and a million-seller.

And it became his biggest hit single.

After he died Rolling Stone magazine did a feature cover story on him. The April 7, 2017, issue said about the song:

> "It was the biggest smash of Berry's career –
> Number One in the U.S. and U.K. – yet it
> wasn't like anything else he'd recorded:
> Both the melody and lyrics were juvenile,
> but Berry regarded it as one of his best
> songs because it made him newly rich."

I liked hearing that.

Good for The Chess Brothers.

Good for Chuck Fucking Berry.

Good for me. I helped him figure out what to do with his Ding-A-Ling.

But my relationship to Chuck Berry and his Rock & Roll music went back many, many years, way before his Ding-A-Ling, all the way back to the days of "Heartbreak Hotel" and Elvis the Pelvis.

Alan's father with Alan on graduation day,
June 1956. The ribbons were for track:
100- and 220-yard dashes.

2 The Way They Make Records, Part 1

For whatever reasons, at age 15 in 1956 I found myself stuck in my final year of a four-year run at Rumsey Hall, a boarding school in Washington Depot, Connecticut.

I passed many equivalency exams over the years, including one for four-year college. Rumsey Hall was and is a truly great school. As it turned out, it was all the formal education I would really ever get.

I just didn't want to be at school. I wanted to be in my hometown of Torrington, Connecticut, running the streets with my buds. And from time to time I would up and leave and hitchhike into town, about 25 miles away. There wasn't much anybody could do about it short of throwing me out — which they wouldn't do for their own reasons (never mind why) — so the school learned to live with my fairly regular and highly unauthorized excursions.

Even though my best friend and roommate, Johnny Troy, was the nephew of the school headmaster, John Sherry, Johnny and I were 8th grade outlaws who continued to perpetrate significant foolishness throughout what we considered to be our too-long tenure at Rumsey.

Johnny didn't want to be there anymore than I did. We ran illegal card games for nickels and dimes and sold Kool-Aid at five cents a tiny paper cup to sweaty, dehydrated, perspiring young athletes who had to pass by our open Fitch House window on their way back from the fieldhouse and athletic field. At a cost of two quarts for a nickel, our profit margin was considerable.

The arrow points to the Fitch House window where
Johnny Troy and Alan ran their Kool-Aid business

We even found a way to rig the spring semester of the school competition between the evenly split school population of Blues (Johnny and I were Blues) and Reds. Despite an overwhelming Reds lead, the Blues won — and the Reds went ballistic. Johnny's uncle came down from his office and looked into it, including a very tough interview with the two of us, but nobody could ever figure out how we did it.

"Are all the work recommendations signed by teachers?" Johnny asked.

Sherry had to admit they were. Everything was done properly, was in perfect order, and he had to let the results stand. The Reds remained furious, while we snickered, quite out in the open. The prize? Our winning Blues got to go into town for a movie with tons of free popcorn and candy, while the losing Reds had to stay and clean the entire campus for graduation. We never told a soul how we did it.

All the cute girls I liked were Blues.

Lisa and Alan at 8th grade prom, June 1956

My first-ever crush in life was Lisa Sherry, daughter of John. Thankfully, Lisa was a Blue. She didn't know I existed until 8th grade when she agreed to go to the prom with me, but only because her top pick had not asked. Good enough for me. She was so incredibly beautiful.

Although Johnny and I played fair with all the regular kids, in what turned out to be a lifelong ambition of mine, our card games cheated the hell out of the bullies. I hated, and still hate, bullies.

It remains a delight to outsmart and scam them.

We never told anyone how we did that either.

There was no television at Rumsey Hall back then, but just about every room had a radio. Johnny was a sports nut who wanted to grow up to be a sportscaster, and I liked music and just wanted to grow up and get the hell out of there. So we kind of split our radio time between sports and the popular hit music of the day. One day a song came on the radio the likes of which I had never heard before. Haunting. Aggressive. Nothing like the popular Big Band singer recordings of the era. Production absolutely buried in reverb, which was also something that was totally new. A stunning vocal unlike any other. Musically, it was completely new territory.

"I don't know what that is, but it's going to change the way they make records forever," I said to Johnny.

"What time does the game come on?" he asked.

"No. Listen. You ever hear anything like that before?"

"Um, no, not really. Why do you care?"

To this day I remember how much Johnny, who was the smartest of the smart, didn't care. I was flabbergasted. The record was "Heartbreak Hotel" by a then-unknown singer named Elvis Presley.

And that was how it started.

That quickly.

One moment in time.

One record.

There were earlier Rock & Roll-type records, to be sure. Big Joe Turner's Jump Blues "Shake, Rattle & Roll". Bill Haley and the Comets' Rockabilly "Rock Around The Clock". Chuck Berry's genre-crossing hit "Rock & Roll Music". But the phenomenon side of Rock & Roll. Wow. The screaming girls. The crazy worldwide pandemonium. That was born from the reverb-heavy song "Heartbreak Hotel" delivered by young Elvis the Pelvis.

That one record did indeed forever change the way they made records.

Chuck Berry said it best: "It's gotta be rock and roll music if you wanna dance with me."

The house where the original Bop Shop started is still there,
but the tree is gone

3 The Bop Shop

Graduating from Rumsey Hall in June 1956, I returned to Torrington and moved in with my dad and stepmother. We lived in a nice two-family house on a tree-lined lane aptly named Brightwood Avenue.

There was a very large basement, shared by both families, but as the other family was my Uncle Earl and his crew, no one complained when my best friend, Roger Kunzig, and I took over the basement area for ourselves.

Roger and I were so close to the characters on the TV show *Happy Days* that when it came on the air in 1974 we couldn't believe those characters weren't created with us in mind.

Roger was The Fonz almost literally. He looked like him, dark-haired and handsome. He was a tough character who wore the same white t-shirt and black motorcycle jacket as Arthur Herbert Fonzarelli, and had the exact same haircut he combed incessantly, just as Fonzie did.

The girls dug Roger the most.

Roger Kunzig, circa 1964

I was Richie Cunningham. Book smart, well read, and supposedly college-bound. Will Hunting to streetwise Chuckie Sullivan. Tod Stiles to Buz Murdock in *Route 66*.

But we didn't need Arnold's Luncheonette. We created our own version in the big ol' basement in the Brightwood Avenue house. We called it "The Bop Shop".

I played drums, set on a riser, to music blasting from stacks of 45s loaded on a large automatic record player perched atop a wood crate sitting right next to me. Even then I studied the people who were there and pre-programmed for "the room". The records dropped in the order I loaded them.

We assembled a loosely constructed shack which we turned into the office. Covered all of the lights with red Christmas cellophane. There was a large tree in the front yard with a branch shaped like an arm where we hung our sign:

The Bop Shop.

From the bottom of that we attached two eye hooks from which hung an additional sign. "Open" on one side and "Closed" on the other. As soon as we put up the "Open" sign, the place filled up after school. Ten cents to get in.

A turned-around bookcase was the bar. Iced Kool-Aid was a nickel a drink. Cigarette loosies from behind the bar, also at a nickel apiece. With cigarettes readily available at the corner store at twenty cents a pack, once again we enjoyed a lovely mark-up.

A third friend, Frank Toussaint, was our bouncer, but Frank was so big he never needed to bounce anyone: Everyone behaved nicely when he was around. The kids danced, made out a little on the couches, and we had a great thing going. Guys, gals, Rock & Roll music, a glowing red-light nightclub just for us.

I've loved the idea of teen clubs ever since.

Teenagers by definition need a place to be with each other, to move away from the nuclear family and learn how to interact socially among themselves outside of school.

The Bop Shop fulfilled that need in our neighborhood.

There were rumors we had card games for money going on in the little office we built, but those are just rumors which I will neither confirm nor deny. Eventually my slightly to the right of Attila The Hun stepmother suspected the rumors were true, that we were having a little bit too much fun. She abruptly closed us down.

After The Bop Shop closed we moved on to a small place, The BelAire Luncheonette. It was very Arnold's. But, for as long as it lasted, The Bop Shop was ours. Elvis, Chuck Berry, Fats Domino, and Little Richard blasting.

Rock & Roll music. Drums.

Red lights. Girls.

A place to be. A place to make a little bank.

We knew halls, churches, and other venues promoted dances for teenagers, but we never thought about whether there were other little teen clubs like ours anywhere else. It never occurred to us.

Turns out, historically speaking, there weren't. Teen clubs didn't appear in America until the mid-1960s, almost a decade later. Were we ground zero for teen clubs?

Probably not.

I always figured there had to be tons of other kids doing exactly what we were doing, but who never got publicized anymore than we had. I can't prove it, but it was a first for me, I'll say that: A Teen Club DJ. Playing drums along with the records.

To say we were slightly ahead of our time would be a bit of an understatement.

Turk Coury with his wife, Dawn, circa late 1950s

4 The Great Turk Coury, Part 1

I'd heard about it when the Bobbysoxers rioted in Times Square in 1944 over Sinatra. I'd seen it in the newsreel footage of a young Elvis a decade later. When Presley appeared on *The Ed Sullivan Show*, the whole world saw and heard it live. But I'd never seen it in person, and never imagined I would: The hysterical screaming from teenage girls over the stage persona of a music artist. It was a true, new radio and television worldwide phenomenon.

A psychiatrist once suggested young girls' bodies were changing, hormones raging, all somehow creating a kind of emotional hysteria channeled directly at the stage.

Turk Coury was 16 that summer of '56 when we started public high school in the fall. I was 15 and had graduated from Rumsey the previous June and was — at least temporarily — staying with my dad and stepmom.

It was the year I took up playing the drums and the year we built The Bop Shop. It was also the one year I was sort of in public high school. I say *sort of in* because with an advanced boarding school curriculum, I'd already had all those courses at Rumsey. Four years of French, two years of Latin and algebra. I paid little attention to classes in high school, went every day, mostly, and did the pop quizzes in class, but never bothered with homework knowing I'd ace any final exams. I had just plain had enough after years in boarding school.

Back to Turk. His real name was Thomas Coury; he was called Turk because of his Mideastern heritage. He was already famous — a small, darkly handsome fellow, and fierce, known to be a no-fear-of-fighting country boy no one wanted to tangle with.

He also didn't care anymore about school than I did and at 16 already had a pencil-thin moustache, a driver's license, and access to a car. At night he and his buddies drove forty miles to New York State where 18 was the drinking age.

The first bar over the state line was The Log Cabin. Filled with rough farmhands and other rural tough-guy types, they didn't care how old you were, within reason. If you had the money, they'd serve you. There was another place a few miles up the road in the small town of Millerton simply known as Hole In The Wall. Filled with rugged locals who didn't like boys from Connecticut, you could always find a good fight if that was your intent. The fights between the young Torrington boys trying to get their macho on and the regular gang at Hole In The Wall were the stuff of legend.

Turk regaled me with stories of his adventures the previous night — stories of racing hot rods across the state line, drinking, fighting, and chasing girls.

Then I became sort of famous, too.

There was a contest to sell magazine subscriptions to benefit the school. I badly wanted to sell these subscriptions because each day they had these stupid little prizes such as no homework the next day or permission to chew gum in class.

Cool stuff like that.

But in Torrington, a blue-collar manufacturing city nestled snugly into the Naugatuck Valley and surrounded by the Berkshire mountain range, most of the residents either were, or descended from, immigrants who came over through Ellis

Island at the turn of the century. So every kid in school had a million relatives they could sell subscriptions to.

I had one relative to sell to: My dad. He had relocated there for his job, assistant treasurer of The Torrington Company, a manufacturer of ball and needle bearings primarily for the airplane industry and the employer of about one-fifth of Torrington's thirty thousand residents. So I asked him who bought the magazine subscriptions for the company waiting room. He explained the role of a purchasing agent and set up an appointment for me for the next day after school with The Torrington Company's man.

It turned out the guy must have wanted to make Dad happy because he bought subscriptions for lots of different magazines for the next zillion years.

There were five or six other large manufacturers in Torrington; this fellow knew all the other purchasing agents from all the other companies and set me up with appointments. Either he was popular with his contemporaries or I was a great salesman because they also bought lots of subscriptions for the next zillion years.

At the end of the contest the closest kid to me had sold maybe two hundred dollars in magazine subscriptions. I sold almost three thousand. That made me famous but, since all the other kids had known each other since grade school and I was the outsider from some hotsy-totsy boarding school, I was not particularly popular.

At the end of the contest the ten top sellers won a trip to New York City. We had a choice between going to a New York Yankees game or a Broadway show. I figured I could hear the Yankees on the radio anytime so, to my credit, I chose the Broadway show *No Time For Sergeants* that made Andy Griffith a star.

But the fun part of the contest was figuring out how to win every day by bringing in the orders and doling them out a few at a time and then winning the daily homeroom prize for the entire duration of the contest.

Turk was amazed by this and we became good friends. I already thought Turk Coury was the coolest cat in the world, but to everyone's complete surprise, including mine, he actually became even cooler. In just one night, Turk Coury became the ultimate in cool, creating a legend remembered to this day. Here's what happened:

The Warner Theater is still there. Newly remodeled, it is now the primary concert venue for all of western Connecticut.

It was November 1956 and 20th Century Fox had just released Elvis Presley's first movie, *Love Me Tender*. To promote the movie they held an Elvis imitation contest at the movie's premiere at our eight-hundred-seat Warner Theater. Every kid in town was there. It was pretty neat.

A dozen or so kids came out on stage and lip-synched Elvis songs, hips shaking, playing air guitar.

Suddenly, no advance warning, out came the final contestant and it turned out to be none other than my homeroom friend, Turk.

He strolled across the stage wearing blue jeans hanging low on his hips, the collar of his shirt turned up Elvis style, an acoustic guitar slung over his shoulder. There was no microphone. When he got to the middle of the stage he pulled the guitar down, did a bit of a jump, landed with his legs spread wide apart, and let it loose with "You Ain't Nothing But A Hound Dog".

The theater exploded.

He sounded exactly like Elvis. Exactly. He danced just like Elvis. Exactly. Every shake of the hip and move of Elvis' fancy footwork. And, though smaller, from a distance he was the spitting image of Elvis.

So there it was. Eight hundred kids, including me, screaming at the top of our lungs. Full-blown Elvis hysteria. They screamed after he finished, took a bow, and left the stage. The great Turk Coury won a 45 RPM record player. Since he was married with a kid on the way, he immediately sold it. I'd never seen anything like it before and was sure I'd never see anything like it again.

I was wrong.

Famous Jazz singer Dakota Staton

Alan with Snazz, Peter Hartbarger and Linda Susan, 1987

Baltimore radio legend and WITH morning man, Jack Gale

5 Rock & Roll Music

Late in the afternoon on the sunny Friday afternoon of October 4, 1957, the Russians launched Sputnik, the first artificial Earth satellite. It rocketed into an elliptical low-Earth orbit. I was visiting a friend in a hospital in downtown Baltimore. I was 16.

The neighborhood surrounding the hospital wasn't so great — downtown Baltimore was just on the outskirts of the somewhat sleazy red-light entertainment area collectively known as The Block. A parade of old-timey storefronts, a few closed, a few just abandoned.

Walking along the street, suddenly music was coming from a nondescript storefront. I stopped. Although the sign told me nothing except they sold Rolling Rock beer, it was obviously some kind of nightclub. But live music in the middle of a Friday afternoon?

So, acting like I knew what I was doing, in I went.

The place was pitch dark. I could see and hear the band tearing up some rockin', stompin' Jump Blues on a brightly lit stage behind the bar at the end of the very large room.

Although I couldn't see anything else very well, outlines of tables, filled with patrons, were clearly everywhere. Adjusted to the darkness, I saw something else.

I was the only white person in there.

Slowly forging ahead, making my way between tables, I eventually perched myself on the only open stool at the bar. The bartender looked at me like I was on fire.

"What the hell do you want in here?" he demanded.

"Um, do you sell Coca-Cola?" I asked sheepishly. He shook his head and walked away without speaking.

Next to me was a hip-looking fellow wearing a beret and a pair of very dark sunglasses. I couldn't see my hand in front of my face and this guy was wearing shades.

"What are you doing in here?" Shades Cat challenged.

"Um, I like the music?" I ventured. The bartender brought me a Coke. I paid cash, maybe a whole dime.

"You play music?" Shades Cat challenged again.

Good question. The answer was that I played drums — sort of — but just along with records, never with a live band.

"I play drums. A little."

"Oh yeah?" He looked up at the stage. The band was between songs. He yelled at the band frontman as he pointed at me, "Yo! Let the white kid play."

The frontman looked at me suspiciously. "Whatdya play, Kid?" he asked.

"Um, I play drums, a little." He did not look thrilled. "Alright, come on up here."

The thing was, I didn't have that many records at home. True, I had Elvis, Bill Haley, Fats Domino, and everything Chuck Berry ever did. But my collection was limited to those early Rock & Roll records, so I was praying hard they would kick it off with a song I knew.

I sat down behind the drums and, as one does, adjusted the height of the snare drum and waited, thinking *please, oh please, let this be something I have at least heard before.*

The frontman paid me no never mind. He just stepped to the microphone and started.

"Just give me some of that Rock & Roll music!"

Oh yeah! Chuck Berry — I had the record! Played it zillions of times. I kicked it off and away we went. The drummer was hitting on the girls at the bar and didn't seem to be in a hurry to return. The bass player not only kept smiling at me, encouragingly, he kept bobbing his head to the groove, keeping me right on the beat in every song.

I love bass players.

The rest of the band basically ignored me and didn't seem to mind I was there. I played one full set which, as it turned out, was the last of the afternoon. Everybody was so nice. They wanted me to come back. Wow, 16 years old and I had found a friendly place where people were nice to me and I was welcomed to play drums with a live band.

As it turned out, another of those damn boarding schools was right around the corner and it was a long time before I was able to get back to that club. When I finally did get back to Baltimore a little over a year later, I headed straight for it but it was closed, the storefront boarded up.

Still, the feeling never left me. That Friday afternoon when Sputnik circled the globe and I first played drums with a real live band. Thank God for Chuck Berry and Rock & Roll.

As you read in Chapter 1, fifteen years later I'd meet Chuck Berry in person, and be able to return the favor.

Rock & Roll Music...and a big Ding-A-Ling.

The Champs

6 The Champs, "Tequila", and The Redhead.

There I was. Sixteen and in Baltimore visiting my mom when the high school had final exams and I missed them, so they flunked me out of my first and only year of public high school. That pissed me off, so I just said screw it, quit altogether, and moved down to Baltimore where I had sat in on drums with a real live band one Friday afternoon and found out all about the famous area of strip clubs known as The Baltimore Block.

But, because I wasn't 18 yet and of legal age, it turned out there was one more boarding school in my future, this one in eastern Pennsylvania. They let me have my drums and we put on talent shows, I played music, and, all in all, it wasn't so bad. As boarding schools go, if you have to be in one, at this one I had a pretty good time.

Although the boys and girls had separate campuses, they held occasional record hops where boys were allowed to dance with girls. At one of these dances I found myself truly enamored with an adorable little redheaded cutie with a pretty face and a ton of freckles. But she didn't dance to slow songs, only to the jitterbugs. Her favorite song was the 1957 classic "The Book Of Love" by The Monotones, a real mover at a speedy 175 beats per minute.

So I got a buddy of mine who knew how to dance to come out in the hallway and teach me the basics of the jitterbug. When I felt like I knew enough to be able to do a decent dance, I immediately walked over to the adorable little redheaded cutie and asked her to dance. She had a lovely smile and couldn't have been nicer.

"No, thank you, but thanks anyway."

I was crushed. But at least now I could dance.

The school had a part-time staff member who, as I remember, was named Charlie Love. His real job was being the drummer for a big-name recording group, The Champs, who were from the area. (The real ones who played on the records were from California; these Champs were the East Coast touring version. But I didn't know that then.)

Mr. Love toured a lot with the East Coast Champs. This group was licensed to play music of The Champs. Based on the strength of that West Coast group's huge hit record, the instrumental "Tequila", they did well. But when he wasn't on the road he worked part-time at the school. Mr. Love knew I played drums and, from time to time when he had a few free minutes, would show me a lick or two. He could tell I wasn't very good yet, but he saw I could keep a steady beat and wasn't truly awful.

At some point we had a big dance where all students from the other campuses, including the gals, joined us. The school booked a live band, Charlie Love's touring version of The Champs, to play. Given that the East Coast Champs were from the area, and that their own drummer worked at the school, if their schedule was open that night they probably gave the school the brother-in-law price.

I was so hoping Mr. Love would let me play a song with the band. Just one, even a slow one, would have been awesome. And he did! And not just one song either, a whole set. Not "Tequila", mind you; they both opened and closed the night with that big hit and he wasn't about to let me fool with it. I was grateful. "Tequila" has a different beat and I wasn't confident I could play it anyway.

But a whole set? Wow! This was a big-time record act and I played every song in set two. They were all pretty straight-up Rock & Roll and I got through it just fine. In fact, I even learned a few new tricks.

Once again a friendly bass player kept me honest.

I love bass players.

After the set was over I was sitting with my buddies, beside myself with excitement. The Champs. A whole set! Wow! And then all of a sudden there was someone in front of me. It was the little redheaded cutie, and she had brought all those freckles and that lovely little smile along with her.

"Hi," she said, and she told me her name. "I've changed my mind and I'd like to dance, if you still would."

Oh yes, I surely still would. And so we danced the night away. I learned a lot more than a few new licks on the drums that night. I learned what John, Paul, George, and Ringo were busy learning over in Liverpool:

Playing in a band is a good way to get girls.

"Tequila" would later be nicknamed The Big Shoe Dance in the movie *Pee-wee's Big Adventure*.

7 My Truly Awful Phony ID Card, and The Mob

In 1959 I was just 18 but looked younger, living in Baltimore and haunting the infamous Baltimore Block, a red-light district with nightclubs, most of which were straight-up strip joints with names like The Flamingo, The Circus Bar, Boots 'N Saddles, The Gayety Show Bar, The Oasis, and The Midway. There were a couple of burlesque theaters, a bunch of storefront pizza joints, and a few cheap steakhouses. People strolled sidewalks and streets, and even during the week the automobile traffic in that little area at night was wall-to-wall.

There were no club DJ's then and all the music the girls danced to was live from Jazz trios. The drinking age was 21; most of the clubs refused to serve me.

I figured if I tried during the day I had a better chance of getting served. I made what had to be the world's worst phony ID card. A duplicate Maryland driver's license on which I typed a phony birth date over the real one, using an early version of whiteout over a pastel pink background. It was truly awful.

But I set out on a blistering hot Saturday afternoon, trying every club on The Block to no avail, and by the time I walked into The Flamingo I was tired, hot, sweaty, and not in a very good mood. I practically screamed over the music at the bartender for a cold Rolling Rock, "Cold as you got!"

The Flamingo was very dark and the bartender, who I later learned was known as Minky, barely glanced at my truly awful phony ID card in the darkened room and dug down into the cooler. The Rolling Rock was cold as ice and, now served, I stayed until closing, making as many new fast friends as I could. Night after night I came back, solidifying my status as a legal customer. The bartenders never asked for my truly awful phony ID card again as I became a regular.

One of the bargirls, an older gal named Jean, took a liking to me and sort of looked after me. When my dad came to town for a visit, she entertained him all night and told him what a cool cat I was. Dad was very impressed. He liked pretty girls, too. She was a bargirl philosopher.

"Whenever something don't seem right, don't feel right in this life," she advised, "put your hand on your wallet. It's always about the money."

That turned out to be pretty good advice.

"Treat a hooker like a lady and a lady like a hooker." She said that a lot, especially when the booze had sent her into that sweet little alcoholic fog she drifted through as the night wore on. "And never, ever, let 'em think you're a trick."

That last one, in any situation: *Best advice ever.*

The Mob was at the height of its power in those days, owning almost every club in town. A few months later this big fellow came in; maybe, 6'2" or 6'3", which in those days was gigantic. He had the deep scowl, the gravelly voice, the whole bit. He was in his mid to late 60s, and looked a little like the famous movie actor, Anthony Quinn.

He also looked really pissed off. He walked straight up to me and said, "In my office. Now!"

I almost fell off my stool but followed him dutifully to a dark, dingy office in the back of the club amid cases of liquor and other supplies. He sat down at a small wooden desk, lit only by a single small desk lamp, motioned for me to sit in the chair next to it and said, "Sit down and lemmie see this goddamned goofy ID card you got."

Right away I knew somebody ratted me out but had no idea who. I handed it to him. He looked it over and shook his head in anguish. "[Several expletives deleted.] This is the worst [more expletives deleted] thing I have ever seen."

I was alone with him in this tiny, dark back office, and seriously considered he might shoot me. But instead he opened his top desk drawer. At the front there was a huge stack, an inch or more thick, of blank Maryland driver's licenses. Driver's licenses did not have pictures on them back then. He slipped one of the blanks into the typewriter and filled it out using the information from my outrageous phony ID and gave me a new birth date making me 21. He handed it over and ripped mine into tiny pieces before throwing it into the wastebasket.

"Here, use this," he said. "Now get the [expletives deleted] out of my office."

It was an offer I did not refuse. I rocked around many blocks with that ID until I was 21.

It was never once questioned.

8 The night I had sex with Blaze Starr

The band at The Flamingo was cool. It was an unnamed all-black Jazz trio. I knew all the cats pretty well and they often let me sit in and play drums — not when the girls were dancing, mind you, but between shows.

Sol Goodman's infamous 2 O'Clock Club was a sleazy little basement club located a block or so up on the other side of the street from The Flamingo. One night the manager of the 2 O'Clock Club came into The Flamingo looking for me.

The 2 O'Clock Club became famous when notorious sex show promoter Goodman, who also owned the Globe Burlesque next door, changed the name of one Fannie Belle Flemming to Blaze Starr *(previous page)* and made her his celebrity headliner. Turned out their drummer hadn't shown up and someone told him there was a kid at The Flamingo who could play a little bit — and had a union card.

He wanted to know if I could — would — play the night for 15 dollars. I guess he assumed I read music because I had the union card. With my shiny new phony ID I had seen Blaze's show many times by then and honestly, musically, playing the show wasn't a huge challenge. The bass player, as bass players always do, kept me in the pocket.

I love bass players.

Talk about Rockin' Around The Block. Blaze by then was this huge internationally famous star and for an 18-year-old kid who wasn't even old enough to be in the place, the whole night was a great adventure. When the manager handed me my pay at the end of the night, Blaze was with him.

She gave me a little buss on the cheek and whispered in my ear. "You don't read a note of fucking music, do you?"

"No, ma'am, I sure don't."

Blaze Starr had streaming red hair, carried around 38 DDs, and had a huge, beautiful smile.

She leaned in close and whispered, "Good job, Kid."

I was 18. I got kissed on the cheek by Blaze Starr. When you're 18, in that era, a kiss on the cheek from someone like Blaze Starr pretty well passes for sex.

Blaze eventually bought the 2 O'Clock Club. She retired from The Block in the 1970s when the clubs went all-nude, and in 1983 from stripping altogether. A part-time gemologist, she made gemology her full-time career thereafter. The movie *Blaze* was about her affair with Louisiana Governor Earl Long. Paul Newman was Long and Lolita Davidovich played the title role. It was a box office hit in 1989.

In the early 1980s, in Baltimore on business, I went back and visited The Block. Almost 25 years had passed. The Block had changed, but even though slimmed down by puritan politicians, it was still immediately recognizable; many of the old clubs were still there.

Memories of my youth flooded over me. Good times. Jazz times. Early Rock & Roll times.

I went into The Flamingo. That hadn't changed at all. It was just as sleazy as ever. Bargirls, the so-called "B" girls, lined the bar. You buy them a drink and they will talk to you. If your drink is $5, theirs is $20, and they get a stirrer with whatever they are drinking. At the end of the night they turn in the stirrers for cash, maybe $10 per.

My favorite bartender, Minky, had recently retired; they said he was living in a condo right up the street. A beautiful gal came up and rubbed herself all over me. But I knew the rules: Never let 'em think you're a trick.

"You seem like a nice girl," I said to her. "So I'm not going to charge you for that." I turned to my drink.

She followed me around all night. I ain't no rookie. I mean, back when I was a kid, I had sex with Blaze Starr one night, right over there across the street, up The Block a bit.

Blaze Starr died on June 15th, 2015, due to complications from a severe heart condition.

She was 83.

9 Purnell Rice & His Jazz Crew

1959. I had never heard of Purnell Rice.

The big, fancy, much-of-it-neon sign hanging on the side of the large nightclub resting on the corner of a major thoroughfare and a sad side street in the middle of inner city Baltimore said "Purnell Rice & Jazz Crew. Formerly with Dakota Staton".

Staton was a Jazz singer of some renown. Dakota was later to become the mother of Candi Staton, an even better known '70s R&B and Gospel singer who did "Young Hearts Run Free", a hit Disco classic in 1976.

But at the time I had only vaguely heard of Dakota. Dakota Staton or not, this Purnell fellow was clearly a man of some significance. And so was the club, which, neon sign still blazing, remained open and packed hours after the legal closing time had passed. As I understood the arrangement, nobody in law enforcement ever bothered them. Apparently the fix was in.

Purnell Rice was the drummer in the house band, a wailing six-piece Jazz combo of big-time players. One night after The Flamingo closed, I was taken there to see Rice by my good friend, the bass player in the all-black Jazz trio that was the regular house band.

My friend was a tall, skinny, good-looking black man. Sharp, married, a serious sort of fellow who worked at the post office during the day and played bass at night. I wish I could remember his name, but I can't. He befriended me, looked after me, and kind of took me under his wing.

For the purposes of this little tome, we shall call him Edward. His name was almost certainly not Edward, but I remember him as an Edward-looking sort of guy.

We were good friends. He took me to his house to meet his wife and to a big house party with all his friends and relatives. He even tried to hook me up with his sister, a very pretty gal 7 or 8 years older than me. She had zero interest in kids, white or black. Often Edward would take me to smoky little illegal house clubs, located in the basements of row houses, deep inside the Baltimore inner city.

Sometimes these house clubs would stretch two or three houses long, with the basement walls knocked out to join their spaces together. They all had a bar, usually a piano player, sometimes a trio, and often colorful lights with, if nothing else, a lot of red. They reminded me of The Bop Shop.

There would be pretty ladies and cool gents and usually a few guys huddled together in some corner consuming some kind of illegal substance Edward would not ever let me see or even get close to.

Everybody welcomed me.

Edward had his post office gig and I worked days at a bank pushing punch cards through IBM machines, so on weekends, Friday and Saturday nights, after The Flamingo closed at 1 AM, Edward often took me into the Baltimore inner city to this open-all-the-time, big-time nightclub featuring Purnell Rice & His Jazz Crew.

Once again, at any of these places, I was the only white guy in the house. Edward always wanted me to sit in, part of his mentoring of me to become a better, more experienced drummer. To me that was nuts, this Rice guy was incredible. He could outplay me with one finger. But my friend Edward insisted and, unbelievably, Rice quite easily gave up his stool and let me take over. It wasn't my impressive drumming that motivated him; he just liked to chase the girls at the bar.

Once again a friendly bass player kept me in the pocket.

I love bass players.

To me this was all crazy. Here I was playing in a big-time, big-city nightclub with one of the hottest Jazz bands I had ever heard. Wailing. Packed club. Hot chicks. Cool cats. Loud. Busy. Wheels changing colors sequentially as they lit the room through the smoky air. Beautiful ladies. Men making moves. It went down 'til dawn and sometimes beyond.

Edward took me there often and I was always allowed, even encouraged, to sit in. Purnell used to take me into the kitchen and play some wild and crazy riff on the countertop. Then he'd hand me sticks and say, "Here, play this."

I tried, but are you kidding me? He'd throw his hands up in despair and say the same thing every time, "Man, white people can't play drums."

I was beginning to believe him. But Purnell liked to chase the ladies and so I played and played, white kid or not. The guys in the band got used to me and boy did I ever learn things every time I sat in.

You can't buy that kind of experience.

Through the years I often thought about Purnell Rice and wondered why he hadn't become bigger, more well known.

Not until 50 years later would I learn Purnell Rice was considered one of the greatest Jazz drummers of all time and, in addition to Dakota Staton, he had played with Billie Holiday, Lena Horne, Dinah Washington, Sarah Vaughan, Count Basie, Eddie "Lockjaw" Davis, Eddie "Cleanhead" Vinson, Fats Domino, Leo Parker, Earl Grant, Red Prysock, and many others. It's Purnell Rice playing on "Handclappin'", the Red Prysock Jazz dance classic.

All that wouldn't fit on that sign hanging out front of the club. Maybe this would fit the sign:

Alan White — Formerly with Purnell Rice

He was 33 when I knew him.
He died at 50.

"Long Lean Lanky Larry Dean, the Dean of Rhythm and Blues,
you dig", popular WITH radio DJ and one of Alan's heroes

10 Turk Coury, Part 2 — The Big Dance

When I finally got out of boarding school I moved to Baltimore and lived with my lovely, totally delightful Aunt Algie. She was a tiny little thing, only 4'11", and she was just the nicest person ever.

She loved her nephew Alan.

I got a job at Loyola Savings & Loan pushing punch cards through IBM machines, a skill I picked up working for minimum wage at The Torrington Company in a job my dad had gotten me between my quitting high school and moving to Baltimore. Loyola Savings & Loan was a pretty good job, only six hours a day, and it paid $50 a week, about $424 in 2019 dollars.

Those were the years I haunted The Block at night, acquired my phony ID card, sat in on drums with the cool trio at The Flamingo and with Purnell Rice's band at the after-hours club, and that one time with Blaze Starr. These were very good years — Rock & Roll years — the period of time in Baltimore covered by the movies *Diner* and *Hairspray*.

Top 40 radio WCAO and R&B station WITH were rocking it. I loved listening to "Long Tall Lean Lanky Larry Dean, the Dean of Rhythm and Blues, you dig". Because WITH had a white morning man, the hysterically funny and legendary Jack Gale, I didn't even realize WITH was a black station until I went to a hop. I was the only white kid there. Dean himself was black.

The music was great. I was already thinking of someday becoming a DJ. I found a girlfriend, a college girl I was crazy about, and life was good. For a while. Then the college girl graduated and moved back home to Buffalo. Even knowing her parents would try to break us up, I followed her.

Classic.

I still remember sitting in a bar in some Buffalo 'burb called Tonawanda betting drinks on which way the states would fall in the 1960 Presidential election. I assumed Nixon would sweep Kennedy like a messy floor and lost my ass that night, one state at a time.

What I learned about politics was never to engage in wishful thinking when it comes to predictions. Using that formula as a mantra, I've not been wrong with a prediction in a Presidential election since.

Eventually the college girl's parents succeeded in breaking us up and, heartbroken, I moved back to Connecticut.

I picked up a weekend gig playing in a band on Friday and Saturday nights in the big room, which held over 300 people, at the Berkshire Lodge Hotel right over the line in New York State, where the drinking age was 18. All the Torrington kids went there, so the place was packed every Friday and Saturday night.

Although I don't remember the name of the band, or even if it had one officially, the frontman was a tall, skinny, hugely talented black kid named Eddie Smith. If there wasn't already a Chuck Berry, he would've been it.

Eddie Smith was tearing the place up and I was delighted to be playing drums, my first real, regular paying gig. Eddie Smith played mostly rhythm, all chords. The lead guitar was a guy named Mike Stoffi.

Mike was a country boy and didn't take any guff from anybody. One night he had a run-in with some joker and Mike laid him out like an undertaker. As a result, the hotel management barred him for 4 weeks. But the guy who managed the club part of the hotel knew he was needed, so he urged Mike to find a creative solution, and boy did he ever.

Mike drove a nice 1957 Ford convertible. He parked next to an open window directly aside the stage. Then he ran his guitar wire through the window into the amp. With the top down, he sat on the top of the back seat, playing lead from outside. If anything, the band got more popular because if it. Thankfully we never had a rainy Friday or Saturday night while he was barred from the club.

One night I ran into Turk Coury there. "You're getting pretty good on those drums," I remember him saying.

We had a beer on my break and talked about his night at the Warner Theater and old times in homeroom. He had put together a great band around town called Turk & The Bop Kings and, although they had recently broken up, he was still my hero — the coolest guy ever.

One day about six months later, after the hotel had fired the Eddie Smith band following another fight, I got a call from Turk. He tells me he put together this new band but they broke up because the rest of the guys wanted to only play Country and he wanted to play Rock & Roll with maybe a little Country thrown in.

It seems he had a high school gig booked up in Copake Lake, New York, and would I play drums for him? Are you kidding me? The great Turk Coury? You bet! I didn't even ask him how much it paid.

So when the big night rolled around he picked me up in his '53 Mercury, we threw my drums in the trunk, and off we went to the big high school dance. Turk only played rhythm guitar, just chords. So, while we rode along on the way to New York State, to make conversation I happened to ask who was playing lead guitar.

"Well," said Turk, sheepishly, "that's the other thing. I couldn't find anybody else. It's just the two of us."

So there we were, looking like a couple of ants set up on this huge stage in a gigantic gym. There was no amplifier, no microphone. Just Turk's acoustic guitar and my drums and his voice. Looking at our non-amplified setup and comparing that to the huge room, we wondered how in the hell we were going to be heard.

But then, Turk turned to me, smiled, shrugged, and did what he had done at the Warner Theater. He jumped, landed feet spread wide, threw back his head, and wailed —

"Some people like to rock. Some people like to roll..."

And the freaking place went wild. The guys were jumping up and down and yelling. The girls were screaming. Once again it was like he was Elvis.

We never took a break. Turk just kept firing, song after song after song. Mostly fast songs, but ballads too. The crowd never stopped screaming at the beginning of every new song.

When it was over we went to someone's cottage on Copake Lake and I drank a lot and met a really cute girl and we drank and played music all night long and soon it was daybreak and most of the crowd had gone home and we drank for a few more hours anyway.

What I learned that night was about magic. Magic so real it was always present. Turk was just about always the center of attention in any room he was in — men, women, children, even animals always flocked around him. What I didn't realize was the way it would translate on the stage.

Turk Coury was never the best singer in the world and while his rhythm guitar was wildly energizing, he often played the wrong chords. In later years he even stopped imitating Elvis and just sounded like himself.

But he was the most electrifying entertainer and had more stage charisma then anyone I ever saw. He did to crowds what Elvis and The Beatles could do, but with no hit records.

It was natural, magical, consistent — and inexplicable.

And on that occasion, I was the drummer in a for-real magical mystery, albeit a two-piece, band. I'm told that to this day there are people who still get together every so often and reminisce about the night Turk Coury destroyed the high school gym in Copake Lake, New York, with an acoustical guitar and an overly enthusiastic and very loud drummer. They say that dance is the stuff of legend around them parts.

For Turk and me, it was just the beginning.

Alan, 23, afternoon drive DJ
at WHVW-AM 950, Poughkeepsie, N.Y., 1964

Mike, Alan, and Turk in 1960 as
Turk & The Party Cats

11 The Brass Rail, the Great Turk Coury, Part 3

It was so hot that, if you had one, you could have fried an egg on the hood of the car. Pleasing my father again, I found myself — for a third time — taking the IBM Programming Aptitude Test in Poughkeepsie, New York. IBM and I had long ago resolved my logic and creativity scores would be off the charts, but my mathematics skills and potential as a programmer would continue to be non-existent. Dad was correctly convinced that computer programming was the next big career opportunity in the American workforce. He was relentless in pursuit of trying to get me in the door.

He was right, too. Plastics was a few years away and Mrs. Robinson was still happily married. Computer programming was indeed the next big employment wave.

The neon signs in the window of a nondescript bar called The Brass Rail on Main Street said "Cold Beer" and "Air Conditioned". Since I had neither in the car, I slid the into a curbside parking space and made a beeline for a cold Rheingold. The bartender's name turned out to be The Squirrel. He was a big, burly, balding, Mel's Diner kind of guy. He brought me a cold beer and a warm smile.

As I drank my way through this Friday afternoon I met some of the regulars in what was clearly a mostly gay bar. There were two Freddies, White Freddie and Black Freddie.

Black Freddie was bisexual and often announced that no matter who came through the door, white or black, woman or man, if they were cute, they were his. White Freddie swished around cheerfully.

There was a beautiful young woman in her early 30s named Shirley. It was rumored she had cirrhosis of the liver and was drinking herself to death *à la* Nicolas Cage in *Leaving Las Vegas*.

There was this other young woman, pretty but hefty, with very large breasts she had lovingly nicknamed The Girls. It got to the point The Girls became her own name, as in, "Has anybody seen The Girls around here today?"

There was a smallish, dark-haired, foul-mouthed woman in her late 40s stomping around behind the bar, muttering obscenities, supposedly under her breath, but mostly loudly enough to be understood by all.

"What's her problem?" I asked The Squirrel.

"Oh, that's Rosie. She's the owner and we're supposed to have a Rock & Roll band in here tonight and tomorrow. Every Friday and Saturday night. And I guess they called her earlier this afternoon. They got some other gig and they aren't gonna show up and so now she's furious."

"A band?" I asked as I surveyed the shotgun bar. "Where would you put a band in this place?"

"You can't see it now because all the lights are off, but we have a huge back room way back in there. Every Friday and Saturday night all the Vassar girls come here with their dates from all the other preppy colleges like Yale and Harvard and such and this place gets pretty busy."

"Who's the band?"

He told me their name and I had heard them once. A loud Rock & Roll trio fronted by a singing drummer, a wild-looking fellow with crazy blonde hair and only one tooth, an upper, right in the middle of his mouth. They weren't very good but they were loud, and in Rock & Roll that often passed for good.

"I might know a band," I ventured to The Squirrel. So he sent Rosie over.

"How many in the band?"

"Um, just two of us. But I'm not sure I can even reach the guitar player."

"Nah, for Christ's sake you can't play Rock & Roll with two people." And off she went.

Didn't matter to me. What did I care? I had a serious long-term relationship going with the Rheingold Brewing Company, and I wasn't sure Turk would be interested anyway. We'd played a couple of gigs at a middle-of-nowhere Country bar called Lee Van's Tavern, but I hadn't seen him in a while. So I sat at the bar and let the long afternoon slip away.

Then Rosie was back. "Maybe you should call your friend. I gotta do something."

"How much does it pay?"

"Sixty dollars."

I did the math. Two nights at $30 a night, that's $15 a man (about $125 a man in 2019 dollars), which is what we got at Lee Van's and which was pretty much the going rate for a musician back then.

"He's not going to want to pay for drinks, I can tell you." I knew Turk well enough to know that. If he was making money for a bar he couldn't see them charging him for drinks.

"Fine. We'll take care of the tab. Call him."

So I went to the pay phone and called Turk and got lucky. He was home and picked up the phone on the first ring and thought it sounded like fun and he needed the money anyway since he now had two kids.

"I'll swing by your father's house and pick up your drums. I can be up there by around 8. Ask her if that is okay."

It was. We set up in the larger-than-expected back room in time and started playing about 9 o'clock, just as the college-age kids were beginning to arrive.

"Some people like to Rock…"

And suddenly this Friday night was just like the high school gym in Copake Lake. The boys yelled and the girls screamed and everybody danced. We played two two-hour sets with a short break in between, a break just long enough for me to go over to the sleazy hotel next door and get to know The Girls a little better.

When we arrived Saturday night, the place was already crowded. By the time we got underway there was a line outside the front door. The place was just nuts that night. Hot and loud and wild and crazy — Rock & Roll crazy. Off-the-hook nuts. When there are people digging the music it's always more fun to play, and this was what playing drums behind Elvis himself must have been like. We just killed them. Both nights. All night.

When we finished up Saturday, Turk went over to get the money from Rosie while I packed up my drums.

He was back in a flash with a puzzled look on his face.

"How much did she say?"

"$60. I *know* she said $60."

He just stared. "Yeah, well she gave me $120."

We were both silent for a moment. "She meant $60 a night," I finally said.

"Jesus."

"Does she want us back?"

"Yeah, I already booked us. Every Friday and Saturday night. That's more than I'm making at the factory job for the whole week."

"Turk, I've been telling you ever since Copake Lake that you should be doing this for a living."

"Tell you what," he said. "I'll take leader's pay and we'll split it $70/$50." (That was about $594 for him and $425 for me in 2019 dollars).

We were there almost three years and The Brass Rail was packed to the rafters every Friday and Saturday night for our entire run. We were instantly the hottest band in the area.

After a few months, Turk wanted another guitar player, so we added my old friend from the Eddie Smith band, the Stratocaster lead guitar playing Mike Stoffi, and we were three. Turk & The Party Cats came to be.

Rosie happily paid the additional money and we were all of a sudden professional musicians. I often stayed at the rundown hotel next door to The Brass Rail where The Girls lived. The Girls and I became great friends.

Turk bought a Silvertone amplifier from Sears, the high-end model which came complete with a reverb unit. He ran both his guitar and his microphone through that and it sounded great. I upgraded my partial snare and kick drum kit to a full set, complete with a serious Ludwig chrome snare and a solid set of Zildjian cymbals.

Turk played chords, Mike played lead, and I played loud.

Eventually I had the image of an intoxicated cat holding a bubbly champagne glass painted on my bass drum head, backlit by a red light inside the drum.

It was funny because I had always wanted to be like the drummer on *The Ed Sullivan Show* and play in the orchestra pit behind great singers. The whole time I played with Turk I never felt like I was in a band — I felt like I was that pit drummer playing behind Elvis.

We added a Wednesday night at another popular college hangout, the Williams Café, owned by a guy named Bill Pappas. He was very creepy, but the place was big, he paid well, and it was packed every Wednesday.

The way we would get a new night was as much fun as the gigs themselves.

One time when we went out looking for a Thursday night, we hit a bar called The White Stag. It was Country, complete with deer heads mounted behind the bar. It was way out in the middle of nowhere about halfway between Torrington and Poughkeepsie, just over the state line where the 18-year-old New York drinking age kicked in.

The way it worked was we would go in and just start drinking with whoever was there. Then I would say something like, "Hey Turk. Go get your guitar, man."

And then he'd say, "No, nah."

Invariably someone would say, "You play guitar? Yeah man, go and get it."

And he'd say no and they'd say yes and finally he'd appear to give in and go get his guitar. It was a setup. He had drumsticks in his guitar case. The plan was I would turn a tray over a bar stool, making a little snare drum.

I still remember the White Stag night. It was a Thursday, the night we were looking to book. There must have been about ten or fifteen people drinking when we arrived.

We ran the game and while Turk dragged his guitar case in from the car, I rounded up a nice tray and got that set up on a bar stool someone had climbed off to make room for me. Then all of a sudden Turk was back and he handed me the sticks, slung his guitar around his neck, jumped up on the bar, threw his head back and wailed "Some people like to rock, some people like to roll."

And then he danced his way along the length of the bar, not once knocking over a drink. People ran for the pay phone.

"Martha, y'all get gotta over here. You ain't a-gonna believe what's going on in here right now." Within an hour there were maybe fifty or sixty people.

Needless to say we booked the Thursday.

Our Sunday night was at The Green Lantern, a nice little place in rural southern Massachusetts. We were working five nights and I was making the equivalent of about $1000 cash money in 2019 dollars and Turk was making the equivalent of about $1400.

Turk had only recorded one record and that was back in The Bop King days, before The Party Cats. The song was "Kathy", which he wrote himself and recorded at Bell Sound in New York using studio musicians.

But he never liked the way it came out, never pursued the record deal, hated cities, and just could not be talked into any further interest in recording or pursuing a national career.

Fifty years later I would clean up the single remaining acetate demo from that 1958 session, entitled simply "Kathy", and put it up on YouTube. He was visiting at the time and approved the edited version, fascinated by the computer technology used to digitize and re-master the recording.

I'm sure part of his refusal to get involved with the record business was that he liked being this country boy in touch with nature and away from cities and all that, but I have always suspected a lack of musical training, and therefore musical confidence, was a part of it too. I talked him into becoming a professional musician but never got to first base trying to convince him to record and seek a national career.

Turk Coury was a powerful personality and, like Elvis himself, once he got something in his head, that was it. You couldn't tell the man anything.

We went to play a one-night fraternity party at Rensselaer Polytechnic Institute in Troy, New York. On the way up in the car a song came on the radio like nothing I had ever heard before. It had harmonies, even handclapping rhythm, like no record I had ever heard. I will never forget the moment I turned to Turk and said the exact same thing I had said to Johnny Troy all those years ago, "I don't know what that is, but it's going to change the way they make records forever."

We were rocking the frat party like it was *Animal House* when the kid running the party came up to us and asked us to take a break. No one had ever done that before so Turk asked, "Sure, but how come?"

"Oh," the kid said, "The Beatles are coming on the radio."

"What's The Beatles?" Turk asked.

"It's a new band from England and they are incredible."

So we all gathered around a big floor radio and listened as Joey Reynolds on WKBW in Buffalo introduced "I Want To Hold Your Hand", The Beatles' first hit record.

It was, of course, the same record I had heard on the way up in the car. Turk just looked at me with a small smile.

"Wow."

Wow, indeed.

By the time the summer of 1963 came along we were probably the best-known band in the general area of northeastern Connecticut, southeastern New York, and southwestern Massachusetts. When we eventually left The Brass Rail we booked a nice weekend gig right on the water at a club in Putnam Lake, New York.

Mike Stoffi tired of music and wanted to get back to his main career of raising horses. He left the band and was replaced by a less aggressive guitar player named Dave Gallitello, who played both lead and rhythm.

He was a much better musician than Mike and musically it probably made us a better band, but it also changed our sound from Rock & Roll to more middle of the road. Turk was even doing Tony Bennett and Frank Sinatra songs.

One night late in September of that summer of '63, Turk came to me and explained he had finally booked a gig at Vassar College he'd been trying to book for a long time and since it was so important, he wanted a drummer named Buddy Dio to play instead of me.

I knew Buddy Dio; he was a great Jazz drummer, ten times better than me or anyone else around those parts. But he was a terrible drunk who played over everything, including all the vocals. Not only did I think he was the wrong drummer for Turk, my feelings were hurt.

I was angry and quit the band.

However, by then I had become a decent drummer and within a week I was asked to join a Four Seasons sound-alike band based in Poughkeepsie called The Thunderbirds.

Their lead singer, a guy named Tommy something-or-another, not only looked like Frankie Valli, he had the same clean and pure falsetto and everybody in the five-piece band sang except me. The band was tight and we sounded exactly like the Four Seasons on all their songs.

The Thunderbirds were interested on going on the road and were working on a record deal.

But November 22, 1963, changed everything.

Motorcade moments before
John F. Kennedy is assassinated in Dallas, Texas

12 The Day They Killed the President, Part 1

November 1963. I was working at a Catholic hospital in Poughkeepsie just to have something to do during the day. My night job was still playing drums on weekends for the Four Seasons sound-alike band, The Thunderbirds. The day gig was in the hospital stockroom where we kept track of incoming medical supplies. It was my job to get them where they needed to be, whenever they needed to be there.

We did not have a TV in the stockroom, but the radio was on all day. I had always thought I might like being on the radio and, as a kid, whenever I was lucky enough to be living at home, my dad would bring home his office Dictaphone and I'd use it to practice being a DJ. But I hadn't ever followed through with the thought.

There was a fellow named Large Sarge on the local station whose signal came in the best, WHVW Live 95, located at 950 on the AM dial.

WHVW was a small 250-watt daytime startup station but for some reason their signal covered the entire Hudson Valley. Large Sarge was so talented and popular he had, almost by himself, put the brand new station on the map.

He had an amazing radio voice, deep and full. He was just a fantastic radio personality — funny, witty and smooth. I loved listening to his show.

Here's the saga of how Large Sarge got the WHVW radio job. It's a real humdinger.

Back when he was in high school, he and some technically-oriented buddy ran an illegal mobile bandit radio station set up out in the woods. Just before they signed on the air they would jam their powerful, but illegal, homemade transmitter signal over the top of both of the two most popular Top 40 stations coming into the Poughkeepsie radio market, WABC from New York and WKBW from Buffalo. Then they would announce to those stations' listeners that they were signing on the air, and at what dial position.

Then Sarge would DJ Rock & Roll music in the old AM Top 40 personality style. He'd read Coca-Cola commercials out of magazines. Their illegal bandit radio station became so popular the local record store owner bought commercials.

Finally, after a good long run, worried the FCC might eventually triangulate them, they gave it up.

A few years later, around 1962 when AM radio station WHVW first signed on in Poughkeepsie (actually the Poughkeepsie suburb of Hyde Park), station owner Tom Durfey, a former college professor, had heard of the legend of Large Sarge and the bandit radio station's wild success.

Knowing the local record store had already bought commercials, Durfey went to the store owner to track down Large Sarge. He found him, offered him a job and, as soon as he put Large Sarge on the air, Durfey's new station took off like a rocket.

It was a late Friday morning when the AP wire service at the radio station went absolutely nuts. I still remember exactly what Sarge said:

"According to The Associated Press, the President has been shot in Dallas. More details as they become available."

That was it. The AP bulletin was all he had, so Sarge played a record. It turned out that was all he could do. I didn't know it at the time, but Sarge was alone at the station. The News Director, a very good one named Jim Tyrell from WBZ in Boston, was out to lunch along with the rest of the station personnel, so all Sarge could do was run back and forth from the AP machine in the back of the newsroom to the DJ booth, alternating updates and music until Tyrell could make it back.

Like the rest of America, the hospital was locked into a kind of walking zombie shock. Nuns and nurses and patients were crying. There was a TV in the waiting room and another in the hospital office, but I was alone in the stockroom with only WHVW and the voices of Large Sarge and Jim Tyrell.

The news was terrible, of course, but that afternoon listening to Large Sarge, Jim Tyrell, and the WHVW radio coverage of the assassination, I was mesmerized. It was my eureka moment. Radio was something I was going to try. I had no big education and terrible math skills, but I always had the gift of gab, the gift of language. Combined with my love of music, broadcasting was a decent option.

My father had finally given up on my becoming an IBM programmer and graciously offered to front me thirteen weeks in DJ school, including room and board. The stupid club owner where The Thunderbirds were playing insisted we be open the night of the assassination so we just rehearsed all night because, of course, not one single customer ever came in.

But, inspired by the broadcast of the events that day, later that night I gave the band two weeks' notice and took Dad up on his generous offer. In January of 1964, I began thirteen weeks at the famous Columbia School of Broadcasting in Washington, D.C.

Like everyone else, I wondered who could possibly be responsible for the assassination of JFK.

Less than a year passed before we — Large Sarge, me, and WHVW — would become one of the very first news outlets in America to discredit the government's lame assassination cover-up known as The Warren Report. [See Chapter 18 for this story.]

Alan at the Columbia School of Broadcasting, 1964

13 Dean Anthony, Broadcasting School, and Ronnie Dove

The privately owned Columbia School of Broadcasting was located in three small rooms in the same nondescript downtown office building housing the Washington Redskins' central offices.

There was a tiny office for the owner of the school, a lovely, large-sized, prematurely silver-haired, quite handsome fellow we called Mr. Jansen. There was a main classroom with standard classroom desks which easily accommodated the 15 or 20 students in this thirteen-week class, and another small room divided into two smaller sections; one with a very early video camcorder and a cheesy backdrop setup, and a studio for basic audio production.

All of us stayed at the same place that came with the price of the broadcasting course, a large complex of row houses located very near Dupont Circle. I think it was Hartnett Hall. They were nice, clean, basic rooms, and came with two meals a day in a dining hall across the street.

Among the students was a fellow named Gil King who had done part-time weekend announcing at a small radio station in Grand Rapids, Michigan. But he also played keyboard and wrote songs. He produced a terrific record, "Footsteps", which had it ever come out would have been a surefire hit. Nice kid but going nowhere in radio. I always thought he was probably wasting his time, but he might very well make the big time as a music producer and/or songwriter.

There was a guy who kept very much to himself named Tom who had a great, professional voice but very little personality. He wanted to be a newsman and, unlike the rest of us, had little interest in music or Top 40 radio. I sometimes think I've seen him on network news but none of us knew him well and so many years have passed, it's impossible to be sure.

There was a kid named Larry who not only had a voice that sounded like a chicken with its throat cut, he also had a horribly thick Southern accent which he couldn't even begin to shake. Nice kid. We all liked him. But no way José.

And then there was David Kimmel.

Kimmel didn't care about music or Top 40 radio either. He was a sports nut, particularly college basketball; he wanted to become a sports announcer. David was one of the funniest people I ever came across, then or since. He was like the ad lib king of the world who kept all of us in stitches most of the time. Even our crusty old English teacher often succumbed to his quick-as-a-wink wisecracks as off-the-cuff funny as Steve Allen's. He had a decent but somewhat high-pitched voice, a lousy complexion, was significantly overweight, and wore thick, horn-rimmed glasses. But Kimmel was hysterical.

One night Gil King had wrangled a date with some pretty little gal, but she would only agree to go out with him if he came up with a date for her girlfriend, who was said to be very, very beautiful.

Gil and David were pals, so David went with Gil to be the beautiful gal's date. Kimmel didn't want to do it; there was a game on or something else better he wanted to do. Gil only got him to do it by stressing the proposed date's supposed incredible beauty. In order to get Miss Beautiful to agree to this blind date they told her David Kimmel was the funniest man alive. On the night of the big date they picked up Gil's date first and then went to collect Kimmel's gal.

When she got into the back seat, she took one look at David and said: "Okay, Pal. Be funny." David's instant no-hesitation response?

"First you be beautiful, then I'll be funny."

That was David Kimmel.

The teachers were what mattered.

Mr. Jansen himself taught us basic broadcasting, how to find a job, and a curriculum of useful and interesting broadcasting generalities. He was a nice man whom we all liked; we found his lessons useful.

There was an older man who taught us English — particularly pronunciation and specifically difficult foreign word pronunciation. He taught us how to write foreign words phonetically, grammar, and basic copywriting skills. He was a crusty old dude like the hall monitor you used to hate; none of us really liked or related to him much. But what he was teaching was invaluable and we needed to know it. So we lived with the grouchy old cuss; most paid attention.

There was a very nice, very gay man whose name I do not remember, who was there to teach us writing, specifically comedy writing. He had at one time written for big-time TV and movies and had an impressive background in Hollywood. He regaled us with stories of Hollywood and taught us how to think funny. We adored this guy and couldn't wait for his twice-a-week classes. Funny man. Between this fellow and David Kimmel, those classes were absolutely hysterical.

Big Ol' Fat Ol' Dino

And then there was Dean Griffith.

Dean Griffith (named after D.C.'s Griffith Stadium) was a stock radio station name at Washington's number one Top 40 radio station, WPGC, where Dean was the program director and afternoon drive DJ. He turned out to be the fifth and final Dean Griffith.

He was Dino on air. "Big Ol' Fat Ol' Dino, losing a pound a day 'til it all melts away." But that wasn't real either. He was actually skinny — maybe 5'10" and 160. *Dino* was just another stock station gimmick. His real name was Sal Jovino. He was a great Top 40 DJ running a great Top 40 station, and that was what we wanted. Rock & Roll radio, baby!

Even though we didn't know his real name then, Sal as Dean Griffith also taught three or four mornings a week; those classes were the ones we most looked forward to.

Sal/Dean told how The Beatles first broke in America on competitor station WWDC. It turned out popular WWDC personality Carroll James had a secretary who went on vacation to England. While she was there she was exposed to The Beatle phenomenon, which had already exploded in Great Britain and across Europe.

Upon her return to the States she brought back a copy of "I Want To Hold Your Hand" to her boss. James programmed the record immediately for across-the-board station play. Overnight it became the station's number one request.

In Top 40 radio the format says you talk and do all your business over the introduction and fade, the front and back of each record, and although WWDC wasn't a pure Top 40 station — they were a little more middle of the road — they followed the format pretty closely.

So Dean taped WWDC 24 hours a day until he found an occasion where, coming out of a newscast, they played "I Want To Hold Your Hand" cold, no talking on either end. Dean immediately pulled the song from the reel-to-reel tape and put it onto a tape cartridge. These cartridges looked a bit like eight-track tapes and generally held one song, or one commercial, or one station promo, or one jingle, and were commonly used in every station in America.

He made the stolen "I Want To Hold Your Hand" the WPGC pick hit. This made WPGC only the second station in the nation to play The Beatles.

Dean taught us how to read a commercial, a newscast, and particularly how to intro and outro records. He was a nice guy and had lots of cool stories, but he was also a strict teacher who demanded we pay attention.

He'd laugh along with Kimmel's constantly hysterical ad libs, but he'd also shut him down so we could get serious and actually learn something. Dino favored those of us who were taking this schooling the most seriously.

Often Dino would do station remote broadcasts, where we were always invited to show up. While the other guys were busy screwing around on their downtime, I went to every single remote. On one occasion Dino and I were sitting side by side at some shopping center lunch counter in Maryland waiting for the station to throw it to him so he could read a commercial. Suddenly he handed me the copy and said: "Here, you read it."

What? This is the number one radio station in a major market in the middle of the afternoon, I've never been on any radio station before in my life, and you want me to read this? What? The look on my face must have been one of horror.

Dino just laughed. "You do it all the time in class. This is no different. Forget all the zillions of people you figure are listening. Just read the commercial as you do in class."

So I did. And it came off without a hitch. I read it and when I was done the guy running the board back at the station hit a jingle and segued directly into a record. Dino nodded and said, "Good job."

One Sunday afternoon I had been out at a movie and was on my way back to Hartnett Hall when I saw a bunch of police out in front of a row house. I pulled over, parked, and walked up the first police officer I saw, little pad and pen in hand.

"Hi, Alan White. WPGC News," I lied. "What happened?"

He told me what he knew — a couple of guys had gotten into an argument and one had shot the other. The one who was shot had been transported to a hospital and the shooter was in custody.

I had the WPGC hotline number so I went to a pay phone and called the station. Gentleman Jim Hanlon was on the air.

"Cool," he said. "When this record is over, I'll throw it to you." And he did.

"There has been a shooting in Northeast Washington and WPGC reporter Alan White is on the scene. Alan, what happened there?"

So I told him. I had it all written out — where, when, how, whom; all the news reporting basics. I remembered to speak slowly and in my deepest news reporter voice. He taped my report and ran the story all day and into the evening.

Monday in class, Dino pointed out my enthusiasm. I was one proud potential broadcaster. First a live commercial and now a live news report. Nobody else had been on the air at all. Going forward those two on-air moments helped me prepare for broadcasting in a way no classroom experience ever could.

But music was still my thing. Naturally I went to every cool club in Washington to see every hot band in the area.

My favorite place was The Rocket Room, a smart, upscale club located next to the bus station in downtown D.C.

The band playing there most often was Ronnie Dove & The Belltones. Dove *(top of next page)* was a Swing singer with a monster voice in the Bobby Darin mold. He was simply amazing. For one thing he was ridiculously handsome with jet black hair and gleaming white teeth. For another, The Belltones were one hell of a band.

His shows at The Rocket Room were every bit of Bobby Darin, who would later become his mentor.

Another club was Rand's. They had an R&B band fronted by Big Al Downing, who had formerly been with The Chartbusters. The drummer was a fellow named Mitch Corday (*right*) and, man, he could really play.

One of the things about Washington, D.C., was that the area had some of the top bands in the country during that era, with Big Al Downing's and Ronnie Dove & The Belltones being two of the best.

As my thirteen weeks of broadcast school wound down, Corday and Dove and I exchanged phone numbers. Ronnie was on his way to Nashville to record his first record. I promised to play it wherever I landed in radio.

When the broadcasting course was done, Mr. Jansen threw a big party for us at his lovely ranch house out in the suburbs of Maryland. I don't know where he got them, but there were a bunch of pretty girls there. We drank until sunrise and that's all I'm going to say about that.

Later in the summer I got a job working with Large Sarge at my favorite station, WHVW in Poughkeepsie.

Around 1965, Sal Jovino left behind "Dino" and moved on to become "Good Guy Dean Anthony" at WMCA in New York, where he hosted an all-night show, playing his highly popular Actors and Actresses game until the station went all-talk in 1970. He died of cancer in 2003 at age 68.

Ronnie Dove eventually put eleven records, all ballads, into the Billboard Top 40, but none reached the Top 10. His first big hit was "Say You" and as I had promised him, I played it at WHVW. He continues to perform in and around his hometown of Baltimore to this day.

Mitch Corday opened a music management booking agency called Paramount Artists Corporation and two years later recruited me to be his primary agent. He died of cancer around 2005.

I never heard of, or from, any of my classmates at the Columbia School of Broadcasting again, but to this very day I keep thinking I'll see David Kimmel doing standup comedy again, someday, somewhere.

Disco: The Vinyl Years

Broadcast House, WHVW-AM 950

14 Just Get On The Payroll: WHVW-AM 950

When we completed our 13 weeks of broadcasting school, we had short reel-to-reel audition tapes.

They were pretty awful, just the reading of news and commercials. No DJ'ing of music. No music at all. No personality. Just dry copy.

As we were advised to do, I sent my tapes out to stations in my area, which was western Connecticut and eastern New York State. All I got was a bite from some small Connecticut station in the middle of the nowhere. I went in for an interview, read some news and ad copy and left, correctly assuming I had not gotten the job.

Getting nowhere fast, I finally went up to my old haunt in Poughkeepsie, got a cheap room and did some day drinking at The Brass Rail, the club Turk Coury and our band The Party Cats had played for such a long time.

On a lark I applied at the station that had inspired me to go to broadcasting school in the first place, the station where I had heard Large Sarge and News Director Jim Tyrell cover the assassination of JFK, WHVW-AM 950.

No openings for a DJ, but they did have an opening for a salesman. My dad had a saying, "Just get on the payroll." As I had always been good at sales, I jumped at the opportunity.

The Sales Manager, an energetic, friendly Italian in his mid-thirties named Bill DeCesare, immediately took me under his wing. We went out together, pitched clients, and I made demo tapes of what their commercial might sound like.

One guy we pitched said, "Nobody listens to that station."

Bill said, "Well, I'll tell you what then, I'll give you 25 free spots as a sampler. How about that? Would that be okay? Do I have your permission to put them on the air?"

The guy says, "Sure, I guess so."

So we go back to the station and, even though I thought he was crazy, I produce the spot Bill wants. Then we take it back to the prospective client.

"I got it in all the best time slots," Bill promised as I pushed the play button on the portable cassette tape recorder.

Whatever you do stay away from this place. This place is awful, the owner is mean and nasty and they'll cheat ya to beat ya.

This is professionally produced and has music under it and everything. The guy goes nuts.

"You can't put that on the air," he rages.

"Why?" Bill asks. "You said I could, and besides…nobody listens to our station anyway."

I thought the guy was going to punch him, but instead he breaks out laughing. "Alright, you got me."

He bought a nice schedule.

This went on for about two weeks and then the station manager said they wanted me to do morning news. The News Director, Jim Tyrell, who I had admired so much covering the assassination, does the news on the hour and half hour and I am to do the quarter hours, 6:15, 6:45, 7:15, 7:45, and so on. Then I am off to my sales job.

As it turned out, Tyrell was a raging alcoholic who often was so hung over with the shakes I had to read his news. But sick as he was, he wrote all the news copy himself; he was a terrific writer. Sometimes I made phone calls for him, but he wrote all the copy.

He came from Boston powerhouse WBZ and regaled me with stories of Major Market Radio. It went unsaid that he was only in a smaller market like Poughkeepsie due to his drinking. He drank every night, usually at some political event. He was on top of every local political development. But he often had the shakes so bad he could barely move.

That situation went on for another few weeks. Then they wanted me to follow Sarge, who went off at 5 PM, with a DJ show until sign-off. During the spring, summer, and autumn months, that was a 3- to 4-hour afternoon drive show.

That went on for a few weeks and then they wanted me to do a six-hour Sunday afternoon DJ shift. And when the station manager was out of town, which was a lot, they added a Saturday morning talk show called "Open Line".

I was a very busy boy — and all for $60 a week.

One day I came back to the station after sales calls at about 11:30 in the morning.

"What are you doing here?" the receptionist asked.

"Um, I work here?"

"No. You're at Big Ben at noon for a remote."

What? I had never done a remote. Nobody had told me. I'd seen Dino do them at broadcasting school and had hung out with him as he did, but I had never done one myself.

Big Ben was the first box store I had ever seen, as big as any Walmart I've ever seen. Huge. They were a major sponsor.

I jumped in my little green Dodge Dart convertible and, breaking every posted speed limit, raced the 20 minutes to Big Ben. When I arrived the manager was there to greet me, there was a microphone with a very long, maybe 100-150 foot wire, and absolutely nothing else.

"Some guy was here and he hooked up that wire and left," the manager says. I glance at my watch. 11:50.

"Do you sell radios?"

"Sure."

"Get me one. Fast."

So he races to the electronics counter and comes back with a transistor radio, which he is smart enough to have turned on and has working. I hurriedly dial up the station.

"And now, ladies and gentlemen," says the midday announcer, just as the station signal locks in, "we join DJ Alan White who is live from Big Ben. Take it away, Alan."

And I was on. So I just start talking.

"Alright. We are live from the fabulous Big Ben store and waiting right here to see you."

Some lady strolls in and I walk right up to her.

"Hi, we're on the radio together on WHVW. How are you today?" And then she and I went shopping together.

I talked to everyone who came in the store.

"How are you, sir. I dig that tie. Let's go shopping."

It went like that all afternoon. Four hours of it. I never missed a beat. Not one second of dead air; the station was thrilled. When it was over the manager said, "Man, that was great. You can talk to anybody about anything. I didn't know anybody could do that."

"Neither did I!"

15 The Voice Of God

By June 1964, I was on the air at WHVW with my afternoon show following my original broadcast hero, Large Sarge, and still playing drums on weekends.

Sarge and I had such fun together at WHVW. He and I were about the same age (around 24 years old) and were DJ'ing the only Rock & Roll Top 40 signal in the Hudson Valley area. Our ratings at one point were higher than all the other area stations combined.

The other WHVW DJ's were forced to play middle-of-the-road music, or MOR. But when Sarge signed on and the kids got out of school, then we rocked it. Sarge did 1 to 5 PM and I did 5 PM until our legally required sundown sign-off. We both played Sarge's Top 40 music format, which drove the MOR-

Large Sarge (Johnny Donovan) in 1982, long before he became "The Voice of God"

oriented Program Director Dick Neiden absolutely nuts. But Sarge was so popular Neiden couldn't stop us. Weekends we rocked all the time because the kids could listen all the time.

Our real competitor was WABC in NYC, and we eventually beat them in the ratings by doing a lot of local stuff — local sports reports, local news, playing local records, etc. We made stars out of a great local British-style band, The Teddy Boys, by playing their pretty decent British Invasion-sounding record to death. We promoted local Rock & Roll shows with name recording artists at a local theater, whose manager was my best drinking buddy.

One of the best things we pulled off was when Sarge figured out the WABC music format.

He programmed WHVW to play each record one record before WABC played it. When they did their news, we played our #1 record. When they played their oldie, we played our pick hit.

We were a daytimer — meaning we were only licensed to be on the air from sunrise to sunset. So when we signed off we didn't want our listeners going to our biggest competitor. To keep folks from waking in the morning with their radio dials set to WABC's position, AM 770, we sent our listeners to another powerhouse Top 40 signal (which didn't get into Poughkeepsie during the day), WKBW 1520 in Buffalo, right as I played the national anthem and signed off.

WKBW was a local Buffalo station during the day, but it went to 50,000 watts at night and you could hear it up and down the Eastern Seaboard. Sarge and WKBW superstar nighttime DJ Joey Reynolds knew each other. Joey would welcome all our listeners by using our names and call letters just as he knew our listeners were joining his show.

We finally got a ratings book that beat WABC. I remain very proud of that, and I'll bet Sarge is too. Sarge and I were best friends, we spent a lot of time together and he was one of the nicest guys I ever ran with.

Sarge's relationship was with broadcasting, though, while mine was with music. His goal was WABC, period. Mine was music and adventure. His stated goal in life was to marry an 18-year-old gal and work at WABC, both before he was 30. Apparently he accomplished both things. I did music and had many adventures.

Sarge moved on from WHVW shortly after I did and went on to New York stations WBAZ in Kingston and WENE in Binghamton, and WMID in Atlantic City, before landing in New York City, first at WOR-FM.

At WOR-FM Sarge picked up the Johnny Donovan moniker. A year later he was at WABC, first following Cousin Brucie from 10 to midnight, eventually moving to the midday shift which preceded superstar DJ Dan Ingram's highly rated afternoon drive show.

In about 1980 Sarge called and asked if I knew Ross & Wilson, the highly rated morning team at Z93 here in Atlanta. I said, "Sure, I know Brian Wilson really well and I book at lot of personal appearances for him, why?"

Turned out, Ross & Wilson had signed to do the WABC morning show (Brian hadn't yet told me) and Sarge wanted to know if I thought their shtick would work in New York.

It had been decided that if Ross & Wilson couldn't recover WABC's lost ratings, the station was going to change to an all-talk format. Johnny (Sarge) had been considering the Production Director's job and needed to know whether or not he should come off the air and take it.

I asked for the night to consider this and called him back in the morning. "No," I said. "No way. They are two really nice and very talented guys, but what they do isn't going to work in New York City."

I believe Brian intrinsically knew it as well, but he was from New Jersey and grew up with WABC, so he just couldn't pass up the opportunity to work at the station he grew up with. As I had predicted, Ross & Wilson didn't work out on

WABC and the station went all-talk. When WABC finally did give up music programming, Johnny stayed with the station for over forty years, becoming Production Director until his retirement in 2015.

He remains the "The Voice Of God", or as everybody else knows it, the announcer for *The Rush Limbaugh Show*.

Large Sarge and Alan in Ocean City, New Jersey, in 1964

16 WHVW and The Big Show

WHVW was a small-signal, directional AM daytimer at 950 on the dial. It was some kind of engineering axiom: The lower you were on the dial, the better the signal got out. So 950 was pretty good.

For some reason involving transmitter location and signal direction, WHVW covered almost the entire Hudson Valley, thus the shortened call letters "HV", which is the way to which the station was routinely referred.

News Director Jim Tyrell was an ace at local politics and went to every local political event, primarily because they drank big. A raging alcoholic; still he was great on the air and drank well with the boys. He had every nuance of local politics covered: Inside rumors, gossip, and scoops.

Those were the days when few women worked outside the home; midday radio shifts from 9 AM until 1 PM were traditionally aimed at housewives. We had one fellow, a roommate of mine for a time, named Richard B., doing a midday show he called *The Richard B. Spree.*

He was a practicing pseudointellectual whose musical tastes ran to Broadway, but he was smart, had a great voice, and was a pretty boy who photographed well for his station press shot.

All the New York stations were sponsoring big theater shows with big-name recording stars. Sarge and I got to thinking we should maybe do the same. It would be great station promotion and make ourselves a bit of cash.

Other than Sarge himself, my best friends and drinking buddies in those days were a fine fella named Lenny Mays and his wife, Kathy. Len was the manager of the Juliet Theater, a 600-seat art house located so close to the Vassar campus that even during exam-related campus restrictions it was still considered to be on campus.

Len Mays was a tallish, late 20s fellow with thinning reddish hair, terminal acne scars, and a huge IQ. He was possessed of a terrific sense of humor, was a great friend of mine, and he and Kathy and I perpetrated a good deal of craziness together. We drank together almost every night.

He was also a client of mine who ran ads on the station for his films. He was all about Sarge and me, and WHVW, so he gave us the brother-in-law rate to rent the Juliet Theater for our proposed show.

The Juliet Theater, now owned by Vassar College, in about 2015. The marquee is gone and there is a restaurant inside now, but they have a screen in the back which shows old art movies just as the Juliet did back in the day.

We planned the show for a Monday, December 28th, 1964, between Christmas and New Year's when we knew the kids would be out of school. We billed it as the Gala Holiday Rock & Roll Show.

My old Washington, D.C., friend from broadcasting school days, the impossibly handsome, world-class crooner Ronnie Dove, had gotten himself a big hit record with "Say You", which WHVW had played to death. Since I had his phone number, we figured he would be our big headline act.

But he was booked. That was something that had not occurred to us. We were already committed to the theater, so I called another friend from my time in D.C., the onetime drummer for The Chartbusters, Mitch Corday, who had opened the booking agency Paramount Artists Corporation. He was eager to book our show and got us The Chiffons, who had two huge hits ("He's So Fine" and "One Fine Day") and were a much bigger act than Ronnie Dove.

The Chiffons

He also made us book a whole package deal, which included his Chartbusters and a new act, a band called The British Walkers *(below)*. He required a 50% deposit. The Chiffons were $300 and The British Walkers and The Chartbusters were $150 each: $600 total. So we needed $300 for the deposit. I was making $60 a week and Sarge wasn't making much more, and neither of us had the cash.

So we went to the station owner, Tom Durfey. He thought it was a great promotion. The station put up the deposit and came in for a 25% share of the profits.

As much as we didn't like giving up 25%, with the station as our partner Sarge and I were both able to jump on the event like it was the second coming. We could run as many spots as we wanted. And boy, how we wanted. The station was beginning to sound like one big promotion for the show, with the occasional hit record scattered in.

Corday's British Walkers had a pretty darn good British Invasion-sounding record "I Found You" which we were playing, as the saying goes, like it was the national anthem. We had local British Invasion band The Teddy Boys, and were all over their record, too. The Chartbusters also had a small hit called "She's The One" and we were playing that as well. And of course the two big Chiffons hits — "He's So Fine" and One Fine Day" — from a couple of years back were inserted back into the music rotation as though they were current.

We printed up show cards and posted them all over town. We had flyers on the counter of the local record store. We were promoting fools. Everywhere you turned there was something about our show.

We had four shows planned: 11 AM, and 2, 5, and 8 PM. On the day of the show, I got to the theater early. Lenny Mays and I set up the box office admission sign, concession stand, whatever needed to be done. Lenny double-salted the popcorn and unplugged the water fountain. We were officially ready to go in time for the first show at 11 AM.

All the acts were backstage except the The Chiffons, who we had installed into a makeshift dressing room upstairs behind the movie projection booth. There was a powerful follow spotlight at the back of the theater, the stage was lit for a live show, and we were ready to Rock & Roll.

Four people showed up. They sat in the front row.

Backstage, both Sarge and my old friend and electrifying live performer Turk Coury were rallying the troops.

"Hey, let's use this as a rehearsal," Turk said to the gathered acts. "The next show we'll be really tight."

And then he said something which I carried with me for the rest of my professional life: "If only one person comes, it's not their fault nobody else came. They deserve the same show we'd do if it were a sellout."

Everybody got behind the idea and we did the whole thing, including running The Chiffons down the aisle and up onto the stage with the band vamping their hit hook and the powerful spotlight following them.

At the 2 PM show we had 12 people. At the 5PM show we had about 20.

Each time the performers rocked like it was a sold-out house while Sarge and I tried to figure out how we were going sneak out of town and move to the Islands since we had no way to pay anybody anything.

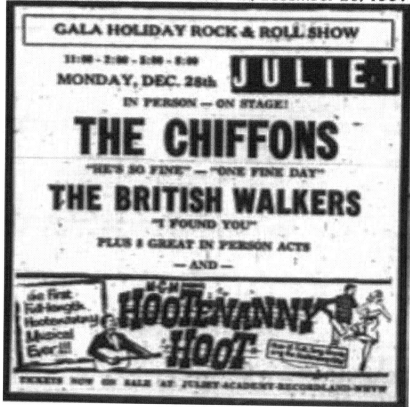

Poughkeepsie Journal - Saturday, December 26, 1964

Following the 5 PM show, Sarge and I gathered up The Chiffons and drove them back to the station in my little Dodge Dart convertible. Sarge interviewed them on the air. I still remember lead singer Judy Craig telling Sarge all about a new record she had just heard and what a gigantic classic it was going to be. She was over the moon for this record. From her lips to God's ears. The record was "You've Lost That Loving Feeling" by The Righteous Brothers.

The station was a 20-minute drive from the theater. But as we neared, we ran into heavy traffic backed up wall-to-wall.

"What the hell is this?" I griped. "Rush hour was over a long time ago." We were still 3 or 4 blocks from the theater.

I looked at Sarge and he looked at me.

"You don't suppose?"

"Move over and drive!" I screamed to Sarge and jumped out of the car and began to run toward the theater.

When I got there I couldn't believe what I was seeing. Traffic was shut down. The streets were filled with kids. The line at the box office was forever. Lenny was standing by the box office trying to control the chaos.

I opened the door of the box office and grabbed the little sign reading "Admission $3.00" and took out the 3 and replaced it with a 4.

"You can't do that," said Box Office Girl.

"Three dollars was in advance. It's $4 day of the show."

"But we charged $3 all day," she grimaced.

"Matinee prices," I grinned.

And so, at four bucks a pop, we sold out the show in minutes. We put a dozen or so ticket buyers in the projection booth. The aisles were lined with kids. If the fire marshal had shown up, we'd have been closed down for sure and, if an actual fire had broken out, everybody would have died.

Lenny and I were in the office where we had a big cardboard box like what wholesale rolls of paper towels come in, but it was filled with mostly one-dollar bills we didn't have time to count. Len had no safe, so we just left the box in the office and locked the door.

Given the acts had done this three times already, this was a very well-rehearsed show. Sarge and Turk had worked out a sort of vaudeville act where Sarge would come out to introduce an act and Turk would come out onto the stage pushing a broom.

Sarge: What are you doing?
Turk: I gotta sweep.
Sarge: No, we gotta show going on here.
Turk: I sweep at this time every day.
Sarge: No, we have a show.
Turk: What kind of show?
Sarge: You know, a music show, where people sing and
          play instruments.
Turk: I sweep better than I sing.
Sarge: No, not you. We have people who sing.
Turk: Either I sweep or I sing. Can I borrow that guitar?
Sarge: No, we have people who sing.

Turk ignores this and picks up the guitar, which had been resting quietly against the curtain, and hands the broom to Sarge, who turns his head to the side and does a perfect Jack Benny. Then the crowd is silent, wondering what the hell is going on, when Turk straps on the guitar, walks up the microphone, throws back his head and does his thing.

"Some people like to Rock, some people like to Roll..."

And the crowd goes absolutely nuts as he launches into his dead-on impression of Elvis. When Sarge introduced The British Walkers, we were stunned by the response. The kids reacted like they were The Beatles, screaming right into and throughout the first song.

Led by me and an usher, The Chiffons came running down the aisle just as we had rehearsed it, the follow spot on them all the way while The Chartbusters, who were the excellent backup band, vamped their hit hook "Dulang, Dulang, Dulang. Dulang-Dulang".

The crowd never stopped screaming. After the show I had a quick meeting with the acts, offered each of them a little bit more money, and added shows at 10 PM and midnight. All the shows sold out and the big cardboard box of money in the office was filled to the top.

"If only one person comes, it's not their fault nobody else came. They deserve the same show if it were a sellout."

For me, ever since that day, Turk's great motivational ad lib has been written in stone. Later on we did two more such shows. For the second we brought back The British Walkers and The Chartbusters and featured The Crystals as our big-time headliner with almost precisely the same result.

The Crystals:
Alan's good friend
Barbara Alston
is on the far right

For the third show we headlined Jimmy Jones, who had two big smashes — his signature 1959 hit "Handyman", later covered by James Taylor and others, and "Good Timin'".

Jimmy Jones
(Photo courtesy
of The Michael
O'Harro
Collection)
Jones died at 82
in 2012

But as it turned out we unknowingly scheduled our show on the same day as IBM (home office in Poughkeepsie) had an open-to-the-public Rock & Roll show scheduled in their corporate auditorium featuring Herman's Hermits, Freddie & The Dreamers, Chad & Jeremy, and The Rolling Stones.

General admission: $1.00.

We got killed.

Sarge and I decided, what with big-time promoters now entering the business with a lot more capital than we had, we'd retire the show idea and just do record hops and outdoor live-music shows at local fast food restaurants.

The Jimmy Jones show was to be our last theater show. Until it wasn't.

Poughkeepsie Journal - Friday May 7, 1965

SPRING SWING SPECTACULAR

RECORD HOP

FEATURING THE FANTASTIC FUN-FILLED

"FUGITIVES"

WITH

LARGE SARGE AND **AL WHITE**

AT

CARROLS DRIVE-IN

DUTCHESS TURNPIKE

TONIGHT — 7:30 P.M.

In the Event of Rain the Hop Will Be Cancelled at 8:00 and Held the Following Friday

17 You Can Never Go Home Anymore

Sarge motioned for me to come into the production studio. "Listen to this and tell me what you think."

I could see the Red Bird label and I suspected it was a new Shangri-Las record. And boy was it ever. Another death record. Moving, emotional, beautifully produced, and just as bubblegum as any of the others.

It was "I Can Never Go Home Anymore".

Producer George "Shadow" Morton had long before turned the girls into actresses as well as singers, especially the lead vocalist, Mary Weiss. On this record she runs away from home, but when she wants to go back, her mother has died.

"And in the end, the angels picked her for a friend, and that's called Sad." Lots of dying strings.

"What do you think?" Sarge asked.

"I think it's a smash, a Top 5 record."

"I do too. You thinking what I'm thinking?" he asked.

"Yeah maybe. If we can get a price on the girls, I can get the theater," I ventured, adding, "Let's call Larry and see."

So we called The Shangri-Las' manager, a fellow named Larry. "$2500. Gotta get $2500 for 'em," says Larry. "The record's a smash." He was practically screaming.

"Are you crazy?" I shouted. "They've been getting $500."

"The record's a smash," Larry repeated.

"What record?" I'm grinning at Sarge. He's grinning back.

"'I Can Never Go Home Anymore'! You guys ain't playing it?" Larry cannot believe it.

"Never got it, Larry," I lied. "It's not on the charts or anything. I mean, send it to us, sure, but anyway we can't afford that. It is a small theater. You know, we thought, maybe $500. So never mind. But do send us the record."

He prattled on for a while, telling us some more about how the record was going to be a monster hit, a million-seller, a #1 record, and how he had to get $2500. And then, never one to lose a gig, he settled for the original $500.

We booked it for 12 weeks in advance, when we figured the record would be hitting its peak. $500. We could make some money at that price. We didn't wait for him to send another record: Our copy went on the air the next morning as our pick hit of the week. One more show starring our favorite gals, The Shangri-Las.

By the time we were four weeks away from the show, the record was huge. Top 10. The Shangri-Las were appearing at a club not too far away from us one Saturday night and I suggested to Sarge we'd better go see them and make sure the date was still good.

"No, no. I gotta get $2500," Larry screamed over the music.

"Larry, we have a deal. $500."

I understood his point, but I was still trying to enforce our original, hard-fought deal. We go back and forth for a while screaming over the music until finally we found a deal both of us could live with, $750.

All three shows sold out.

Poughkeepsie Journal - Friday, November 26, 1965

Wednesday, December 29th at the . . . .

LIVE IN PERSON

The SHANGRI - LAS

PLUS SPECIAL GUEST STARS

★ BILLY CARR   ★ THE JULIETTES   ★ THE BARONS
BIG HIT "WHAT'S COME OVER THIS WORLD"

★ THE MARK IV   ★ THE SCEPTRES   ★ LEWIS & CLARK

★ Direct From Long Island THE NOTATIONS

| 3 SHOWS 2 P.M.—7 P.M. and 9 P.M. | $2.50 IN ADVANCE OR $3.00 AT DOOR | TICKETS AVAILABLE AT RECORDLAND AND JULIET BOXOFFICE |

Only a Limited Number of Tickets are on Sale

18 The Day They Killed the President, Part 2 — The Warren Report

I was pulling a Sunday news shift on September 27, 1964, the day The Warren Commission Report passed over the AP wire. It was a slow news day and so, even as long-winded as it was, I speed-read it in its entirety. I was absolutely astonished: It was complete and total bullshit, revealing absolutely nothing new. Sarge was on the air spinning records when I walked into the DJ booth and told him about it. He asked, "You want to do a special on it?"

"Really? You bet I do. Can we?"

So he called his dad, who handled all the advertising for the largest dairy in the area, and got him to agree to sponsor a special. We did 30 minutes. I read the supposed highlights. It said nothing everybody hadn't already heard. Every section seemed to end with the phrase, "We can find no evidence that...blah, blah, blah."

I still remember my closing: "Apparently The Warren Commission can find no evidence of anything, and this reporter can find no evidence they even tried. This is Alan White for Impact Central News. And now back to the Large Sarge Show."

Still, how curious that this would happen after I had heard the original report of the assassination, before I ever became a broadcaster, right here on this very station. The Warren Report was regarded as factual by the public and the mainstream media alike for a very few weeks, and then cracks began to appear. Soon thereafter the public and the media alike turned on it and began to call it out for what it really was — bullshit.

I remain proud Sarge and I called bullshit on it from the first day it came out.

The Warren Commission with President Lyndon Johnson

The Warren Commission

Earl Warren

Gerald Ford

Richard Russell

John Cooper

John McCloy

Hale Boggs

Allen Dulles

Arlen Specter
(Assistant Counsel)

David Belin
(Assistant Counsel)

J. Frank Wilson of "Last Kiss" fame

19 The Last Kiss

It was a song written about a real-life death, which oddly was surrounded by real-life death.

White, giant-haired James Brown copycat Wayne Cochran, once wrote a song about a girl dying in a car accident, which he based on an actual fatal car accident in Barnesville, Georgia, near where he lived.

The song was one of several teen tragedy songs from that period. Cochran titled the song "Last Kiss" and recorded it with his band, the C.C. Riders, and released it twice, once in 1961 on the Gala label, and again in 1963 on James Brown's label, King Records.

Neither release was a hit.

However, in 1964 "Last Kiss" was covered by Texas singer and recording artist J. Frank Wilson and his band, the Cavaliers. It became a huge hit, beginning in the summer of 1964, reaching #2 on the Billboard Hot 100 and becoming a certified million-seller.

I was doing afternoon drive on WHVW that summer in Poughkeepsie. The Coral Reef Supper Club, located across the river about halfway between Newburg and Kingston, was one of my major sponsors. Coral Reef was in a huge freestanding cinderblock building and was a major nightclub only about 90 miles from New York City. On weekends they featured top-name recording artists. J. Frank Wilson, with his huge hit version of "Last Kiss", was a natural booking.

One Friday afternoon I got an unexpected phone call from the Shangri-Las' manager, Larry, a casual acquaintance. He explained that Wilson had himself been in a car accident, his manager and record producer Sonley Roush had been killed, and country singers Bobby Woods, Jumpin' Gene Simmons ("Haunted House"), and Wilson himself had been badly injured. Larry had taken over management of Wilson and booked him into Coral Reef for the three-day weekend.

"He has a broken leg and he's in a cast but he can still sing and he needs to do this gig," Larry explained. "I'm on the road with The Shangri-Las this weekend and I need someone to go over to Coral Reef and babysit him. Could you possibly do that for me?"

"Sure." And so I did.

Wilson was in a great deal of pain and was day drinking when I got there after my DJ shift late Friday afternoon. He greeted me at his motel room door, drink in hand but in good spirits. Nice guy. I liked him right away. He explained how he was in such pain from his broken leg that he had to be loaded up on booze to move around and do the gig. So I went to a nearby liquor store, bought a couple of bottles of Chivas Regal, and joined him.

I stayed in the twin-bed motel room with him all weekend and we drank hard for 3 days and 2 nights. He wasn't feeling any pain and neither was I. That much liquor and emotional intensity brought us close. I genuinely liked the guy and felt deep sorrow for his circumstance; I was right by his side every second of the time we spent at Coral Reef.

The Coral Reef owner, Neil Lapidus, was a friend of mine. There was no problem with J. Frank being in a cast as long as he could do the shows. He did all the shows, and he was fine. The crowd screamed when he began the opening line of "Last Kiss" —

"Oh, where oh where can my Baby be?"

He sang it like it was just another song. Only it wasn't.

During that 3-day weekend it became clear to me that J. Frank Wilson was deeply haunted by the coincidence of his huge breakthrough hit being a teen tragedy death record about a car accident, and then, just as the record had reached its chart zenith, he was in a fatal car accident himself where his manager was killed and he and his friends were badly injured. He couldn't shake it. Not even for a moment. It was in every breath he took.

It was consuming him.

As we said our goodbyes that Sunday night I wondered if he would ever find a way to be able to deal with all of it, if he would ever be able to shake the liquor which was numbing him and hold himself together. Would our paths ever cross again? Would I discover how he made out?

It turned out, quite coincidentally, that I would.

It would be three years later and would involve "The Killer" himself, the famously alcoholic Jerry Lee Lewis.

20 How You Book Talent

Frank Barsalona *(previous page with Little Stevie Wonder)* was a talent agent from the major NYC talent agency GAC (General Artists Corporation). He left and founded Premier Talent Agency in 1964. His vision was to book Rock & Roll artists the other established agencies were ignoring in favor of the movie, TV, Broadway, and adult music artists they had been booking all along.

That same year I was a Top 40 DJ in Poughkeepsie, New York. As a side business, I booked talent into nightclubs that bought advertising from the station. It quickly came to my attention that Premier Talent Agency was *the* agency that handled Rock & Roll (read Pop music) artists. We did a lot of business throughout the year.

One day during the summer of 1965 I drove into New York to Premier's offices on 57th Street to pick up 8x10 glossies of The Shangri-Las for a show I was promoting. It was late in the day and all of a sudden Frank Barsalona appeared.

Frank said to everybody in general, "Everybody. Into my office. Now. You too," he said, nodding my way. Did he think I worked there? I went into the office anyway and Frank told us this story.

The Motown record and management company always liked to have all their artists signed to different agencies so they could make those agencies compete for the privilege of booking Motown acts.

Premier Talent Agency specialized in British Invasion artists and did not have a Motown act. One day Motown called and asked if Frank would be interested in booking Little Stevie Wonder. Frank was all over it. "How much?"

"We *have* to get $750 a night."

Within 48 hours, Frank had 30 dates booked, all in a row and all routed perfectly from one city to the next and all for $750 a night, for a grand total of $22,500.

Motown was ecstatic. They thanked him profusely. Then they called back.

"You know Frank, we were thinking. If you could get $750 a night for Stevie 30 times in a row, how many times could you get, say, $1000?"

"Aw man, don't do this to me guys. I mean, I've got this all booked. 30 in a row."

"You can call them back."

So he did — and all the dates held, all 30 — at $1000 a night. Again, Motown was ecstatic.

"That's great. You're a genius Frank." And then they were back. "You know, Frank, we were thinking..."

That became 28 dates, at $1500 a night. Motown kept at it. They were relentless. Frank was furious and, at the same time, absolutely determined to keep Stevie Wonder on the Premier roster. Long story short, the tour wound up at 23 dates at $2500 a night for a grand total of $57,500.

When Frank finished the story he stood up. As he rolled down his shirt sleeves to put on his jacket and head home, he said: "And that, gentleman, is how you book talent. Now get the hell out of my office and go sell something."

I only met Frank once more, at an after-work press party about 3 years later, sometime early to mid-1968 when I was a hot, young, very experienced talent agent working at a similar Rock & Roll agency, his biggest competitor, Action Talents.

Somebody introduced us, but he didn't remember me until I reminded him of the Stevie Wonder story.

"And so now you're over there with Betty Sperber stealing my acts. I created a freakin' monster here." He was smiling.

"You stole The Music Explosion from us," I replied truthfully.

"I did, didn't I?" I was glad he was smiling. "Well, you stole The Shangri-Las from us."

"I had them when I was with Paramount Artists."

"Paramount Artists? In D.C.? I heard they only had one agent. That was you?"

"That was me." Now I was the one smiling.

"Wow. How many agents you got over at Action Talents?"

"Right now we're just getting started, so there's just me."

"You're kidding. Just you? Where the hell did Sperber find you? Man, we gotta talk."

But before I could answer, he was pulled away. I never saw or heard from him again.

Frank Barsalona went on to turn his Premier Talent Agency into the largest Rock & Roll theatrical agency in the world. He died in 2012 after a long bout with Alzheimer's disease, at 74.

He was married to the same woman for 46 years.

Alan White is Mr. Disco

21 Disco Dis Way

WHVW sales manager Bill DeCesare and I formed a partnership in 1965. We bought the old rural New York State tavern The White Stag — where I had played with Turk & The Party Cats for so many years — and converted it into a big-city-style nightclub, The Rumpus Room.

It was six or so miles from the Connecticut border, where the drinking age was 21. The drinking age was 18 in New York. A slam dunk.

In 1964 I first learned about the concept of discothèques from the gals at Vassar College. The Vassar gals knew me, both from my time as the drummer for Turk & The Party Cats at The Brass Rail, which packed out with Vassar gals and their boyfriends every weekend, and as the voice of afternoon drive radio at WHVW.

One day a Vassar gal called and asked me to DJ a discothèque dance at Vassar.

"Sure, I'll be happy to do it if you'll tell me what a discothèque dance is."

So she did, explaining in monosyllables that the word discothèque is French and literally means records (discs) being played in a club instead of live bands. A little research informs that the first discothèque anywhere was the Whisky à Go-Go, established in Paris in 1947 by Paul Pacine.

Vassar Girl explained discothèques were huge all over Europe and they had special records recorded just for that purpose. "I don't have that music," I said.

"We do. The girls picked up the music when they were in Europe over the summer," she replied.

So station engineer and DJ Lance Michaels *(above at the WHVW studio board in 1965)* rounded up sound equipment and a couple of turntables, and I DJ'd the dance. As I remember it, the music was sort of Al Green on steroids. R&B, with a very solid groove. As far as I have ever been able to tell, that dance at Vassar College in 1964 was the first discothèque event ever held in America. I have always believed were it not for The Beatles, discothèques would have sprung up worldwide a decade earlier than they did.

Although I always enjoyed doing radio, parts of it were a little boring. You are alone in a small sound booth, away from the madding crowd, sitting, waiting for records you've heard a hundred times to end. Oftentimes, you are the only person in the station. I liked both being around people and playing drums in a nightclub, but I also liked being a DJ. I told Dad that, in a perfect world, I could move my record hop into a nightclub and DJ for the dancers.

Like The Bop Shop…only better. It was the standard in those days for clubs to have two bands.

"No, we don't need two bands," I told Bill DeCesare, my Rumpus Room construction-oriented partner.

"Build me a DJ setup from some old equipment at the station and we'll get us an amplifier and a couple of big speakers. I got this. We'll add the name Discothèque to the advertising. It's a hip new thing in Europe. Trust me."

And so, that's what we did.

Poughkeepsie Journal - Friday, September 3, 1965

We built a DJ setup and bought stage lighting from a theatrical outfit, Times Square Lighting, in Manhattan. We still had a live band, Tommy & The Ones, but I spun records before they went on, during their breaks, and at a late-night chill set after the band had quit.

As it turned out, The Rumpus Room became one of, if not the very first, discothèques in America. Note the date and the word discothèque in the upper-right corner of a 1965 Poughkeepsie Journal ad on the next page.

Poughkeepsie Journal - Friday November 26, 1965

Rock 'n Roll   Discotheque
RUMPUS ROOM
WHERE THE ACTION IS!
SWING WITH
Turk and the Party Cats
WEDNESDAY NITE
•
STUDIO UNIT IV
THURS. - FRI. and SUN. - NITES
•
THE ONES
On Saturday Night
RUMPUS ROOM
Rt. 343   Dover Plains, N. Y.

Around this same time the Whisky a Go-Go, taking its name from Paul Pacine's 1940s Paris club, was doing the same thing in L.A. Although the club billed itself as a discothèque, the Whisky a Go-Go, like The Rumpus Room, featured a live band led by Johnny Rivers, with one of the go-go girls, a scantily-clad dancer known as DJ Rhonda Lane, spinning records from a suspended cage between sets.

Around the same time or slightly later, DJ Jack Alix, from WEAM radio, the highly rated Arlington, Virginia, Top 40 station dominating the Washington, D.C., market at night, was spinning records when The Newports, the house band at The Rocket Room in Washington, were on break. But that was short-lived and they stopped doing it long before I arrived in D.C. in 1966.

Just by coincidence, because I had given up the radio gig and I was DJ'ing the club for a living, and because I was a professional DJ and not a go-go girl, I quite inadvertently became the first professional club DJ in America.

1965. Who knew?

View from The Rumpus Room DJ booth

The Rumpus Room idea began to spread to New York through a club owner friend of mine, Neil Lapidus, who operated a major club called Coral Reef about 90 miles upstate from New York City proper.

He had copied my Rumpus Room idea and, as he was well known in the city, particularly out on Long Island, before long the idea began to spread. Discothèques began springing up all over New York over the next few years. Some early Discos, by coincidence, took up The Bop Shop idea to have a drummer to play along with the records, and although the concept soon faded, it was a cool idea while it lasted.

It wasn't a mad craze. It was just that increasingly bands of the era all thought they were The Beatles and, dressed like overworked farmhands, they wouldn't play hits. People came for hits. These bands played their originals.

In addition, sound amplification was beginning to become an important force and most bands played so loud that glasses shook on top of the bar. Add to this the fact the musicians' union kept pricing bands out of financial viability, and the playing of records in a club began to make both financial and creative sense.

As the originator of The Library chain in Philly, Len Stevens, once told me after I counseled him to go to records, "I fired the band and hired a record player." Thanks to the musicians' union, bands refusing to play hits, ear-shattering guitar volume, and a wardrobe right off the farm, as a consultant I put a lot of clubs into the Disco business.

All through the early years, when I needed a day job, I worked as an IBM machine operator. I even went to IBM school to learn how to wire (program) the various machine accounting devices, printers, calculators, etc. Computers were so new that businesses had to wait a long time to get their units programmed.

One time during this period, 1960-ish, my dad took me to

the defense contractor Pratt & Whitney in Hartford, where he knew people and I saw an early Univac mainframe computer in action. The thing took almost the whole floor, which had been strengthened to handle the increased weight.

The programmers Dad introduced me to wanted me to play chess with it. It had no monitor. They typed in my moves and it printed out its moves. I'm a decent chess player and beat it easily. The computer printed out: "The computer cannot win. The computer will not play." And shut itself off.

The programmers were backslapping and laughing hysterically — it was exactly what they had programmed it to do, but evidently I was the first guy who had beaten it.

It also played music, tinky-tinky-tinky melodies you find on greeting cards, but all quantized into perfect rhythm. To me it was obvious right then and there:

Someday music and computers would merge.

AT&T at that time was sort of the Elon Musk of its day, working on everything futuristic. One of their big projects was making electronics smaller. Televisions of the era were huge but coming down in size every year, just as pretty much everything else was. Anybody involved or around this stuff could see where we were headed. Honestly, it was pretty obvious. I predicted drum machines to my bandleader, Turk Coury, in 1961. He thought I was crazy, but it was not very hard to foresee and, in fact, by the mid-1970s Turk himself was working as a solo act and playing guitar along with a very early drum machine.

Although the true digital age didn't begin until Bill Gates, Steve Jobs, and the Internet, Billboard magazine had a section where they talked about MIDI (Musical Instrument Digital Interface), i.e. a digital music section, as far back as the mid-'70s. MIDI is a protocol designed for recording and playing back music on digital synthesizers and is supported by many makes of personal computer sound cards.

Originally intended to control one keyboard from another, it was quickly adapted to the personal computer.

By 1969 I wound up moving to Philadelphia to go into business with 1960s recording star and former Dovells lead singer Len ("1-2-3") Barry.

LEN BARRY

We were gonna make records. Len was a white Motown-style singer, so I assumed that was the sort of records we would make: White Motown records.

But Len had a slightly different sound in mind. Dance records for clubs, which were beginning to be called Disco records. What Philadelphia Salsoul Disco legend Vince Montana would later famously call Motown in Tuxedos.

The same studio musicians we used, with a very young Daryl Hall *(left, with John Oates)* on a Hammond B3, later became the famed Philadelphia Disco orchestra MFSB, officially standing for "Mother Father Sister Brother" (unofficially Mother Fu*king Soul Brother), a pool of more than thirty studio musicians backing up Harold Melvin & the Blue Notes, The O'Jays, The Stylistics, and The Spinners among others.

Our first Disco record was by Atlanta superstar Grover Mitchell *(right)*, who we discovered during a two-week Len Barry gig at Atlanta's "Kittens Korner" in late 1968. It was a cover of Anthony Newley's hit song "Who Can I Turn To" from the hit Broadway play *The Roar of the Greasepaint, The Smell of Crowd*. It was produced by Len Barry for John Madera Productions and released on United Artists Records in late 1968, one year before the concert at Woodstock.

The arrangements for that record and the follow-up were inspired by Stevie Wonder's classic hit record "For Once In My Life". In Philadelphia, studio talk said that was "getting close" to a record. With "For Once In My Life" you could make an argument that Stevie Wonder created the first Disco hit and didn't even know it.

The follow-up, also by Grover and on United Artists, was a re-cut of Johnnie Ray's classic "Cry". Both were terrific records, but neither was a hit. These days you can find both on YouTube.

Len Barry eventually did catch a hit with the third record, a funky offbeat Disco-like novelty instrumental "Keem-O-Sabe", recorded with essentially the same studio personnel as the previous two; also on United Artists.

Len named the band The Electric Indian.

I didn't know what a discothèque was when we did The Bop Shop. I didn't plan to do a discothèque dance at Vassar in 1964. I didn't plan to call The Rumpus Room a discothèque in 1965. And it wasn't me that planned to make Disco music in Philadelphia.

That was Len Barry. I just happened to be there.

In 1973, after a divorce and a year of almost constant litigation, I sold the management consulting firm I founded and operated and left Philadelphia to go to work with my old pal, the wildly popular major market Top 40 DJ Peter Berry, The Flying Dutchman *(left)*. Dutch was at WFBR radio and was the #1-rated morning man in my old stomping grounds of Baltimore, Maryland.

The deal was, as I had learned in Poughkeepsie, there was more money doing personal appearances in clubs than there was on the air, but it was being on-air that gave you the celebrity to fill up the clubs. And since morning men have to get up at 3 AM to get ready for their show, they find it really hard to do the club appearances that bring in the big bucks.

So what we did was, Dutch would advertise a personal appearance on the air at some venue from 8 to midnight. Then he would show up promptly at 8, give away some promo records, and be gone and headed to bed in ten minutes. I would finish up and DJ the night. Very clever.

And we got away with it.

Dutch and I were really good friends and we had a terrific time doing this for the next year or so, but eventually Dutch got a better job offer in a different city and moved away.

I decided to stay in Baltimore and found a stereo store which had connections in Europe, where they were looking for an American to test out their new mobile DJ board. They arranged for me to buy the first one off the assembly line for the brother-in-law rate as long as I agreed to report on its performance. With an adjoining sound system, the Shure Vocal Master System, I began to book myself into clubs.

The first board didn't perform very well and after I pointed out the various flaws, they came out with a second version. That one worked very nicely. I still have both the second board and the Shure sound system.

I spent most of the mid-'70s DJ'ing in Baltimore and at one point, while gigging there in 1975, somehow got booked on

Maury Povich's *(left)* Washington, D.C., TV talk show *Panorama*, billed as the first Disco DJ. On the same show was a hip British rock journalist named Nik Cohn who had a book called *Rock Dreams*, a collection of reproduced oil paintings of various rock stars for which Cohn had written hip liner notes.

Me and my
first board,
1974

My first mobile DJ setup that I believe was the first all-in-one

The three of us were all roughly the same age and talked about the 1950s, questioning whether it was more like *Happy Days* or the James Dean movie *Rebel Without A Cause*. It was a fun conversation and in the end we agreed that it was probably a little of each. At the end of the segment Maury turned to me and asked, "So Disco is next?"

"Bet the farm," I answered.

Maury turned to Nik Cohn and said, "You know what you ought to do? You ought to rewrite *Rebel Without A Cause* into a Disco movie. We all laughed. Years later, exactly that happened. Cohn indeed did rewrite *Rebel*, not into a movie, but into a short story, *Tribal Rites of the New Saturday Night*, which he sold to New York magazine.

As it turned out Cohn was good friends with Australian talent manager and producer Robert Stigwood who, as it happened, was the manager of the Bee Gees. In a transatlantic phone call with Cohn, Stigwood explained he was looking for a story to make a musical with the Bee Gees and wondered what Cohn had written lately.

"Nothing," said Cohn. "Just a short story for New York magazine."

"Well, send that to me," said Stigwood.

So Cohn did. Upon receipt of the article, Stigwood immediately optioned it and turned it into the movie *Saturday Night Fever*.

It wasn't my idea to write that story, it was Maury's. And I didn't write it, Nik Cohn did. But it is also true that if I had not been booked on that segment, the subject of Disco would never have come up, and *Saturday Night Fever* would never have been written. Disco continued to follow me.

(Following page: Poster from the movie Saturday Night Live. Bee Gees, *lower right. Author Nik Cohn, upper left.)*

By 1977, I was resident DJ and Music Director at Jeryl's, the Powers Ferry Road discothèque, the #1 club in Atlanta throughout the Disco era, fast becoming a virtual legend.

Above:
Jeryl's billboard, 1978,
with (left to right)
Adria, Jack Pepper,
Jeryl Hensley,
and unknown

Left: Alan at Jeryl's in 1978

Jeryl's was located between the two apartment complexes, Sundown and Riverbend, which Penthouse magazine had graciously labeled the two hottest singles apartment complexes in America. Jeryl's was on the first floor of a series of three large office buildings. In the beginning we featured top local radio DJ's at night and, since I talk and basically do a radio show in a club, I DJ'd happy hour when interacting with the crowd was essential. Since the radio DJ's had no idea what music was hot for play in the clubs, I also programmed the music for them at night.

All the music I selected for play at Jeryl's went into a single wooden box organized in order by BPM (beats per minute). The radio guys all played from that box, in whatever order they chose.

When the movie *Saturday Night Fever* came out, I rushed to a matinee, staying to the end to see the music credits, wondering if any of my friends had a writing or production credit. "Based on a short story by Nic Cohn."

What?

Nic Cohn? Without a *K*? Are you kidding me?

Only then did I realize that *Saturday Night Fever* was a dead rewrite of *Rebel* with Travolta in the James Dean role, Donna Pescow playing what was essentially Natalie Wood's part, and the kid who goes off the bridge in the Sal Mineo role.

With an 18-year-old drinking age and no strict DUI enforcement, the monster success of *Saturday Night Fever* turned Jeryl's into standing room only almost every night. We were such a hit that we no longer needed radio DJ's to draw a crowd and, with the exception of Atlanta radio legend Gary McKee, who appeared every Wednesday night throughout the entire run, we got rid of the radio DJ's and I moved to nights. We hired a lovely, bright, upbeat, energy-filled actress/model named Barbara Woods to take over my happy hour show. I trained her to do what I had been doing — a record hop in a club and, as her middle name began with a *J*, she took on the moniker of BJ The DJ.

Barbara "BJ The DJ" Woods, 1978

I got a Gold record for helping to break local singer Alicia Bridges' Disco classic "I Love The Nightlife". I remained as resident DJ and Music Director at Jeryl's for the remainder of the run of the club, and Jeryl's remained the top club in Atlanta throughout the Disco era.

Over my objections and against all my professional advice, Jeryl's went Urban Cowboy and closed soon after. I eventually went back on the road doing some DJ'ing, general business consulting, and other unnamed monkey business.

As I got older, since I knew the music from almost the beginning of the music business, clubs that catered to an older crowd were perfect for me. Atlanta nightclub entrepreneur Johnny Esposito and I rebuilt his earlier Big Band-only club, Johnny's Hideaway, into a club that played the greatest dance music throughout all the years, and again, we often had standing lines, even during the week. Johnny did the promotion, and I designed the music format. It became a legendary club for the over-40 crowd.

Alan and sound engineer Michael Rahn running the weekend bikini contest poolside at Shooters & Bootleggers in Fort Lauderdale in 1984

DJ Alan White,
Johnny Esposito,
and Alan's ex-wife
Miriam Cwietneiwicz
in 1991

Although it is a very different club from what it was when Johnny and I were there, it is there to this day and still packed every weekend, almost 40 years later, though I'm not allowed in there these days. The new owner barred me — the bouncer said "for life" — apparently because I mentioned their name in an Internet conversation about clubs which could automate their music programming on a computer and eliminate a live DJ. That cracked me up. The discussion wasn't even about them. It was about dance music automation, programming, and computers.

Music and computers. Just what I knew would happen.

I put the record-collection filing system on a computer in the early 1980s, and 20 years later the music was on a hard drive, too. These days 100,000 songs fit onto a small computer hard drive. All a DJ has to carry is a computer bag and out pops a party of his mixing.

Old-time beat mixing DJ's of the '70s and '80s often criticize the EDM (Electronic Dance Music) DJ's of today, saying all they do is push buttons. It is sad to hear that from a bunch of old-timers missing their heyday of beat mixing vinyl records together and being pretty blind to the new world of DJ'ing. I feel sorry for those guys.

These days there is a DJ who goes by the name of Deadmau5. He is the top and highest-paid DJ and music producer of the EDM era. How the Deadmau5 show is put together and presented is unbelievably complicated as well as incredibly brilliant. It is so much more than pushing a button. Deadmau5 produces his own music, designs his own multimillion-dollar light show and produces his own tours.

He pushes a zillion buttons.

His real name is Joel Zimmerman *(right),* and he got famous wearing a huge mouse head which cost a million dollars and lights up with a very sophisticated LED technology display.

He is an outspoken, off-the-wall, 24-hour-a-day workaholic mastermind who is that rare combination of musician, songwriter, producer, computer genius, and P.T. Barnum. He works in a multimillion-dollar, two-story cube of high-definition LED screens, constantly flashing a massive digital light show to the music.

He calls Madonna "Grandma" and chastises her for promoting drug use at her show. He doesn't do drugs. He is as

old-fashioned as my youth, smokes incessantly, and reportedly drinks like a fish. Deadmau5 *(left, in costume)* commands hundreds of thousands of dollars per show and his net worth is said to be in the hundreds of millions. What he is doing is ahead of the cutting edge.

Deadmau5 is The Man.
I love this guy.

I love what this Disco dance music has turned into.
Computers, music and lights.
All doing a highly synchronized, digital dance.

I had wandered from The Bop Shop and the computer I beat at chess, to The Rumpus Room and Times Square Lighting, to The Flying Dutchman and Maury Povich and *Saturday Night Fever*, to Jeryl's and Johnny's Hideaway, to a bunch of Atlanta hot spots and then to Nemoe's, a recently-closed hot spot nightclub in the Atlanta suburb of Norcross, Georgia, where I booked the bands, promoted the club, and DJ'd opposite the cover bands.

I didn't plan on making an offhand comment which would eventually turn into *Saturday Night Fever*.
Disco was truly following me. Forget Forrest Gump.
Just call me Forrest Disco.

The Paramount Artists building at 28th and M streets
in Georgetown, circa 1966-1967
(Photo courtesy of Bobby Poe Jr.)

22 Paramount Artists Corporation

Mitch Corday was really Leonard Gentile of Carbondale, Pennsylvania.

Mitch was a highly unusual person in every way one could imagine. He was absolutely a terrific drummer and every band he played with, such as The Chartbusters (the revised Poe Cats with Vernon Sandusky and Big Al Downing), was happy to have him.

When Mitch left The Chartbusters, he and founding Poe Cat and Chartbuster lead singer Bobby Poe started a professional booking agency and talent management company, Paramount Artists Corporation, in Washington.

Back in the '50s, Bobby Poe and the Poe Cats had been the backing band for Rockabilly queen Wanda Jackson on her two big hits "Let's Have A Party" and "Right Or Wrong". One of the first, if not *the* first, interracial Rock & Roll groups in America. In 1965 they had a small hit themselves, "She's The One", with Vernon Sandusky and new musicians under a new name, The Chartbusters.

The Poe Cats, Bobby Poe center, with Wanda Jackson, in about 1958.
In the upper left corner is Vernon Sandusky and next to him
is Big Al Downing. (Photo courtesy of Bobby Poe Jr.)

Bobby Poe & The Poe Cats, circa 1958
Left to right:
Big Al Downing, Vernon Sandusky,
Joe Brawley, and Bobby Poe
(Photo courtesy of Bobby Poe Jr.)

I had known Mitch Corday since my broadcasting school days back in 1964, through his booking of our shows at the Juliet Theater in Poughkeepsie, and in early 1966, with my partner running my discothèque nightclub, The Rumpus Room, in New York State. When he recruited me to come onboard with Paramount Artists in Washington, D.C., as an agent, I accepted the challenge.

Mitch had a thing about names. He always wanted everything to sound like it was something big. Paramount Artists worked. People thought we were somehow connected to the movie studio and/or record company.

Starting at lower left and proceeding in an arc to the right: Vernon Sandusky, Johnny Dubas, Frank Dillon, and Mike "Pokey" Walls

The name of his primary band, The British Walkers, worked too. British Walkers were actually a famous shoe brand. But Mitch dressed the band like The Beatles and people somehow thought they had heard of them as a British band, a part of the British Invasion. We booked them for big bucks.

Same with The Chartbusters, which was a popular radio station and music business term for a hit record. And maybe the best of all was Little Willie & The Hand Jives, fronted by Big Al Downing's younger brother, the high-energy, piano-playing Don Downing.

Our publicity flyers said: "Hear Little Willie & The Hand Jives perform *the* big hit *Little Willie & The Hand Jive*." Not *their* big hit, mind you, **the** big hit. The actual hit record was by The Johnny Otis Show. We booked Little Willie & The Hand Jives for good money too.

Don Downing,
aka Little Willie
(Photo courtesy of
The Michael O'Harro
Collection)

Once, at Georgetown club The Roundtable, we had a four-piece band called The Counts Four. When Texas recording artists Count Five caught their hit "Psychotic Reaction", we added a sax player and put a sign in the window which said "Hear The Counts Five sing '*the*' big hit Psychotic Reaction."

Mitch had a band called The Surf Boys for a minute; we once got an offer of $5000 from a promoter for them to do a show in Manila. As the promoter obviously thought he was booking The Beach Boys, for me it was a bridge too far.

I wouldn't book the date.

Mitch said, "Fine, I'll book it."

But he never did.

Mitch Corday had kind of an interesting language all his own. Instead of saying "talk to someone" he'd say "say your words", as in "call The Shangri-Las and say your words." He once told one of the musicians in The Chartbusters: "You can't be a Rock Star with short hairs."

Mitch Corday and his
girlfriend, our secretary
Linda, in 1966
(Photo courtesy
of Frank Dillon)

Mitch didn't drink at all and Bobby Poe didn't drink much. They both worked hard, but they never really worked smart. Chartbusters lead guitarist Vernon Sandusky carried Bobby who, as band manager, got an equal share of The Chartbusters' gigs even though he wasn't in the band any longer. Bobby's role was on the management and recording side, and he was always trying to figure out how to get that one big hit record deal which, sadly, he never did.

Other than Jack Boyle at The Crazy Horse in Georgetown and Riley Carter at The Roundtable, with whom Bobby and Mitch had solid relationships, even locally I managed the booking end of Paramount with places like The Rabbit's Foot, and the Bombstein Brothers' wildly popular Rocket Room, and for the gigantic roving singles club called JOPA (Junior Officers and Professional Men's Association).

I booked all of the road gigs, clubs, colleges, concerts, and private events, and had recording star contacts from my days in radio. When I found out all the big New York agencies were dropping these artists as soon as their record fell off the charts, I started signing and booking national acts like The Shangri-Las, Len Barry, Dee Dee Sharp, Jimmy Jones, Bobby Lewis and The Kalin Twins, among others, in direct competition with the only other agency booking them, industry leader Premier Talent in New York. I set up big Jerry Lee Lewis and Shangri-Las tours. It was my thing. I have always been able to sell just about anything of value. Mitch concentrated on managing his pet act, The British Walkers.

The original British Walkers: Roy Buchanan (white guitar), Bobby Howard (far right) (Photo courtesy of Bobby Poe Jr.)

It was through The British Walkers I met Mitch Corday. The British Walkers were a terrific British Invasion-style band from Washington, D.C., and the surrounding Virginia area that Sarge and I booked for our first Rock & Roll theater show when I was a DJ at WHVW in Poughkeepsie a couple of years earlier. The original British Walkers had white R&B sensation

Bobby Howard singing lead. He was tall and handsome and dressed like a Beatle. He looked the part.

He was from Virginia and had a thick Southern accent but learned how to say *'ello luv* in the most British Liverpool way and, other than singing, that was all he ever said on the microphone. Smart man.

They had the man Eric Clapton has called the world's greatest guitar player, Roy Buchanan, on lead guitar. Buchanan and Howard had written their first recording, the song "I Found You", which we played to death on WHVW and, with the help of Joey Reynolds at WKBW in Buffalo, made into a regional hit.

The original British Walkers were a sensational band.

Mitch set up Paramount Artists by basically stealing the client list and contact information from famous Philadelphia booking agent Norman Joyce's card file systems. But even with the contacts, clever as he was, Mitch was a terrible agent. He could sell it as well as anyone, but it took him a week to make a single booking call and "say his words".

Other than The Chartbusters, the only thing Paramount ever had that was truly special was The British Walkers. And even then, only the original band with Bobby Howard and Roy Buchanan. When Howard and Buchanan left, Mitch replaced them with other talented musicians, but it was never the same. All the other versions of the band with American musicians were okay musically but were never *special*.

Mitch had gone over to England and lived there for almost one year while he looked for legitimately British members for the band. He brought them back. I could not book them because they paled in comparison to the originals.

During my two years at Paramount, I learned what it was to be a theatrical agent, made a decent living and, in a pre-computer-age town where gals pretty much staffed the government and outnumbered men 30 to 1, I had a lot of fun.

Alan at
Paramount
Artists, 1966
(Photo courtesy of
Frank Dillon)

Eventually Bobby Poe got tired of being poor and started a R&B record tip sheet, the Soul Music Survey. It was very successful almost immediately, but pretty soon the Black Mafia came to him at Paramount's Georgetown office demanding protection in the amount of $1000 a week, sent to a post office box in New York.

Bobby ignored them.

When they came back, it just so happened Bobby was out of the office, so they beat up and almost killed Mitch Corday, who had absolutely nothing to do with the Soul Music Survey. They broke both of his legs and he spent months in the hospital. Mitch was always very paranoid and that attack just made it worse. One day after he got out of the hospital, Mitch Corday just up and left Washington, without saying a word to anyone, and Bobby Poe never saw or spoke to him again. I heard through a writer, who had called me for some Roy Buchanan stories for a book he was working on, that Mitch eventually owned a used car lot in upstate New York.

Mitch and I were never particularly friends, but he was clever, he hired me, and I respected him. Oddly, I learned a lot from him about what is possible. Mitch Corday believed that if you were clever enough, with enough hard work, anything could be done. Although he never did get what he really wanted, which was big hit records so all the young girls would fall at his feet, he did accomplish some amazing things. I've always agreed with him: With enough hard work, anything can be done.

I still carry that attitude with me to this day.

Eventually, based on all the name artists I had signed and booked at Paramount, I got recruited to Action Talents in New York City, a startup booking agency led by Betty Sperber that was part of Buddah Records and ready to take on Rock & Roll booking industry leader Premier Talent.

Bobby sold the Soul Music Survey to the Black Mafia for pennies, started a different tip sheet, the Pop Music Survey, which was very, very successful almost at once and, finally, Bobby got rich.

During my Washington years, from sometime in early 1966 until very late 1967, Mitch Corday and Bobby Poe were major professional forces in the D.C. music scene and beyond.

I was to run into Bobby again in the mid-'80s at one of his gigantically successful Pop Music Survey conventions at a major hotel by the airport in Atlanta. He blew off the heavy convention admission and made me his guest. I had an amazing and most interesting time.

I got a letter to him shortly before he died. He was too sick to read himself, so it was read to him by his son. He sent word through his son that he was happy to hear from me.

Bobby Poe died of throat cancer on January 22, 2011.

Mitch Corday died of cancer sometime around 2005.

The Chartbusters' leader, Vernon Sandusky, 80, went on to play guitar for Roy Clark for the next 20 years and was eventually inducted into the Oklahoma Music Hall Of Fame. He has nine children, all girls, and lives in Edna, Kansas.

Much respect to these guys.

Mad About Music billboard ad, 1974

23 Poverty Sucks

When I first started working for Paramount Artists Corporation as a booking agent in 1966, the first person I met was a tall, darkly handsome playboy-type fellow named Michael O'Harro. I was 25. He was maybe a year or two older.

Michael O'Harro was an unusual person. He was both brilliant and a total hustler with a capital H. A triple-A personality. He had a white-hot flash temper, but it totally cooled in a matter of mere seconds every time it exploded.

He worked all the time, mixing dating beautiful women in with his business, which was, as it turned out, partying with and dating beautiful women.

There was a very Hugh Hefner aura about Michael and although Mike was the pretty boy, he and Hefner even looked a bit alike. Unlike Hefner, however, who liked to live in a mansion, when I knew him Mike lived in a rented room. But he drove a beautiful, brand new Corvette.

It had all started for him while he was still a junior officer in the Navy and decided it would be a good idea to throw a big ol' party as a way to meet girls. As he put the party together, he sat down to figure out how much money he should charge in order to cover his expenses: Pay for the hall, the entertainment, the food, and the booze.

But he figured all wrong.

When it was over he found he had not only covered expenses, he had a very handsome profit. So, not being a complete idiot, he jumped on the idea and ran a bunch more parties the whole rest of the time he was in the Navy and, in doing so, made beaucoup bucks.

When he got out of the service, Mike met his future partner, another Navy veteran named Jim Desmond.

Desmond *(below, right)* was a pirate-looking fellow, roguishly good looking, with a patch over one eye. He was quiet and friendly, an unassuming Type B personality, the polar opposite of O'Harro *(below, left)*.

With Jim Desmond as his partner, Mike started a sort of roving party club for singles 18 to 25, which they called the Junior Officers and Professionals Association, or JOPA.

Guys were supposed to be Junior Officers in the military or college graduates. Girls just had to be 18.

Michael O'Harro, Jim Desmond, and the JOPA office staff, circa 1966

They charged $3 to get into their parties. Draft beer was free. Memberships were also $3, but just for the men the first time they came; memberships were free for the gals all the time. In 1966 Washington, D.C., government paperwork was handled by humans, almost always female, who did the clerical work. As a result, women outnumbered men in the town by something like 30 to 1. For guys, that ratio was like a license to steal, and JOPA was the bank.

By 1966, when I got there, JOPA had 30,000 members.

One of the primary reasons for the success of JOPA was that Mike promoted a wide variety of events and parties. He constantly held them at interesting new venues. One party I booked was a six-hour JOPA cruise on the S.S. Potomac, with 1,100 single party people and Little Willie & The Hand Jives booked as the band.

S.S. Potomac JOPA Party

Little Willie (Don Downing)

Mike promoted Tuesday, Friday, and Sunday parties. Occasionally there were parties and events on other nights.

A typical JOPA party

The only regular party was held every Sunday night at the famous Bayou Club. The Bayou was a hugely successful club located down by the river in Georgetown, where a popular band, The Telstars, held forth.

Although The Telstars occasionally played the Sunday night JOPA parties, Sunday was their regular night off, so routinely I booked The British Walkers, The Chartbusters, and occasionally The Newports *(left)* for the Sunday night JOPA events.

On Sunday nights in Washington, D.C., in 1966 and 1967, everybody who was anybody went to JOPA.

The Bayou Club probably held about 400, maybe a bit more, but most other events were held in ballrooms of large hotels. Attendance was often in the thousands.

For the next two years I became Michael O'Harro's personal booking agent, booking most, if not all, of the bands and the many recording artists for his events.

The Shangri-Las at JOPA

Alan gives
Dee Dee Sharp
last-minute
instructions
at a JOPA party

Alan gets some inspiration from girlfriend
Dana Perrone at a JOPA party in 1967

For a JOPA anniversary party, I booked The Coasters. Mike agreed to pay their asking price of $750.

If I remember the numbers correctly, we had 5000 people at $5 a head in a gigantic ballroom in a Marriott hotel across the river in Virginia. The Coasters looked out at the crowd and did the math. They were furious. From then on, whenever I booked them, I changed my name and used an alias.

Michael O'Harro, along with Jim Desmond, had literally, singlehandedly, invented roving singles clubs.

Today these singles clubs are known as meetup groups.

The Coasters perform at a JOPA event

As time moved along, Mike expanded his enterprise into two clubs, both of which he named The Gentleman II. The first Gentleman II was at the corner of 18th and M streets in Washington, and the second was on Charles Street in my old stomping grounds of Baltimore, Maryland. As far as anyone knows, these were the first two bars in America to be referred to as singles bars.

He eventually bought and operated a club in the seaside resort of Rehoboth Beach, Delaware, where fresh from a romantic breakup, I spent a lot of time, drank a lot of booze, and did a lot of sulking. Mike graciously supported my whinefest through that dark little period.

I left Washington at the end of 1967 and moved to New York to work at Action Talents. I didn't see my friend Michael O'Harro for a number of years.

In 1974 I found myself in Baltimore DJ'ing in clubs, paying the bills, and having a blast. I had a partner, a gal named Bonnie Frazier. Bonnie was a hot blonde who ran the board and engineered the records while I picked out the tunes and ran my mouth. Bonnie was maybe 5′ 10″ and strong and willing enough to help me move equipment in and out of venues. We were having some serious fun.

One club we were interested in booking in particular was an Emerson's Steakhouse, located on Charles Street in downtown Baltimore. When I called to find out who was in charge of entertainment, I was stunned to find out it was my old friend Michael O'Harro.

"I got this," I told Bonnie.

"You know this guy?" Bonnie was clearly impressed.

"Yep. Old friend of mine. Real good guy."

Talk about coincidence.

Only then did I realize this Emerson's Steakhouse Charles Street location was nothing other than the old Gentleman II venue, totally reimagined, redesigned, and remodeled. It was the very same club where I had met Dee Dee Sharp's mom [see Chapter 30] and talked Chuck Berry into releasing "My Ding-A-Ling" as a single.

Small world.

I called Mike, and he and I and Bonnie met for dinner. He told us how he had sold all his assets, including The Gentleman II (which he had sold to Emerson's) and how he had gone into semi-retirement, if only temporarily, living the high life in Spain.

Now he was back in the game and acting as a consultant with Emerson's. Since he had been living abroad he had been almost completely out of touch, and although he had learned a bit about Disco as he traveled, he still had a lot to learn, so much of the dinner involved explaining what was going on with Disco, and just bringing him up to date on the state of the music scene generally.

He graciously booked us into Emerson's for happy hour, which was what I wanted, and at the money I requested.

I immediately saddled up and worked out a promotion whereby the Mayor of Baltimore, William Donald Schaefer, would come down and give me a proclamation naming me the "Evening Mayor Of Baltimore." *(Below, Bonnie Frazier cues a record as Alan receives the honor.)*

Local television covered the event, Emerson's began to do lots of business after work at happy hour, and everything was just peachy keen. Until it wasn't. I couldn't get money from Emerson's. After screwing around with them unsuccessfully, I called Mike. I was furious.

"There is a snake in this woodpile," I said to Mike. "Something is wrong here. They keep jerking me around."

He didn't think so, and was furious I was furious, but being the class act he is, he got me my money and I moved along. I don't know all the details, but as it turned out I was pretty much right.

A year or two later, the Emerson's president, John R. Radnay, and ex-executive vice president, Eli Levi, were accused of double billing and stealing the company blind. Radnay was sentenced to four months in a federal prison for filing false reports with the Securities and Exchange Commission.

But before that Baltimore Emerson's location closed, with Mike still advising them as a consultant, Emerson's turned it into a Disco, named Dimples.

In early 1975, Mike left Emerson's/Dimples. Later in the year, he opened a different Disco, TRAMPS, at the corner of Prospect and Wisconsin avenues in Washington, D.C. It quickly became one of America's most successful Discos, sometimes called the first Disco in America, but that is wrong by a decade because by then Discos were everywhere. There was even one in a Baltimore suburb! Jumping into the Disco scene, Studio 54 would not be built until late in 1977. TRAMPS was already going strong.

Beautifully designed and professionally operated as only Michael O'Harro could do it, TRAMPS was finished, successful, and already operating in a major American city.

So it stood out.

I don't know if Michael himself ever promoted TRAMPS as the first Disco in America, but I'll bet he didn't do anything to discourage the idea.

As it turned out, even though Disco had been around for years, by 1975 it hadn't even blown up yet. It would take a popular-culture shot in the arm in the form of the movie *Saturday Night Fever* to propel Disco as big as Elvis and The Beatles. On December 16, 1977, the movie was released to theaters everywhere, becoming an overnight sensation and suddenly making slinky shiny retro clothing *de rigueur* in many a woman's closet.

In 1983, as Disco began to fade, Michael and longtime partner Jim Desmond struck again, this time opening the first

Champions Sports Bar, once again in Washington. It was considered to be the first sports bar concept in America. By the time Michael sold the company there were 24 locations.

Michael is an honorary member of the National Football League Players Association, the first non-player ever to be given this status. He has donated $250,000 worth of memorabilia to the Smithsonian Air & Space Museum.

Michael is also founder of the International Discothèque Association which, I am proud to say, honored me with a lifetime achievement award.

JOPA is considered to be the first independent, roving singles club in America. The Gentleman II is considered to be the first singles bar in America. TRAMPS is considered to be one of the premier Discos of the entire era. Champions is considered to be the first sports bar in America.

Michael, who never married, is retired, this time for good, and living happily in his beautiful home in suburban Virginia.

He is still best friends with Jim Desmond.

Michael O'Harro did it his way, and he did it right. Because, as he knew all along, poverty sucks.

Next page: This vintage print-on-paper poster features Michael standing next to a Bentley as he gives his opinion about poverty. Next to Farrah Fawcett's famous poster, Poverty Sucks became the biggest-selling poster in American history.

(Previous photos in this chapter courtesy of The Michael O'Harro Collection, except for the picture of Alan White, which is from the author's personal archives)

24 The Guitar Player

Eric Clapton once said he thought Roy Buchanan *(previous page)* was the greatest guitar player in the world. Jeff Beck was a huge fan. So was I. Don't get me wrong. Roy Buchanan was batshit crazy. At the same time, he could be a really nice guy and was always totally confident of what he could do with a guitar: Absolute magic.

I always liked the guy. I first heard Roy as the lead guitar player in the Washington, D.C.-based band The British Walkers, and booked the band for a show with The Chiffons. You read that story in Chapter 21.

Anyway, several years later I went to work as an agent for the company from whom I had booked that show package, the well-established Paramount Artists Corporation, in Washington. The British Walkers, personnel-wise, were still intact and one of the top bands on our roster.

I was in the office working at my desk when it went down, but the story came back to us in the office almost immediately. Apparently when the driver went across the river to Virginia to pick up Roy at his apartment for a British Walkers tour, he found the door open. When he went inside, he saw Roy with a bow and arrow in his hand, Roy's wife looking horrified, and a fellow with an arrow straight through his shoulder sticking out the other side.

Roy was busy loading up another arrow.

The driver immediately disarmed Roy, removed the arrow from the poor guy's shoulder and stopped the bleeding, then got Roy the hell out of there, into the station wagon, back across the river, and quickly out of town. My boss, Mitch Corday, went over immediately, paid the injured guy a bunch of money, and made the whole thing go away. Let's just say Roy could be a bit impulsive.

After a time Roy left The British Walkers and went to work for The Kalin Twins, who had been making a fine living from their huge 1958 #1 hit record "When".

The Kalin Twins,
Hal and Herbie
(Photo courtesy of
The Michael O'Harro
Collection)

We had them booked into one of Washington's top clubs, The Rocket Room. As part of the act, Roy would open the show by coming out onto the middle of the dance floor, standing in the middle of a solitary white spotlight, and playing the famous Spanish guitar folk song "Malagueña" but using only his left hand. It was an astonishing, dazzling piece of showmanship, which never failed to bring down the house.

On one occasion, I happened to be downstairs under the club where the bands and others gathered when they weren't upstairs playing. I saw Roy and walked up to him and said, "Man, that was incredible."

"Think so?"

"I do."

He picked up an acoustic hollow-body guitar and began to play "Malagueña" with both hands. Everything stopped. The other band members, the groupies who had gathered, the hangers-on — everybody went silent. It got so quiet the Bombstein Brothers, Joe and Sanford, came out of their offices because they thought something was wrong. When he finished there was a huge round of applause.

He put down the guitar, looked at me and asked with a smile, "How old are you?"

"Twenty-six," I said. I was two years younger than him.

"Well, you have a lot to learn if you want to be a great agent. What I did upstairs? That was flashy." A smile. "What I just did? That was incredible." Another smile. "And if you want to be a great agent, you need to learn the difference."

To this day, every time I hear singers or musicians — well-known or not — get flashy by screeching or playing ninety miles an hour, I remember what Roy Buchanan said about the difference between the flash and the bang.

Following his arrest for public intoxication, and after another alleged domestic dispute, Roy Buchanan was found hanged from his own shirt in a jail cell in Fairfax County, Virginia, August 14, 1988. He was 48.

His cause of death was officially recorded as suicide, a finding disputed by Buchanan's friends and family, and by one of his close friends, Marc Fisher, who reported seeing Roy's body with bruises on his head.

The case was never re-opened.

25 Hooked On A Feeling

Driving back to Washington, D.C., one Sunday night during the early summer of 1966 after spending the weekend at The Rumpus Room, my boss at Paramount Artists asked me to stop by a club in Newberg, New York, and pick up commissions from our band, The Chartbusters, who had been on the road for months and owed us mucho casho.

When I got to the club a kid named BJ Thomas *(previous page)* with a huge hit record "I'm So Lonesome I Could Cry" was appearing there along with The Chartbusters.

Although the record was a huge Pop hit, it was a cover of a Hank Williams Country classic. BJ Thomas was clearly a pure Country music artist and maybe a bit out of place in this normally Rock & Roll dance club.

Fortunately for BJ, the sensational lead guitar player and leader of The Chartbusters, Vernon Sandusky, was also a pure Country musician out of Oklahoma. According to reports, that afternoon's rehearsal had gone beautifully.

The Chartbusters were a great band musically, and BJ's backing was going to be perfect. In the dressing room it was decided The Chartbusters would do two songs and then bring on BJ. The Chartbusters went on as scheduled and I waited in the dressing room with BJ, who was nervous and relentlessly pacing. It was driving me a little nuts.

"Calm down man, you got this," I said, encouragingly. "You sing great. You have a great voice."

"I know," he replied. "It ain't the singing. I don't know what to say to these folks."

"Alright, listen. Here's what you do…" I proceeded to give him some good advice about talking.

I watched from the side of the stage as BJ said, "Good evening, ladies and gentlemen. My name is BJ Thomas and I sing a whole lot better than I talk, so if you don't mind, I'm just gonna sing for you tonight."

He opened with his hit "I'm So Lonesome I Could Cry" and the crowd went crazy. BJ sang mostly Country to them for an hour, totally enthralling the normally Rock & Roll crowd. After the show BJ shook my hand and said, "Thanks man, that was some of the best advice I ever got."

Many years later, Len Barry and I went to the Philadelphia Main Line to some big 'ol Folk Rock club where BJ was headlining. We visited with him in his dressing room and talked about how his hit, "Raindrops Keep Falling On My Head", from the movie *Butch Cassidy & The Sundance Kid*, was supposed to be a Len Barry song, approved by Burt Bacharach and the movie producers, and how it got sidetracked to BJ.

There were never any hard feelings between BJ and Len. They had toured together back in the day and were good friends, so the conversation was friendly and direct.

BJ told us how he sometimes wished he never had "Raindrops" because it led him to Vegas and all those Vegas people, and the drugs and hookers and such.

And then it was time for BJ to go on and for us to leave. Len said, "Have a good show BJ, it was great to see you. But Alan and I gotta book. Lots of stops tonight."

And there was handshaking and hugging and the like, but before we made our way to the front door, BJ said, "Hey man, hang in there for a minute and watch the beginning of the show. There's something I want Alan to see."

So we went to the front door and stopped. As we stood at the front of the house watching, BJ was introduced, came out with a big smile and a wave to the crowd and said with a huge grin, pointing directly at me:

"Good evening, ladies and gentlemen. My name is BJ Thomas and I sing a whole lot better than I talk, so if you don't mind, I'm just gonna sing for you tonight."

He threw back his head and laughed.

And so did I, pointing right back at him.

"What was that all about?" Len asked.

"Nothing. Just something from many years ago."

"Hmmm. You know, for the first time tonight, I wished we had gotten 'Raindrops'."

"Yeah, me too. We'd have made a lot of money."

"Yeah, that too." Len grinned. "But I was thinking more about how much better you and me would've handled the drugs and the hookers."

BJ, born in 1942, married singer/songwriter Gloria Richardson in 1968. They had three daughters. Drugs and alcohol nearly ended his marriage and his life. He became a Christian. He's been dominating Gospel music for years. According to reports, BJ has been clean and sober since 1976.

Sometimes, singing ain't everything.

Bobby Hebb in 1967 at a JOPA event
(Photo courtesy of The Michael O'Harro Collection)

26 A Sunny Night

I first saw Bobby Hebb at what was then called District of Columbia Stadium on Monday night, August 15th, 1966, when, along with The Ronettes, he opened for The Beatles. Tickets ranged in price from $3 to $5. The stadium, in 1969 renamed Robert F. Kennedy Memorial Stadium, appeared to be a near sellout of its 50,000 seats.

At the time, Bobby's classic hit "Sunny" charted higher than any Beatles record on the Billboard Hot 100. He was 28 years old. Because of the screaming females, nobody could hear The Beatles. The sound system itself was fine and when Bobby sang "Sunny", he was terrific.

Based on that, a year or so later I booked him for a Friday and Saturday night gig at The Rabbit's Foot out on Wisconsin Avenue in suburban Washington, D.C.

The owner of The Rabbit's Foot, Fred, was a friend and very good client of mine. I had gotten him a good price and, as I had every reason to expect the gig would go well without my presence, I was off doing other business that Friday night.

It was a disaster. Hebb did only original material. The crowd hated him. Fred wanted to cancel Saturday night.

I needed to talk to Hebb…and fast.

So Saturday morning I drove over to the Holiday Inn and knocked on his door. He answered and came outside. I introduced myself as the guy who had booked him for The Rabbit's Foot gig.

I expected flak from an egocentric Pop star, but he couldn't have been nicer. We talked outside his room for a few minutes and he said he understood the issue and promised to do cover songs the crowd already knew.

I suggested he open and close with "Sunny", his big hit.

Apparently nobody had suggested that to him before and he agreed immediately, saying he thought it was a terrific idea. I said I'd see him at the club. And he killed it. He played guitar, opened and closed each show with "Sunny", and every song he played was a big hit the crowd already knew.

He even played some amazing rhythm thing on spoons held between his fingers. The crowd loved him.

After the gig we got to talking about songs and he said he never had any idea which song would be a hit and which song wouldn't. He wanted me to come back to his hotel, listen to a bunch of songs he had written, and use my Top 40 ears to help him figure out which songs would be good singles.

Bobby already had a big background in his hometown of Nashville. He performed on a TV show hosted by Country record producer Owen Bradley, played his spoons thing and other instruments in Roy Acuff's band, sang backup on Bo Diddley's "Diddley Daddy", played trumpet in the U.S. Navy Band Commodores (the Navy's premier Jazz ensemble), and replaced Mickey Baker in Mickey and Sylvia, who had a huge hit with "Love Is Strange".

But evidently no one had ever sat down with him and talked about his songs in terms of radio and hit-making potential. When we got back to the hotel I met his new, young, and white wife. She wasn't particularly pretty, but she was his biggest booster — in this case to a fault. So we sat there for hours and hours and I heard all or part of over 100 songs. As we went along, Wifey pronounced each of them hits, but the truth is there was not a hit single among them.

So we talked about hooks, what exactly they were and how to write them. Bobby was concerned he'd never write another hit as big as "Sunny".

We went out on to the patio, away from Wifey, where we could talk honestly. I told him I didn't think there was a big hit single in the bunch. My advice was to not worry about what would be a hit and what wouldn't be while he was writing.

All the songs I heard were good, well-crafted songs; they just didn't have the hook that would make them hits.

"Just keep writing," I told him. "If it takes 100 songs to get one 'Sunny', so be it. And if there is never another 'Sunny', so be that too."

A hit that big, a song that good, can be a once-in-a-lifetime thing, like a 9th inning walk-off grand slam home run. But it doesn't diminish any of the other home runs a fellow may have hit.

Bobby appreciated the honesty he apparently hadn't gotten anywhere else. If you get a hit as big as "Sunny" you will inevitably be surrounded by yes-men and women, and in his case, there was none bigger than Wifey.

Our paths never crossed again after we parted ways that early Sunday morning, but for years thereafter I wondered how he was faring.

So many artists who have one hit record as big as "Sunny" struggle and become self-destructive trying to chase and re-create that gigantic hit. With Bobby Hebb, that apparently didn't happen. Although he himself never had another big hit record, Bobby, along with comedian Sandy Baron, wrote "A Natural Man", the song which propelled Lou Rawls to the 1971 Grammy Award for Best Male R&B Vocal Performance.

In 1999, BMI listed "Sunny" as #25 on its list of the Top 100 Songs of the Century.

Bobby Hebb continued to live in his hometown of Nashville, Tennessee, until his death on October 3, 2010, at 72, while undergoing treatment for lung cancer at Nashville's TriStar Centennial Medical Center.

27 The Leaders of the Pack

There were always four Shangri-Las. Two sets of sisters, Mary and Elisabeth (Betty) Weiss, and identical twins Mary Ann and Marge Ganser. The group, all teens, was formed in Queens in 1963 and took their name from a local restaurant.

The Shangri-Las *(previous page)* hit the charts on September 5, 1964, with "Remember (Walking In The Sand)", written and produced by a then-unknown George "Shadow" Morton. The original demo, with an unknown piano player named Billy Joel, was over 7 minutes long. Morton faded the commercial release at just over 2 minutes.

Morton's recordings often featured lavish productions with complicated orchestrations and occasionally the use of sound effects. "Leader of the Pack", The Shangri-Las' next hit, landed on the charts in late October of the same year. It ended with roaring motorcycles and breaking glass.

"Leader of the Pack" was one of many teenage "death records" which were popular in the era and went to #1 on the Billboard Hot 100. It was their biggest hit, selling over one million records.

In producing The Shangri-Las, Morton went well beyond Mary's incredible lead voice. He basically turned the girls into actresses for many of their recordings by adding spoken bits and pieces. The Shangri-Las appeared as a full quartet when "Remember (Walking In The Sand)" came out, but late in 1964 Betty took a leave of absence to have a baby girl, leaving the group as a trio for a time.

During the time Betty was having the baby, promotional pictures caused a lot of fans to remember the group as only being a trio. But that was never the case...not really. No matter how they toured or appeared for live shows, The Shangri-Las always considered themselves to be a quartet, the same four lovely kids from Queens.

Betty rejoined them in mid-1965 and the group appeared briefly as a quartet until the start of 1966, when Mary Ann and Marge left at different times, alternately replacing the other. From then on, for live Shangri-Las shows they performed only as a trio.

Around 1967, the lovely blonde lead singer Mary Weiss got nodes on her vocal cords and had to have an operation to have them removed. She had to drop out of the group for a while, but they had lots of dates already booked. Their manager, Larry, called and told me not to worry. Her sister, Betty, was going to wear a blonde wig identical to Mary's famous long blonde hair, take Mary's part as lead vocalist, and Mary Ann (who had left the group due to health issues of her own) would come back to fill out the trio.

I didn't believe it would work so I went to the first gig, a Sunday night show I booked for them at a club in Frederick, Maryland. It was absolutely unbelievable!

I knew them well yet I could barely tell. With the blonde wig, Betty looked exactly like Mary. In taking over the lead vocals, she sounded exactly like Mary too. She had done this before in the studio, although not on any of their biggest hits.

I couldn't believe it.

No one ever knew, not the audiences, not the club owners and really, as far as I know, not anybody. They covered every single date I booked for them as the trio of Betty, Mary Ann, and Marge. I've never seen that reported and, as the girls always kept to themselves on the road, I don't think *anybody* ever knew Betty performed as her sister Mary.

Alan and
The Shangri-Las
around 1966
(left to right)
Betty Weiss,
Mary Weiss,
and Marge Ganser

Their bad-girl image was a marketing myth.

It came mostly from "Leader of the Pack", the fact that the girls came from a tough neighborhood in Queens, and from the kind of outfits they wore when performing. Mary has been quoted as saying the bad-girl image helped push back other musicians from hitting on them on the road.

In reality, from my experience with them, while they were four nice, sweet, lovely teenage girls, and while the bad-girl image was far from the truth, at the same time, when on the road they traveled alone and could take care of themselves.

Mary, who carried the cash while touring, once got into a bit of trouble for buying a gun for protection. While hook-ups on the road were and still are commonplace, that was never the case with The Shangri-Las: The girls kept their own company. To my knowledge, and as Mary has said publicly, they never dated any of the musicians, or anybody else they met on the road.

Sarge and I had promoted shows with them in 1965 and we both knew them and their manager, Larry, fairly well. When I went to work at Paramount Artists, I called Larry and, since The Shangri-Las had fallen off the charts and no one else was booking them regularly, I signed the act and became their booking agent from 1966 through the end of 1967.

They were just kids and often acted like it. They were fun to be around. Sometimes when I'd book a gig Mary would call the office and ask how late television was on wherever the gig was. If it signed off at 11 or even 12 PM, which many stations did, especially in smaller markets, Mary was less than thrilled.

I once booked the girls on a 30-day tour of Kansas. Yep, that's what I said, Kansas. Thirty consecutive days for $1000 a night. $30,000 with no days off, all inside the state of Kansas. Mary was not a happy camper.

"Do they even have television in Kansas?" she asked.

"Maybe," I answered.

They did the tour in a station wagon, the three girls (Mary, Betty, and Marge), a guitar player (Jerry, who also used to play with Dion), and a driver.

I had a $15,000 deposit, from which we had deducted our commission, forwarding the balance to Larry in New York. This meant the girls picked up the rest, in cash, each night after the gig. So they had $15,000 with them at the end of the 30 days. A few days after the tour ended I get a call from Larry in New York.

Him (pissed off and screaming): "Where are the girls?"

Me: "How should I know? They're your act."

It seems the driver came back to New York with the station wagon, but minus the girls and Jerry, saying he had dropped them all off at an airport outside Kansas City. He assumed they didn't want to suffer the long drive and had decided to fly back to New York. Larry was livid — and frantic. He called me every day, and eventually it seemed like every hour. After a few days Mary and Betty's mom called me at the office. She had gotten my number from Larry.

"Don't worry, ma'am," I said, in what I hoped was a reassuring voice. "The girls know how to take care of themselves. And Jerry is with them. I'm sure they're fine."

Finally, after about a week, Mary called me at the office.

"Where in the hell are you guys?" I asked.

"Miami Beach. We're at the Castaways," she said cheerfully. "You ought to see this big yacht we rented. They catch swordfish with it and everything."

"Is there any money left?"

"Yeah, a little."

"Larry is going wild."

"I'm sure. I'll deal with him when we get back."

I was laughing out loud. "Fine. But do me one favor."

"What?"

"Call your mother. She is very worried."

"Oh. Okay. I will. Promise."

"Tell everybody I said hi."

"Okay. See ya."

I called Larry. "The girls are fine. Mary called me. They're in Miami somewhere." Knowing full well she wouldn't, I said I told her to call him. Larry was furious.

"Hey, she told me what she wanted me to know. At least you know they're okay."

He hung up on me. I thought it was funny. Thirty days in Kansas. One could hardly blame them.

The best thing about The Shangri-Las was the way they performed live. They had very complicated records and carried only a guitar player, Jerry, on the road. But every song sounded exactly like the record. The girls sang like birds and Jerry did a fine motorcycle sound effect noise where required on "Leader of the Pack". Their vocal harmonizing was incredible. With two sets of perfectly harmonized sisters, you might think of them as two sets of Everly Brothers, performing as a quartet.

In the 1980s Mary and Marge discovered a bogus trio performing under the name The Shangri-Las and although Betty sat the incident out, Mary and Marge were furious and sued, causing protracted litigation. The remaining original members of The Shangri-Las performed for the last time at a reunion show on June 3, 1989.

Mary Ann Ganser died in Queens, New York, on March 15, 1970, aged 22, reportedly of a heroin overdose.

Marge Ganser returned to school during the late 1960s. She later married, then worked for NYNEX in Valley Stream, New York, and died of breast cancer on July 28, 1996, at age 48.

Songwriter-producer George "Shadow" Morton went on to produce a huge hit with Janis Ian, "Society's Child", and produced what has often been called the first Hard Rock record, the 6-minute, 43-second cover of "You Keep Me Hangin' On" with Vanilla Fudge.
"Shadow" died at 71 on February 14, 2013, of cancer.

As of this writing, Betty lives on Long Island.

Mary Weiss moved to New York's Greenwich Village, then to San Francisco before returning to Manhattan a few years later. She returned to college to study architecture and interior design, becoming a furniture consultant in New York.
Mary had always considered The Shangri-Las to be an alternative, sort-of Punk Rock act, and she returned to music in 2007 as an Alternative Rock artist and recorded for Norton Records. Her second husband manages her music career.
The Shangri-Las. They, and producer "Shadow" Morton, were Punk when real Punk would have been considered Junk.

They really were the Leaders of the Pack.

28 They're Coming To Take Me Away

His real name is Jerry Samuels *(below)*, now 80 years old. At the time he was a cocktail lounge piano player and sometime songwriter. In a phone call he said he was in the studio recording some miscellaneous things one night in early 1966 when, after a zillion cups of coffee and with some time left on the clock, out popped "They're Coming To Take Me Away, Ha Haaa!", an off-the-wall record released under the name Napoleon XIV.

When it came out, ratings were so-so. After some big-market radio stations began to ban it under pressure from mental health groups, the silly censorship drew attention to the record and blew it up. It went Top 5, peaking at #3.

I was running Paramount Artists Corporation in D.C. at the time and, like everybody else, I was trying to sign Samuels, even though I was competing with all the New York managers and agencies.

Jerry and I had a nice conversation; he said he would consider my offer. The one thing I stressed as we wrapped up our conversation was this: No matter who you sign with, do not let them dress you up like Napoleon and send you out on the road like that.

Make them promote you as Jerry Samuels and do the record straight up from the piano. That way after the record's run is complete Jerry Samuels will be a famous, established artist, and you can go forward and build a stand-alone piano career from there.

Sadly, he wound up signing for management with Sid Bernstein, Rascals' manager and sometimes-Beatles promoter, and damned if Bernstein didn't dress him up like Napoleon and put him out on the road. For booking, Jerry signed with Premier Talent. Agent Ron Sunshine from that office once said he was hard to book and they didn't get many offers for his services.

I knew Bernstein a bit; he was a very nice guy and very sharp, but he blew that one because, as I had predicted, when the record ran its course, nobody knew the name Jerry Samuels. Other than a Top 20 song he wrote for Sammy Davis, Jr. ("The Shelter of Your Arms"), he slipped off into Pop music obscurity.

Sometimes they took my advice.

Sometimes they didn't.

Too bad. Real nice guy.

29 Great Balls Of Fire

Jerry Lee Lewis had a reputation for being as crazy as a shithouse rat, but he did not have a reputation for missing gigs. So in 1967 I took a chance and booked him for a 30-day tour. Most of the gigs were clubs, but the crowning engagement on the tour was the last, George Washington University's graduation dinner and dance in the main room at the luxurious Washington Hilton, with British superstar Petula Clark as the dinner concert act and Jerry Lee to play for the dance that followed.

One of the routine gigs was a weekday show at a local restaurant/club in suburban Maryland. It was close enough to D.C. for me to go. As I entered the restaurant I had to walk across the dance floor, where the band was playing an opening set, to get to the outdoor patio where Jerry Lee was sitting with some friends and having drinks.

The singer was way out of tune. As I hesitated for a moment, and looked up at the bandstand, it was none other than my old friend, J. Frank Wilson. He was so trashed he could barely stand upright.

"Is that J. Frank Wilson?" I asked Jerry Lee.

"Yep."

"Man, he is way out of tune."

"The booze got him." That was funny coming from the famously alcoholic Jerry Lee Lewis. "The man needs the gig. And it don't matter none anyway. They didn't come to hear the band. They came to hear The Killer."

Point taken.

And, as much trouble as he caused me later in the tour and whatever dickens Jerry Lee got himself into over the many years, I will never forget that night. I have always had so much respect for Jerry Lee Lewis for carrying J. Frank — even though he was so messed up — because he needed the gig.

Classy thing to do. *Much* respect.

It was a great night and Jerry Lee (*below at a JOPA event, photos courtesy of The Michael O'Harro Collection*) tore the place up. I stayed until closing, met a cute brunette, and became fast friends with Jerry Lee's keyboard player, a nice, hugely talented fellow playing a Hammond B3 organ.

On the day of the final date of the tour at George Washington University's homecoming dinner and dance, it fell upon me to go to the Hilton and wake Jerry Lee up at noon for a sound check.

As I walked through the lobby I saw posters everywhere advertising the Petula Clark dinner concert. I was delighted to see that at the bottom of the poster they also promoted Jerry Lee Lewis and the dance. There were pictures of both artists, although superstar Petula's was rightfully much larger.

Jerry Lee came to the door in his skivvies, let me in, went to the nightstand and poured himself a water glass full to the brim with bourbon. He downed it in two gulps and called his wife. Most touring artists do that first thing.

Call the wife, that is.

"You don't have to hang around, I'll be there," he said to me after he hung up the telephone. So I went back to the office. The kids from George Washington University who had booked Jerry Lee were nice enough to invite me to the dinner and seat me next to a gorgeous blonde who was very impressed someone so young had booked Jerry Lee Lewis and Petula Clark. Actually, I had only booked Jerry Lee. Frank Modica at General Artists Corporation in New York had booked Petula, but I didn't mention that to Blondie.

Looked to be a glorious night coming.

It didn't last long.

I saw my new friend, Jerry Lee's Hammond B3 man, coming briskly toward me. We shook hands. "What's up?"

"We have a problem," he said, seriously. "It's Jerry. He saw the poster in the lobby and is furious that Petula Clark's picture is bigger than his. He is in a rage and he says he is only going to play Country music."

"*What?* He can't do that! These kids came to dance to Rock & Roll!"

"Tell Jerry!"

"Jesus!"

"I have an idea!" said the B3 man. "I toured with Petula last summer in England and I know her pretty well. She is really nice. Let's see if she can help."

But it turned out Petula Clark *(above)* had her own problem. Her husband, Claude Wolff, who was French and knew very little English, was upstairs right in the face of the union lighting people. They were ready to shut down the lights. Petula was very sympathetic to our plight, but she had to scurry off to the lighting room to put out that fire.

I had no plan, no idea what to do except to hope Jerry Lee got over it. Petula was wonderful. She played piano, sang all of her many hits and told stories. The kids screamed when she began the opening notes of "Downtown", her classic hit.

And then it was over and time for the dance. Jerry Lee and the band were all set up. They had several rows of chairs set up at the end of the dance floor, right in front of the stage.

I slid up to the curtain, right next to the Hammond B3. "Is he over it?" I asked, hopefully.

"Nope. All Country songs."

Lordy. I had abandoned Blondie and was looking for fire exits. True to his word, Jerry Lee sat down at the piano and opened with "What's Made Milwaukee Famous (Has Made A Loser Out of Me)". The kids seemed confused. It was stone Country and not at all danceable. And then, all of a sudden, I saw all of the kids' heads turn toward the entrance. And there came Petula Clark, husband in tow, right down to the front row. Students moved out of the way as she and her husband sat down, front row center.

You could have heard a pin drop. Jerry Lee stood up and stared at her. He didn't say a thing. The room remained silent for what seemed like an eternity. And then without warning, Jerry Lee threw his head back and screamed:

"You shake my nerves and you rattle my brain..."

And the place absolutely erupted. It was one of the loudest, most remarkable reactions I have ever seen or heard in my long career. Petula and her husband jumped up and danced along with everybody else. And for the next 90 minutes Jerry Lee Lewis played head bangin', foot stompin' Rock & Roll.

Petula and her husband stayed for about 30 minutes and when they got up to leave, she bowed toward the stage. Jerry Lee saw her, nodded his head, and smiled. Blondie and I reconnected and all was well that ended well.

But that night Jerry Lee Lewis had definitely shaken my nerves and rattled my brain.

Beginning only few years later, Jerry Lee switched full time to Country music and went on to have another huge career, with a string 17 Top 10 Country hits.

Petula Clark is 85 and still married to Wolff. They have two sons and a daughter. She lives most of the year in Geneva, Switzerland.

J. Frank Wilson was never able to overcome the demons of "Last Kiss" and died at 49, on October 4th, 1991, of alcoholism and alcohol-induced diabetes.

Jerry Lee Lewis. Crazy man to the *nth* degree. Big-time drinker. Cousin to Jimmy Swaggart. Married seven times, including to his first cousin's daughter. Savior of tragically distressed singers. Rock & Roll royalty. The Killer. Still alive in 2019 at 83 and living on a ranch in Nesbit, Mississippi, with his family. Concerts booked for 2019.

In 2019, I am 78 and still DJ'ing.
Goodness gracious.
Great balls of fire.

(Following page: Caricature of Alan White circa 1980)

30 The Sharpness of Dee Dee

Dee Dee Sharp *(previous page, photo courtesy of The Michael O'Harro Collection)*, real name Dione LaRue, began a string of big hit records in 1961 including "Slow Twistin'" with Chubby Checker; "Mashed Potato Time"; "Gravy (For My Mashed Potatoes)"; "Ride"; and "Do the Bird".

"Mashed Potato Time" and "Ride" each sold over one million copies and were awarded Gold records.

Dee Dee was smart, aggressive, expressive, engaged with the world around her, and on top of everything in her orbit. She was exactly what her stage name implied.

In a word, Dee Dee was sharp. And she was a monster singer with huge voice which seemed made for radio.

With her Type A personality, she was a powerful advocate for civil rights, which she let her audiences know all about from the stage, lecturing them between songs.

When I started booking her in 1967 she was getting a lot of bookings from some white guy in the Army whose job it was to book entertainment for on-base military clubs. I forgot his name, so I'm going to call him Nick.

Nick was really useful to me. He would book some gig for Dee Dee at a base, generally for really good money, and that would give me an anchor date to work with, which I would then surround with other gigs in the same general area.

Nick was also useful for Dee Dee personally because, at least it seemed to me, she was using him to make her then-boyfriend (music impresario Kenny Gamble) jealous and keep him on his toes. Although I had a girlfriend at the time, she might have been doing the same thing with me, too.

Using the white boys to keep Kenny Gamble woke would be a very Dee Dee thing to do.

Like I say: Sharp.

Dee Dee and I were pretty good friends. Sometimes I would go with her or meet up with her on the road. On one occasion I went to a JOPA party I booked her at The Gentlemen II in Baltimore. She introduced me to her mom, a lovely, friendly woman who drove down from Philadelphia for the show. She stood right next to me throughout Dee Dee's first performance.

When Dee Dee really got going into one of her civil rights rants, her mother turned to me and asked:

"How long has she been doing that?"

"What?"

"The speeches."

"As long as I've known her."

"Hmmm. Well, you won't hear any more of that."

Between shows Dee Dee and her mom hung out in the makeshift dressing room. I never again heard Dee Dee make even a single reference to anything political from the stage.

Evidently, Mom had made her point.

On another occasion I met Dee Dee at a Holiday Inn in Richmond, Virginia, where she was appearing that night at a gig I had booked for her at the famous Sheik Club.

She was already registered and in her room by the time I arrived, and she walked me to the front desk while I registered and checked into my room.

"Sorry, we're all sold out," said the desk clerk.

What the hell? There were almost no cars in the parking lot and most of the little boxes behind him had keys in them. I looked at Dee Dee and she looked at me and we both got it at about the same instant. This guy wasn't going to rent me a room because I was white and Dee Dee was black and he thought we were going to hook up.

It was 1967, and at that time in Virginia, even an interracial marriage was illegal.

"Come here, Skippy," I said to the desk clerk, as I leaned in so he could hear me clearly.

"If you don't find me a room very quickly I am going to come right over the top of the desk and trust me when I tell you if that happens you have had no experience in your life which will have prepared you for what happens next."

A favorite line of mine.

"Hey, look at me," Dee Dee said to the rattled desk clerk. "Look at me. Don't worry about him. You get him a room, and I mean right now, or you'll deal with me, and I'll guarantee you aren't ready for that."

She was almost shaking and obviously furious.

He hesitated for a moment, looked at me, and then spun the registration book around so I could fill it out and turned to fetch a key. "The room next to mine is empty; give him that room," ordered Dee Dee. The desk clerk looked at her and gave out a long sigh. The Sheik Club shows were terrific and we had a blast.

One gig I did not go to was on a Saturday night in Virginia Beach. Dee Dee went alone, without even a guitar player as she was perfectly competent to rehearse any reasonably decent band. On Saturday afternoon I was nursing a hangover and watching a football game at home when she called.

The anger in her voice cut like a knife.

"Do I have to do this gig?" she screamed.

"Why? What's the matter?"

"This club owner is walking around here while I am trying to rehearse this band and he is [n-word] this, [n-word] that."

(They didn't say *n-word* back then. The man explicitly said the word we are talking about.)

"No, you absolutely do not have to put up with that kind of bullshit," I said. "So, here's the deal. All of our contracts, including his, say that the buyer must provide adequate sound, staging, and lighting. So you just don't like the staging or the sound or the lights, or none of it."

I did the math. For not singing, she would get $337.50.

"Good. Great." She was calmer now.

"Now what I want you to do is, gather up your stuff very quietly and just walk out the front door. If they ask where you are going, just say you'll be right back. Do not make a fuss. I'll take care of that when he calls me."

"Gotcha."

She called Monday morning to tell me what happened. As I remember the way she told it, it went something like this:

She gathered her things, as I had asked her to do. There was a huge sign in the window of the club which said "Appearing Tonight: Dee Dee Sharp!"

It had a nice publicity picture of her, which I had sent to the club along with the contract. The sign listed all of her big hit records in very large type.

There was also a much smaller club across the street. On her way out the door, Dee Dee grabbed the sign and walked into the smaller club. She asked to speak to the manager.

"Well, I'm the owner," the man said. "Can I help you?"

"Hi, my name is Dee Dee Sharp and I was supposed to sing across the street tonight, but I had a disagreement with the owner. I was wondering if I could sing here tonight instead?"

"Oh, wow. I know who you are now," the club owner said. "I'm a big fan. But I'm sorry Miss Sharp, we only have a little trio here and we are much smaller club and we could never afford to pay someone like you."

"Sure you can," Dee Dee said cheerfully. "No charge. Two shows. Free. How 'bout that?"

"Well, gosh, sure. That would be fantastic!"

"May I put this sign in your window?"

"Absolutely!"

The trio turned out to be wonderful musicians. Both shows were sold out. The club across the street closed early. I never heard from the owner. All through my days at Action Talents and into the time I moved to Philly, Dee Dee and I remained great friends.

Until we weren't.

She married Kenny Gamble.

And she didn't need no white boys no more.

I saw her a few times after that, just a wave to say hello, but we were never close again. Dee Dee Sharp and Kenny Gamble divorced in 1980. It is said she got a huge share of his reported $100 million Philadelphia International Records music business fortune.

I told you she was sharp.

Dee Dee now lives with her current husband, Bill Witherspoon, in Medford, New Jersey.

31

Where The Action Was

All my life people have told me that since I talk so fast I should be working in New York. So, just for the hell of it, since I was a very experienced theatrical agent, when a job opened up at a new booking agency in New York and I was recruited to interview, I decided to look into it.

Due to the high cost of rent in New York City, everybody had small offices. Especially in buildings like 1650 Broadway *(previous page)* which, according to Ken Emerson in the New York Times edition on August 26, 2001, was the home of the popular music that "reminds the baby-boom generation of its youth, of sock hops and slumber parties, of transistor radios and tail fins, of good girls who said 'no', the nice boys who took that for an answer, and the bad boys who didn't."

It was in that very building I had an appointment with Betty Sperber, head of the new agency Action Talents, on the morning of January 2, 1968. There was a very small reception area with a tiny bench sort of thing for people waiting for an appointment. So I perched there to wait for Betty who, I was told, was in a meeting.

The phones were ringing off the hook and the receptionist, Andrea, in a tiny alcove right across from where I was sitting, was deftly going from one call to the next.

There were two offices in front of me. One, on the left with the door closed, was Betty's private office. The other, on my right, had the door open and I could see three small desks. One desk was occupied by an overweight, ruddy fellow with longish copper hair wearing a ragtag hippie outfit. You could see the huge billboard for the Broadway show *Hair* through the window behind him. He had a plant growing in the window which I later learned was marijuana. He waved me into the office. His name was Chris Bang.

I sat down at the unoccupied desk and met the other person, an attractive, sharp gal named Cynthia Weiss. We were all in our late twenties. We chatted.

It turned out the only agent they ever had was a fellow named Stan Gitt, who was actually the guy who had recruited me to come in for an interview. But he was gone, transferred to their Chicago office. They had a Chicago office?

"We don't!" And the two burst out laughing.

I later found out Stan had gone out to Chicago to hang with some agents they were doing business with, didn't like it there, and returned to his hometown of Philadelphia. Stan had been a small-time agent, actually more of an artist groupie. He had worked part-time for the great Norman Joyce Agency in Philadelphia.

Stan was an acquaintance and thoughtfully referred me to Betty to take his place at Action. Action Talents was — very quietly — a part of Buddah Records. Very quietly, because a record company having ownership in an agency was, absurdly I thought, considered a conflict of interest. Buddah paid at least some of Action's bills including, apparently, Stan Gitt's salary. No one told Buddah that Stan had moved on. Betty, Chris, Cynthia, and probably Andrea, were evidently splitting his check. Chris and Cynthia thought that was very funny.

How the whole thing got started was that Buddah CEO Neil Bogart wanted his artists booked wherever their record was breaking. He and Betty were friends. So he lined up Betty, a talent manager, to create an agency to do exactly that.

At that moment the #1 record in the country was the Buddah release "Green Tambourine" by a group called The Lemon Pipers. They were signed to Action for booking. The record had broken onto the charts thanks to radio play in Ohio and Pittsburgh, Pennsylvania.

"How far ahead are The Lemon Pipers booked?" I asked.

"Well, they're not booked at all," said Chris. "We don't have an agent. Which is why you're here."

The Lemon Pipers, 1968

"What do you do?" I asked.

He laughed. "Well," he said, "I roll a tight joint. And I'm sort of Betty's security blanket."

I turned to Cynthia. "I solve problems," she volunteered. "Like Jimi Hendrix, who was signed to us ever since he played with Joey Dee & The Starliters, which is our act. He became the lead singer and lead guitar player for one of our other bands, Curtis Knight and the Squires, and when he got some recording gig back here in New York he abandoned the Squires at a Holiday Inn gig in Minneapolis with no lead singer, no guitar player, and no money to get home. My job was to figure out how to get them back here. Things like that."

Cynthia was married to Steven Friedland, who had been one of The Tokens and was now doing an offbeat poetry show in Greenwich Village under the name Brute Force (*previous page, lower right*).

He had a record titled "The King Of Fuh" that he wasn't able to do anything with because the lyric "the Fuh King" was thought to be unplayable on commercial radio. The Beatles had tried to release "The King of Fuh" on Apple Records in 1969, which would have been only the eighth release at that point for Apple. It was quickly banned and John, Paul, George, and Ringo only gave copies to friends. You can now hear it on YouTube. Brilliant. Give it a listen and you will see why it was banned.

In the years gone by, I've often wished I had gotten involved with that record, even though it wasn't on Buddah, because I probably had the Mob connections to get it on jukeboxes in the vein of "Baby Let Me Bang Your Box", another double entendre record by Doug Clark and the Hot Nuts about a boring party and a piano sitting all alone in the corner. It broke and became a classic just on jukeboxes, with no radio play whatsoever.

But I never looked into what Brute Force was doing and he got no action on the record until 2018 when Sir Paul McCartney referenced Brute's "The King Of Fuh" tune on his song "Fuh You" from his new CD Egypt Station. Brute Force was, and still is, a kind of strange, funny, offbeat genius. Always been sorry I missed that one.

Anyway, back to the story I started with.

"The Lemon Pipers aren't booked this coming weekend?"

"Nope," Chris said. "Why, you got an idea?"

"I do. Can I use this phone?" I asked, pointing at the phone on the desk where I was sitting.

"Sure."

"How much do The Lemon Pipers want?"

"I heard a $1000 a night would make them very happy."

So I called a friend of mine who owned a chain of about a dozen teen clubs in the Pittsburgh area and who booked recording stars every weekend.

"Alan White! Where the heck have you been?" he asked.

"Well, I'm in New York at the moment and I've got The Lemon Pipers."

"The Lemon Pipers! I've been looking all over for them. Even Ritchie Nader at Premier couldn't get them for me. How much? When are they open? The record is #1. I need them now!" He sounded frantic.

"Hey, they've been in the studio," I lied. "Make a good deal with me and I'll work something out for you this weekend. How many days?"

"Three...Friday, Saturday and Sunday. How much?"

"I have to get like $1500 a day."

"Done. But they have to do shows at a few different clubs each night."

"Fine, I don't care how many shows they do if you provide internal transportation," I said. Internal transportation means paid-for transportation from one gig to the next.

"I have a plane."

"So I've heard."

"So we're good? Three days, $4500?"

"Yep. But here's the thing. I'm new here, so you'll have to wire in the deposit, $2250, by the end of business today."

"No problem," he said.

I gave him the address.

"Ah, I need paper to write this all down," I said to Chris.

He brought me a pad labeled Booking Sheets and, since apparently no one had ever booked a gig before, we figured out how to fill in the sheet together. So I had Friday, Saturday, and Sunday booked at good money. They wanted Ohio, so next I called a friend of mine, former agent and promoter Jeff Franklin, who was running a nightclub in Columbus.

He booked The Lemon Pipers for $1000 a night for Tuesday, Wednesday, and Thursday of the following week and also agreed to wire the deposit by the end of business that day. I had just finished booking the following weekend when Andrea came in and said Betty was ready to see me.

Betty Sperber turned out to be an incredibly sharp, chain-smoking dynamo, with every bit of the fast-talking New Yorker's gift of gab.

Betty *(right, circa 1968)* was relatively attractive, in her mid-forties, with a short hair bob, big-rimmed plastic glasses, and dressed in a miniskirt and blouse. She went from one cigarette to another, lighting a new one from the butt.

We were chatting when Chris came into the office carrying the booking sheets. He set them down on her desk.

"I think you'd better look at these," he said.

The three-day weekend at the teen clubs in Pittsburgh. Three weekdays the following week with Jeff Franklin in Columbus. And the following weekend close by for another $1500 a night. A total of $12,000, $6000 in deposits to be wired in by the close of business that day.

After reading over the booking sheets, Betty looked stunned. "Are these real?"

"They are if the deposits come in by the end of today, which I expect they will. I know these guys."

"Alright, you have to work here." She laughed. "You have to. How much money do you want?"

I gave her a modest figure, which would work out to about $1500 a week in 2019 dollars, and she hired me on the spot.

She wouldn't even let me go back to Connecticut to get my things. They put me up in a nice hotel and sent a driver to my folks' house in Connecticut.

All of a sudden, there I was.

Smack dab in the middle of where the action literally was. I was now an official fast-talking, big-time New York theatrical agent, working for a hot new well-financed agency, led by a super-sharp, well-known New York music business dynamo.

1968 was off to an interesting, action-filled start.

Janis Joplin

32 "Pearl"

It was January of 1968 and I had The Lemon Pipers with their #1 record "Green Tambourine" booked into The Bitter End in Greenwich Village for a three-day run.

When I got to the club Tuesday night, the Pipers were set up and ready to go. The first thing I did was order a drink.

"Chivas and ice, please."

"We don't serve liquor," the gal said, cheerfully.

"I'm sorry?"

"We don't serve liquor. Just fruit and ice cream drinks."

"What the hell..."

"Upstairs is The Tin Angel." She laughed. "We own that too. They have a full liquor license. You might be happier up there."

So up there I went.

When I walked into The Tin Angel, she was just sitting at the bar and I just happened to sit down next to her. She was just a chick on the next bar stool when we got to talking. I didn't know who she was and, at that point, I don't think she did either. I had no idea she was a singer until she asked me to save her drink and hold the stool for her.

"Sure. Where you headed?"

"I'm a singer and I've got a show up the street at The Electric Circus. They don't serve booze there either. Be gone about 40 minutes."

"Cool, I'll save your seat."

When she came back we talked about being a musician, and it was only then I found out who she was.

It was way before Woodstock, and Janis Joplin was not yet a big star. I had only heard of her vaguely in passing, although her band, Big Brother and The Holding Company, had made a little noise. I knew their name a bit, but she was not separately billed. She told me Big Brother and The Holding Company had an album coming out momentarily called "Cheap Thrills", and she was very excited about it. We drank big over those next three days. I don't remember much of it, but here are a few things I can tell you.

#1 — She didn't photograph very well and was prettier than later pictures would indicate. I can understand why Kris Kristofferson was digging on her. The photo at the chapter front is a pretty good likeness of the gal I drank with in 1968.

#2 — She drank Southern Comfort, and the girl could handle her liquor. Back then I could drink a fifth of Chivas a night; she stayed with me, drink for drink.

#3 — She absolutely hated every single person in her high school class and would have liked to have burned the place down. She must have been really bullied there.

#4 — Her favorite Blues song was "The St. James Infirmary Blues". She had a recording of her and the band playing it at an apartment in the Village. We talked about it Tuesday, she brought the cassette in for me on Wednesday, and by Thursday we had moved on to something else.

The tape was raw as hell, but amazing.

We both liked the Jonah Jones version from his "Muted Trumpet" album, and those were the lyrics she sang. I got zillions of cassette tapes the year I was at Action Talents, and

Janis' tape got thrown into the big box with all the rest. When I left New York, I threw the box out. What would that tape be worth historically, never mind financially, these days?

Believe it or not, the Janis I knew was very anti-drug. She bitched about the band lying around their Village apartment, not wanting to rehearse because they were stoned.

She said to me, and this is word for word: "Fuckin' drugs will be the end of Rock & Roll."

We got along great and I liked her a lot.

After those three nights of Comfort and Chivas in the early days of the winter of '68, I never saw her again. The official cause of her death was a listed as a heroin overdose, possibly compounded by alcohol. But many people believe Janis had been given heroin much more potent than normal, as several of her dealer's other customers had overdosed that week as well. I never heard if they caught the dealer.

Janis Joplin died on October 4, 1970.
She was 27 years old.
Just a baby.

33 The Most Beautiful Girl, Part 1

Her name was Paulette. She was a Supermodel who found fame on the mid-1960s TV music show *Hullabaloo*. Betty Sperber managed her.

Paulette was absolutely stunning. She had long brown hair, a slender but full-figured body, big bright eyes, and a beautiful, gleaming-white smile. From that day to this, Paulette remains the most beautiful woman I have ever seen.

She was 18.

Since I was concentrating on my career and had just come off an unsettling romantic breakup, I wasn't really dating, and thus, since I was possibly the only guy in New York not thinking of hitting on Paulette, she would frequently hang out in my office where she didn't feel threatened.

In those days long-distance telephone calls were very expensive and most agents had special, dedicated phone lines that only we answered. That way people could call us "station to station" (meaning number to number) and not "person to person". "Person-to-person" calls were where the operator would get a specified individual on the line for you, and you wouldn't be charged if that individual wasn't available. But those calls were three or four times the cost of a station-to-station call, thus the need for the special, dedicated, private lines which all agents had.

Previous page, top left: George Harrison of The Beatles
Bottom right: Mark Lindsay of Paul Revere & the Raiders

My special station-to-station, private line phone was red. Paulette was in the habit of giving out my private number to many various and potential suitors, probably as a way of blowing them off. Mark Lindsay from Paul Revere & the Raiders occasionally called.

I had had a run-in with Lindsay a few years earlier when he refused to sign autographs for the kids at a concert The Flying Dutchman and I were promoting in Winston-Salem, North Carolina. He not only wouldn't sign the kids' autograph requests, he was rude and arrogant about denying them.

As a result, I didn't like the guy, so when he would call for Paulette on my hotline, I would jerk him around. Paulette didn't like him either, so she didn't mind. In fact, as I recall, Paulette thought it was funny. The Lindsay calls went something like this.

"Hello."

"Is Paulette there?"

"Who's calling?"

"Tell her it's Mark Lindsay."

"What company are you with Mr. Lindsay?"

"I'm with Paul Revere & the Raiders!" he'd say, practically screaming.

"Oh, you're Paul Revere? I'm sorry, I thought you said you were Lindsay...Mark...or something."

"No, no, no. My name is Mark Lindsay and I am the lead singer for Paul Revere & the Raiders."

"Oh, again, I'm so sorry. I just assumed that Paul Revere was the lead singer for Paul Revere & the Raiders."

"No, no. My name is Mark Lindsay. I am the lead singer."

"Good for you."

"Please, can I just talk to Paulette?"

"I'm sorry, she isn't in. May I take a message?"

Click.

One day the red phone rang. I answered. A male voice with a heavy British accent said, "'Ello. Is Paulette about?"

"Who's calling?"

"Tell her it's George Harrison."

What? I'm not usually particularly impressed with celebrities, but that one really caught me off-guard, and I pretty much lost it.

"Um, yeah, George. Um, right. Gosh George, um sure, um hang on George, can you? And let me see if I can find her."

"Sure."

I ran into Betty's office, where I knew Paulette was in a meeting. I didn't even knock. Just barged right in.

"Paulette! It's George Harrison on the phone," I said breathlessly. "George Harrison."

"Oh, how sweet. Take a message for me, will ya?" she smiled back.

"Paulette! It's George Harrison. It's The Beatles."

"Alan, I know who The Beatles are," she laughed. "Do me a favor, please, and just take a message. I'll come explain why to you when I get finished with Betty. Okay?"

"It's George Harrison. Are you sure?"

"I'm sure."

"Okay."

Betty just smiled, and I went back to my office.

"I'm sorry, George, but I just missed her. She just went down on the elevator."

"Oh, bit of bad luck, isn't it?"

"George, can I take a message and have her call you?"

"No, thanks. I'll ring her back, won't I? Cheerio."

And he was gone.

When Paulette finished her meeting with Betty she came back into my office and sat down.

"Let me explain something to you," she said. "When you look like I do, it takes over your life. I didn't do a thing to look like this, and I still don't. I was just born this way. And it is something I have to deal with. People like me have no friends. None. It's not possible. The guys, as I'm sure you know, all only want one thing. And George Harrison, God bless him, and as nice as he is, is no different."

She stared a hole through me and patiently explained.

"Even my so-called girlfriends only want to hang out around me so they can pick off the guys who are trying to hit on me. The only guys who actually do hit on me are really aggressive super Type A personalities. And rich guys who think they can have anything they want. Quiet, more reserved guys, who I might really like, never even approach me. They're intimidated by the way I look. It's just the way it is."

I learned a lot from Paulette that day about what extremely attractive people go through because of the way they look.

"For people like me, the world is just different. That's all. It's just how it is. You understand now?"

"I do. But it was George Harrison. I mean, it's The Beatles. I think Harrison is the greatest."

She laughed. "Then you go out with him."

Paulette didn't stay in the business long and disappeared. Couldn't find anything online about her, either. I would like to think she couldn't stand the life she was headed for and ended up married to some normal guy that worshipped the ground she walked on because he couldn't believe such a great gal as her would choose him.

34 The Peppermint Rainbow

Almost 50 years ago I used to drink Chivas Regal. And lots of it. As a somewhat known and reasonably well-respected theatrical agent at Paramount Artists Corporation in Washington booking top touring bands, I had to be careful where I drank. The last thing I wanted to do was get all trashed and show my ass in some client's club where I did business. For doing business or hooking up with a girl, or both, it was Mike O'Harro's JOPA singles parties, The Rocket Room, or just maybe The Crazy Horse, all clients.

For serious drinking, I found my own little hideaway where how much I drank didn't matter at all. Mac's Fife & Drum was on the corner of M Street and Wisconsin Avenue in Georgetown. They used second-line bands, bands that were serviceable but not terrific, and the club was never really busy. Their sole claim to fame was that The Mugwumps, who later became The Mamas & The Papas, had started there.

To put it in perspective, my bands booked for between $1000 and $1500 a week in 1967 dollars. Mac's paid more like $500 to $600 a week and neither they, nor their bands, were ever going to become my clients.

What they did have was a very interesting five-piece band called The New York Times who were a nice bunch of enormously talented young kids from Baltimore. They were signed to, and represented by, a small-time booking agent named Dick Obits who, although I knew of him, for one reason or another I never came into contact with. However, the kids in the band were just really nice people, and they and I became friends. There were five of them, three guys and two gals. Doug Lewis on guitar, Skip Harris on bass, Tony Corey on drums, and two gals up front, sisters Patty and Bonnie

Lamden. Bonnie sang most of the leads, if not all, but everybody in that band could sing. And they all sang and harmonized really, really well.

Their vocals were stunning.

But they didn't play all that great. Only Doug and maybe Skip were much as instrumental musicians. As I remember it, both girls played mostly chords on a little Farfisa piano organ. Instrumentally, they were weak.

But those vocals. Unbelievable.

The New York Times' two biggest numbers were both medleys, a Mamas & Papas and a Fifth Dimension. On those vocal-driven songs, they absolutely soared.

I wasn't trying to sign them — I was just a fan who came in and drank. It was my personal little drinking spot, one of my all-time favorite vocal groups played there and I became pretty good friends with these lovely kids from Baltimore.

By January of 1968 I had left D.C. and moved on to Action Talents. The Lemon Pipers were managed by a fellow named Mark Barger, whose father owned a large steel mill. He had tons of money and hired New York songwriter and record producer Paul Leka to write and produce records for the band; "Green Tambourine" was one.

Leka's manager, publishing guru Bob Reno *(standing with*

Paul Leka and Shelly Pinz), had an office in the same building as Action Talents. In those early days Paul would often drop by my office and hang out. One Monday morning, not too long after I had arrived in New

York, Paul was in my office looking all down and sulky. Turns out he had a sort of open-ended record deal with Decca Records (now part of Universal Music Group) but couldn't find the band he needed for the project.

I was in the business of selling bands so I said, "I've got lots of bands, Paul. What are you looking for?"

"A Spanky and Our Gang," he said, "only better."

The New York Times instantly sprang to mind. Those vocals. And such nice kids. "Hmmm. You know, I might just have the perfect group for you, but the problem is they don't play all that well. They're not awful or anything, just not great. But the vocals are absolutely incredible. They're like a white Fifth Dimension."

He perked up. "Hell, I don't care if they can play at all. In fact, I would prefer it if they didn't. I'd rather use studio musicians. This project is all about the vocals."

"When do you need this?"

"Now. Today. This minute."

I had Bonnie Lamden's phone number, so I called her. It was 11 AM. As luck would have it, not only was she home, the whole band was over at her house rehearsing in the basement. I told her where I was working and what was going on.

"The thing is, you have to get in the van and drive to New York. Now. This minute. I'll find a place to showcase you tonight, and I'll make sure that Paul Leka and his manager are both there. It's maybe a 4-hour drive from Baltimore, and by the time you get here I'll know where you're playing. You'll most likely have to play the night without getting paid, but it's the chance of a lifetime. I am a little worried about your contract with Dick Obits, but other than that, I believe you guys can do this. But it's up to you."

"Give me 30 minutes with the band and I'll call you back."

I gave her our number. It didn't take 30 minutes. "Yes, yes, yes! We all want to do it! Um, oh, and Alan, my father wants to talk to you too, okay?"

"You bet. Put him on."

"Hi, Mr. White, I'm Bonnie and Patty's father and it's nice to speak with you. I just wanted you to know, that as it happens, I am the Chief Judge for the Baltimore City Court system and I would like to give you my personal assurance that Mr. Dick Obits will never be any sort of problem to you."

Just from the edge in his voice, I believed him. Potential problem averted. I walked into Betty's office.

"Do you have a club where I can showcase a band for Paul Leka and Bob Reno tonight? I don't really know the clubs around here yet. No money and they'll do the night."

One quick call to a guy named Joey at a place called Harlow's on 72nd Street on the Upper East Side and the deal was done. She lit a cigarette from the tip of the one that had burned down. "They start at 9."

By the time I got there it was not going well.

Leka wasn't impressed with the band. Bob Reno was bored and edgy. He hadn't even bothered to order a drink. I moved quickly to the stage. Bonnie, Patty, and Doug came to the front as I nodded in.

"Hi guys, good to see you. Listen, if we're gonna pull this off, I need the Mamas & Papas and Fifth Dimension medleys now. Both of them. *Right now.* Back to back. Nothing else. Just the medleys."

Bonnie smiled, nodded, called the set and I went back to the table. Paul Leka was all in by the second verse of the first song. By the second medley, Reno had ordered drinks for the table and was ready to sign the band on the spot.

And so it began.

I wanted to change the name of the band to get clear once and for all of any possible Obits claim; different brand, different name, nothing he had anything to do with. And so did Leka and Reno, but for a different reason. They wanted something hipper, brighter and more contemporary. We put a ton of names into a hat and the band picked The Peppermint Rainbow. I liked it right away. So did Bob and Paul.

And Decca did, too.

My friend Tony Martinelli, owner of one of the top nightclubs in the history of nightclubs, Tony Marts in Ocean City, New Jersey, agreed to book the kids as his third band until they were ready to go to New York to record.

In the 1983 movie *Eddie and the Cruisers*, Eddie (Michael Paré) and his fictional band rehearse their first record "On The Dark Side" on the roof overlooking the apartments where real bands that played at Tony Marts stayed.

In a funny coincidence in real life, Paul Leka and The Peppermint Rainbow rehearsed their first record "Walking in Different Circles" on that very same roof. Although I liked the song well enough, my Top 40 radio experience told me right away "Walking in Different Circles" was not going to be a big hit. I kept my mouth shut, but I was right. It made only a small dent on the Billboard charts.

But the right momentum was created and the follow-up "Will You Be Staying After Sunday" went right through the roof. Top 40 radio loved it — and it is still popular, as shown by over 1,500,000 YouTube.com plays.

These days "Will You Be Staying After Sunday" by The Peppermint Rainbow is remembered by music historians as a one-hit wonder, a classic of 1960s AM Top 40 Pop radio.

Outclassing Spanky and Our Gang was a fine song by Joel Hirschorn and Al Kasha with Paul Leka's slick production and the Rainbow's soaring vocals. No disrespect to Spanky McFarland intended, but vocally, there was no contest between them.

One Monday afternoon, June 22, 1968, months later, the Rainbow all piled into my office wanting to drag me out, right in the middle of the day. I protested. "I can't do that. I've got all kinds of phone calls backed up here."

"Call Betty," they said. So I hit the intercom button.

"Go with the Rainbow," she ordered, so off I went.

They took me home, gussied me all up and took me to The Royal Box at the Americana Hotel for the grand opening of my favorite act, The Fifth Dimension. I was floored. It turned out the Fifth had worked with the kids on the road and the two groups, which had the exact same personnel makeup of two gals and three guys, had become very fast friends.

In fact, Fifth Dimension lead singers Billy Davis, Jr. and Marilyn McCoo (later the host of the 1980s TV classic, *Solid Gold*) had even dropped by Decca Records one afternoon and made phone calls to radio stations on behalf of garnering airplay for "Will You Be Staying After Sunday". That was a very classy thing to do.

Right in the middle of their show they stopped and made a big fuss over The Peppermint Rainbow. They even introduced and fussed over me a bit for discovering them. After the show we all went to the after-party upstairs in a suite where I wound up conversing with Marilyn McCoo, the good-looking, movie star face of The Fifth Dimension *(below)*.

"Congratulations on the new record," I said.

"Thanks, I sure hope it's a hit," she smiled.

"You haven't seen Billboard yet, have you?"

"No, not this week's."

"'Stoned Soul Picnic' is like #51 with a bullet, first week on the chart. It's a smash."

The whole group went nuts, jumping up and down like little schoolkids, brimming with excitement and creating a delightful memory for me. And probably for them too.

The Peppermint Rainbow went on to have one more small chart record, "Don't Wake Me Up In The Morning, Michael". Then Paul Leka diverted his attention to his new group Steam, giving them his next, and final, chart-topping song "Na Na, Hey Hey, Kiss Him Goodbye" — over Bonnie and Doug's vociferous protests.

Eventually I moved to Philadelphia to manage and make Disco records with Len Barry, and it seemed I would never see or talk with any of those kids again. Not in person anyway. I did see The Peppermint Rainbow on Joey Bishop's late-night talk show. Joey went gaga over the band. I ran into Doug Lewis briefly in about 1972 when he was playing with his new band at Mike O'Harro's Gentlemen II in Baltimore.

But I didn't actually talk with any of them, at any length anyway, for the next 48 years. That is, until 2016 when I spoke with Bonnie Lamden, now Bonnie Phipps, for a nice long, catch-up phone conversation.

Bonnie had become a millionaire CPA and the CEO of a chain of five hospitals. Patty had become a Baltimore City municipal court judge, just like her father.

Betty Sperber reportedly won millions from her lawsuit against Jimi Hendrix, sold Action Talents in the mid-'70s and retired to St. Croix, U.S. Virgin Islands, where she bought The King Christian Hotel and became a treasured citizen.

Betty died of cancer on November 12, 1993, at age 63.

Bob Reno went on to launch Midland-International Records and had huge hits with Carol Douglas ("Doctors Orders", "Midnight Love Affair"), the Silver Convention ("Fly, Robin, Fly", "Get Up & Boogie"), and John Travolta ("Let Her

In"). Eventually he moved to Los Angeles and became involved in real estate. After a failed, and apparently fraudulent, land deal sent him to prison, he died, reportedly of AIDS, in Los Angeles in 2010.

Paul Leka passed away at 68 in 2011.

Billy Davis, Jr. and Marilyn McCoo left The Fifth Dimension in the mid-'70s and have now been married for 46 years. They continue to tour as a duo.

Bonnie Lamden retired, and she and her husband bought a place here in Atlanta at The Four Seasons Hotel as a lovely getaway. She invited me to dinner there. I hadn't seen her in 48 years. She hadn't changed a bit. She lied and said I hadn't either. Visiting with Bonnie was an absolutely incredible night. Yet, in some ways, the visit seems just like yesterday. But it was well "After Sunday".

Almost half a century after.

Alan and
Bonnie Lamden
in 2016

Joey Dee, seated, with The Starliters

35 Joey Dee and Martin Luther King

I was sitting in a smoky bar across the river from Manhattan in New Jersey drinking with my friend and recording artist (who I represented at the time) the great Joey Dee of "The Peppermint Twist" and "Hot Pastrami". The club, not far from where Joey lived, was filled with a completely black clientele. Joey and I were the only two white people there. All of a sudden word began to spread through the club in very hushed tones that Martin Luther King had been assassinated. No details, just that he had been killed.

I cannot describe the chill that came over that room.

As we looked around, we could see the anguish, despair, and anger on the faces of the early crowd. It was both sad and scary. And it caused Joey and I to do exactly same thing, at exactly the same time. Both of our right hands shot up into the air in almost-choreographed unison.

We both said the exact same thing, at the exact same moment. "Check."

About 20 years ago I had an opportunity to speak with Joey's wife, another former client of mine, the super vocalist

Lois Lee. We talked for a half an hour or so and caught up on things.

"All my kids know your name because every year on the anniversary of the assassination of Martin Luther King, Joey tells that same story about you two in that bar in Jersey."

"That's funny," I replied. "I do the same thing. Sometimes I play them 'The Peppermint Twist'."

Lois had one of the greatest and strongest voices I've ever heard. Eventually she retired from the biz, and she and Joey raised a bunch of kids. Lois died from cancer in 2003.

Joey remarried and still performs regularly.

In a 2010 official letter, New Jersey Governor Chris Christie commended Joey Dee & The Starliters for remaining true to their Jersey roots. A big party…I mean, ceremony… followed.

36 Jimi Hendrix

*"If people wanted you to write warmly about
them, they should have behaved better."*
~ Anne Lamott

When I got to Action Talents in New York in January of
1968 — a year and a half before Woodstock and just before he
had his only chart record, a minor hit (#20 in the Billboard Hot
100) called "All Along the Watchtower" — I didn't have an
opinion on Jimi Hendrix.

I had heard some of his music while I was at Paramount
Artists and, since we managed Roy Buchanan, who Eric
Clapton called the greatest guitar player in the world and who
could play circles around Hendrix, I wasn't a particular fan of
Hendrix. One of the first things I learned upon joining Action
Talents was that Jimi Hendrix had been under a management
contract with us, probably from his days playing with Joey
Dee & The Starliters, an act Betty Sperber managed — but
Hendrix broke the contract.

Apparently, as the story went, we had Jimi working as the
lead guitar player and lead singer for one of our bands, Curtis
Knight and the Squires, when he up and left, abandoning
them at a Holiday Inn in Minnesota, right in the middle of the
week, leaving them with no lead singer, no lead guitar player,
and no money to get home.

One of our staff members had to figure out a way to get
the band back to New York, so Hendrix wasn't exactly
popular in our office. One day, not long after I joined the
agency, he came into the office to meet with Betty.

Jimi had someone with him but given the way he was
dressed I figured him for a roadie or a friend or something. He
sure didn't look like a business person.

Like just about everybody, we had a very small waiting area, just a bench really, right outside the two offices, the staff office and Betty Sperber's private office. Our receptionist was away from her desk and I must have been in the restroom because when I came back, although his friend was sitting on the bench in the waiting area, Hendrix was at my desk — and in my chair.

The conversation went something like this:

"Hey man, what's up?"

"I'm here to see Betty."

"Oh, cool. Well, my phone lines are ringing off the hook here so I need to get to my desk. You can wait out in the waiting room with your friend."

He didn't move an inch. "I'm here to see Betty."

"I understand that, but I need to get to my desk to answer these phones."

"I'm here to see Betty."

"Are we going to have problem here?"

"Ah, man," he said sullenly. And he went out into the waiting area and sat on the bench.

I started answering phones, got really busy, and never saw him leave. Betty didn't want to talk about it so I gathered the meeting didn't go well. I never saw him again, and his name never came up again at the office.

I always thought the best thing he ever did was have a great idea at Woodstock: Shred the national anthem through a distortion amp. Not particularly hard to play, but a great idea. To me, even though it wasn't a record, that was his biggest hit.

I might be influenced by the fact that I didn't dig the guy but, to me, he wasn't even the best guitar player at Woodstock. As far as I am concerned, that was Carlos Santana.

Keith Richards was once quoted as saying Jimi Hendrix was a nice guy but he ruined guitar. Given the way he had abandoned his band in Minnesota, I didn't even think he was a very nice guy.

A coroner's inquest concluded that, tragically, Hendrix had aspirated his own vomit and died of asphyxia while intoxicated with barbiturates.

Jimi Hendrix died on September 18, 1970.
Twenty-seven years old.
Another baby, gone.

Jimi Hendrix (right) with Curtis Knight and the Squires
sometime between 1965 and 1967

1910 Fruitgum Company

37 "Simon Says"

Betty Sperber could sell anything.

She was once described by ABC News as a high-powered New York PR woman, and even that was a significant understatement. But she didn't have any real musical instincts and she knew it. Consequently, she often called me into her office to take advantage of my Top 40 radio ears and on this day she did it again.

"What do you think of this record?" she asked, slipping a 45 onto the turntable and dropping the needle. "Neil just signed the act. It's coming out on Buddah."

It was "Simon Says" by 1910 Fruitgum Company. "It's a smash," I said. "That is a big-time Top 5 record. Wow. Whose act is this?"

"Two guys named Jerry Kasenetz and Jeff Katz."

I laughed. "Jeff Katz."

"You know him?" Betty asked, obviously surprised.

I did. Heck of a guy. A hustler...and nice, too.

I knew him when I was at Paramount Artists. He had a band, The Rare Breed, which had a record called "Beg, Borrow and Steal" and since they were all from New York where nobody owns a car because the traffic is just too bad and insurance is too expensive, Jeff brought the band and their equipment all the way to Washington on a train to do a Jack Alix WEAM radio record hop. I didn't know Kasenetz.

Betty wanted to know if I could I reach them.

Yes, I could. I called Jeff at home, caught up a bit and set up a meeting between the boys and Betty. The meeting went well, and it was agreed that we would book the act as soon as the record came out.

The offices next to us housed the production unit for the Dick Cavett morning show. Cavett himself had an office on the fifth floor. I rarely saw him and never spoke to him, but the entire production team was located in a small office space right next to our small office space. There weren't many of them: A producer, an assistant producer, a talent coordinator, and an assistant talent coordinator named Susan Richards.

There was also a totally gorgeous, extremely buxom blonde receptionist/switchboard operator, whose name I do not recall. But she was stunning. That I remember.

Richards was a sort of pal of mine and I once dated the receptionist/switchboard operator, but I didn't know the others. Professionally we didn't have much common ground. The Cavett show was on at 11 AM each morning and was aimed demographically at family-friendly adult women.

They didn't book Rock & Roll acts.

Until one day when they got hung up.

They had no act booked for the following morning and Richards came to me, desperate for an act of some kind for the next morning's show. I figured that was a great opportunity for 1910 Fruitgum Company, whose record had just come out, and so I said, "Well, the 1910 Fruitgum Company record 'Simon Says' is a bubblegum kids record. How about them?"

She didn't think so, but as the afternoon wore on both she and her bosses became more and more desperate and more inclined to book the band. Finally, at the end of the day, they did. Betty was ecstatic but there was one little problem, which we only learned about when we called Jeff to arrange the appearance. The record had been written by a guy named Elliot Chiprut and produced by Chiprut, Jeff, and Jerry, using studio musicians.

There was no actual 1910 Fruitgum Company band.

"Don't worry, we'll have one by tomorrow morning in time for the show," said Jeff, with great confidence. "No problem."

I wanted to cancel, but Betty said not to say anything to Richards and just go with the boys.

Arriving at the office early the next morning I called Jeff and he said they had found a bar band in Jersey. They were going to be 1910 Fruitgum Company.

He said they were on their way into the city as we spoke and they were learning the song, literally as they drove across the George Washington Bridge.

Then all hell broke loose.

AFTRA (the American Federation of Television & Radio Artists), the union which covered TV, refused to allow the band to appear on the show until they officially became members of the union, which cost thousands of dollars and generally took significant time to address all the paperwork.

Betty begged and cajoled, to no avail. The best they would do was allow the appearance, but only if the money was sent to them by messenger, before the show, which was then 90 minutes away. It was frantic in Betty's office as she worked on the problem and I stayed out of her way. I simply tried to keep Susan Richards, who had just learned of the fiasco, from jumping out of her office window. In the end, we made it.

The money got there just in time, and the band was allowed to appear. Cavett was happy. Betty was relieved. Neil Bogart at Buddah was ecstatic.

And all was well that ended well.

Except I was so busy with business I never got to go out with the switchboard gal again. That was a shame. Nice gal.

She probably figured I was a louse for not asking her out again. That one I regret.

I never again booked anything on the Cavett show.

When Cavett was canceled, Susan Richards went on to become the talent coordinator for *The Steve Allen Show*.

"Simon Says" reached #4 on the Billboard Hot 100 in March of 1968. 1910 Fruitgum Company would go on to have one more huge hit record, "1-2-3 Red Light".

But I wasn't through with Jerry Kasenetz and Jeff Katz. Not by a long shot.

38 A Playboy In New York

Betty called me into her office and introduced me to a gnarly little Houston businessman who was apparently representing the music act Gene & Debbe *(below)*. Gene Thomasson was a musician/singer who had some success writing songs in Nashville. Debbe Neville was a terrific female vocalist. They teamed up and put out "Playboy", a sort of mid-tempo Country/Pop ballad, on little-known TRX Records, a subsidiary of better-known Hickory Records.

"Playboy" was on the Billboard Hot 100 in the high 30s and had been stuck there for a while. I had heard the record but wasn't exactly fired up about chasing the act. They seemed to me to be a minor Country/Pop duo, best suited to small clubs in the South.

Betty hadn't heard the record herself, so she played it for both of us and I listened politely. Nice little record, the operative word being *little*. Good melody, strong vocals, not much of a song. Mr. Gnarly Houston had a press shot of the act. Gene was handsome. Debbe was quite pretty.

The issue was how to hype the record and push it into the Top 20, hopefully even into the Top 10. The idea was if we could do that, then we would be able to sign the act. New York Top 40 radio was dominated by only two AM stations. FM stations were insignificant at the time; most of them played only classical music.

WMCA was #1 in New York City itself, but it had a small signal and couldn't be heard outside of the city proper. WABC had the maximum power allowed — 50,000 watts — and a clear channel, meaning no one else was on their 770 frequency. They could be heard at night as far away as North Carolina.

WABC absolutely dominated the Tri-State area. Their afternoon drive DJ, Big Dan Ingram, was a huge #1, and because of that the rest of the station was a close #2, even in the city proper, right behind 10,000-watt WMCA.

"Neither of the New York stations are playing the record," I explained to Mr. Gnarly Houston. "The only way to change that is to bring the act into New York for a free record hop for WMCA."

I kept up the pitch. "The idea is that the act doesn't mean anything for a record hop if the station isn't playing the record. So you book the hop and hope the station goes on the record to draw kids, which they then charge to come to their hop. It's a way of getting around the bullshit payola laws. The station makes money from the free appearance at the record hop, and hopefully the artist gets their record played. It is not a straight up tit for tat. There is no guarantee."

I continued truthfully, "WMCA will often do that, but WABC will not. Ever. WABC is well known to not react to promotion people. But they do react to WMCA. So if WMCA

goes on a record, maybe WABC can be forced on it. Maybe.
Sometimes yes, sometimes no."

Then Mr. Gnarly Houston began griping about how much
it would cost to fly them in for a free gig.

I did not love this guy. By then I didn't care if we signed
the act or not. They weren't exactly destined to become Sonny
& Cher. Betty was interested. The WMCA record hops were all
on Friday nights. Betty was tight with the station.

"Can you book them somewhere here for a Saturday night
to pay for the trip?" Betty asked.

I took a deep breath.

"Well, I can try. It won't be easy since the record isn't
getting played here, and really it is pretty Country, but let me
see what I can do."

Betty almost immediately set up the Friday night hop with
WMCA, and I went to work finding a gig for the following
night to pay for their trip to New York.

I had a little club located on Staten Island where I was
occasionally able to book name acts. I had never been there,
and reports from the artists who had played the club were that
it was a real shithole, little more than a shotgun joint with a
small bandstand in the middle of a U-shaped bar.

And booking-wise they were all over the place. Rock
bands, R&B acts, solo artists. Color didn't matter. Anybody
with a name. They clearly had no idea what they were doing.
If they had a plan, I couldn't figure it out.

But for some reason the guy who did the booking had
been bugging me for a while to get him Mary Wells, who was
not one of our acts. So I called him at the little Staten Island
club and offered him Mary Wells if he would book Gene &
Debbe for the night following the WMCA Friday night hop.
He went for it right away and, to my astonishment, by quoting
the WMCA gig I was able to get hit-record money for Gene &
Debbe for their appearance. More than enough to cover the
cost of the trip.

Then I called on a friend who did book Wells — who would split his commission with us — and arranged for her to appear at the club a few weeks later. It went rather smoothly. Gene and Debbe flew in for the weekend gigs and turned out to be really nice people. Gene was a serious musician and, as I believe I mentioned, Debbe was quite pretty.

I liked them both.

As I drove them to the record hop in Brooklyn we actually heard "Playboy" on the car radio, which was tuned to WMCA. It was followed by a commercial for the hop itself.

"Playboy", the DJ said, was the station's pick hit of the week. We whooped and hollered. Payola, shmayola. This was even better. The record companies didn't actually have to put up any money themselves, they just made their artists do free radio station gigs. And the station played the record so the artist would draw a crowd, which the station then charged admission to see.

The whole music industry, master criminals that we were, walked right around the stupid payola laws. They still do.

Perfect.

The WMCA hop went well. Debbe flirted with me all night. I liked that a lot personally, but I'm not so sure Gene was too thrilled. I couldn't make out if they were a romantic couple or just singing partners, but I didn't do anything to discourage the lovely Miss Debbe's flirting.

As I think I mentioned a time or two, Debbe was quite pretty. The Saturday night gig in Staten Island also went well.

It was as it had been reported to be, an absolute shithole, filled with a rowdy blue-collar crowd who hollered and whooped a lot having a grand, pretty drunken good old time. Gene & Debbe sang their hit and a few songs nobody knew; the crowd seemed to love them.

Debbe continued to flirt throughout the night, I continued to like it, and all in all it was a pretty fun time. Sunday, Gene and Debbe flew back to Houston. Monday, Betty came into my office. "'Playboy.' WABC. Pick Hit."

Boom.

"Playboy" eventually sold over one million copies, spent 14 weeks on the chart, and peaked at #17 on the Billboard Hot 100 in 1968.

Had the New York stations been on the record at the same time the rest of the country was, it would have gone into the Top 5. But even as the rest of the country was going off the record because it had finished its run, just the added play in the Tri-State area pushed the record into the Top 20 and sales topped one million.

As far as Gene & Debbe were concerned, that was that. Until it wasn't.

The Kasenetz-Katz Singing Orchestral Circus

39 The Circus Is In Town

It was not uncommon for Betty to call me into her office to make use of my Top 40 radio ears to get my opinion as to a song's radio-play potential. But on this day it wasn't a 45 RPM single she was cuing up. It was an album. She dropped the needle on track one: The Beatles song "We Can Work It Out" as a massive studio production and gigantic orchestral arrangement.

I listened about halfway through and waved it off.

"What the hell is that?" I asked. "That's incredible."

"It's Kasenetz and Katz again," she said. "They call it The Kasenetz-Katz Singing Orchestral Circus. The idea is that they are putting all their bands into one big orchestra. The ones we know, like 1910 Fruitgum Company, The Ohio Express, and Jamie Lyons & The Music Explosion, who have all had big hit records. And others I've never heard of and who have had no individual hits, or even records that I know of."

She picked up a piece of paper and began reading the names. "Lt. Garcia's Magic Music Box. Teri Nelson Group. The 1989 Musical Marching Zoo. J.C.W. Rat Finks. The St. Louis Invisible Marching Band."

"I've never heard of that last bunch either," I said. "Do they even exist?"

"Probably not," Betty replied. "They like to use studio musicians."

"That's unbelievable." It was all I could muster.

"It gets crazier. Neil has them signed to Buddah and he is going to debut the album with a huge performance by the entire group at Carnegie Hall sometime in early June. Supposedly there are going to be 46 of them."

From left:
Neil Bogart,
Jerry Kasenetz,
and Jeff Katz

"Jesus." I was just staring blankly.

"What do you think?" she asked.

"I'm not sure what to think," I answered truthfully. "I mean, the record is amazing. It's over-arranged and over-produced, but that's what they were going for. Big. Huge. I mean, this whole idea is a gigantic concept."

"Is it a hit?"

I paused. "As a single? I'm not sure. On the strength of the record alone, probably not. The Beatles already had that hit and they did it much better. But this whole concept may carry the record. It depends how it's presented. I mean, Carnegie Hall? That doesn't do much for the kids, but radio? Maybe."

"Neil wants me to book Ed Sullivan."

"Can you?"

"Maybe. Vince (Calandra, Sullivan show associate producer and talent coordinator) is my friend. But maybe not. Can you imagine what union scale would be for 46 people? It's going to take Bob Precht (show producer and Sullivan's son-in-law) to do the deal. It would be a hard sell."

"We'd need to get Sullivan the same week as Carnegie Hall to really break this wide open," I ventured.

"Right. I agree."

We both sat silently for a minute or two.

"This is bigger than we are, isn't it?" Betty asked.

I hated to think anything was beyond our reach. "Yeah, I think maybe it is. But I've got a couple of ideas. Let me make a few calls."

"Okay, go to it."

When I first joined Paramount Artists in 1966, the first thing Mitch Corday had me do was to go to a college block booking conference in Augusta, Georgia.

I couldn't really figure why, because at that point all we did was book touring bands into clubs around the country and the only act we had that anybody had ever heard of was The Chartbusters. And their record "She's The One" had barely made the Top 40, peaking at #33.

But I was glad to go and see what I could learn. All the big agencies from New York were there. The fellow in the booth next me, Ben, from Philadelphia, was the agent for Earl "Fatha" Hines, the legendary American Jazz pianist and bandleader who was one of the most influential figures in the development of Jazz piano.

Both Charlie Parker and Dizzy Gillespie were members of Hines' band at one time or another. Hines had just won the 1966 International Critics Poll for DownBeat magazine's Hall of Fame, so he was red hot. In other words, Ben was doing a lot of business. We became friends. He taught me a lot.

Even though nobody was interested in my Chartbusters, it was a lot of fun.

At the main convention party event, one of the New York agencies brought in a new young comedian named Flip Wilson, who did a fall-down funny routine about Christopher Columbus discovering Ray Charles.

I met and went out drinking with Ric Cartey, who was a well-known agent from the Bill Lowery Office in Atlanta. Cartey, along with Carole Joyner, had written "Young Love", a huge hit record for both teen idol Tab Hunter and Country star Sonny James. Ric was a blast to be around. At one point we had a big meeting of all the agency people and supervisory hotel staff. During the meeting there was significant complaining about the prices of hotel drinks and how they differed from what had been promised.

A man named Ed Garland from the Ashley-Famous Agency in New York stood up and challenged the hotel people about the price discrepancy. I had never heard of the Ashley-Famous Agency, but in his mid-30s, with a squared jaw, movie star good looks, and a thousand-dollar suit, Ed Garland cut an impressive figure.

"Am I right?" he asked the room.

I had the drink price list in my pocket with all the rest of the convention welcoming material and, since none of the big New York agency people were backing Garland up, I stood up and confirmed his accusation.

"I've got it right here," I said, handing the price list to the hotel representative. "You are charging a lot more than what is on this paper you handed out."

Finally, after some more back and forth, the hotel representatives caved and promised us all refunds. Garland thanked me for standing up and backing his play. He bought me a drink at our new, nicely reduced price.

So later, looking to find some major agency assistance for our Kasenetz-Katz Singing Orchestral Circus project, I took a wild shot and called Garland at the Ashley-Famous Agency.

He came to the phone right away. Sure, he remembered me from the booking conference. I brought him up to date on where I was working.

"Action Talents? Little Rock & Roll agency?"

"That's us."

I went right to it. "Listen Ed, what are you doing right now? I need you to do something for me. I need you to come over to our offices at 1650 Broadway. Right now. I have something you absolutely have to hear."

I said it as firmly as I could.

"What are you, nuts? You want me to leave my office and travel through crosstown traffic in the middle of the afternoon? You gotta be kidding."

"No, I'm serious. Think about it. You know me a bit and you know I'm not crazy. You are Ed Garland from the big-time Ashley-Famous Agency. Would I call you up, totally out of the blue, and ask you to come over here through crosstown traffic in the middle of the day if I didn't have an unbelievably good reason?"

He was silent. And then he said, "Hmmm, you know what? Okay. I'll do it. What's the address again?"

"Action Talents, 1650 Broadway, 4th floor. End of the hall."

Garland showed up about 40 minutes later. After introductions, Betty dropped the needle. "We Can Work It Out", cut #1.

Just as I had done, he waved it off about halfway through. "Jesus, what the hell is that?" he asked.

Betty filled him in, then said, "We think this is too big for us. Alan thought you might be one to partner up with us."

"I need a phone," Garland said. Betty pushed the visitors' phone across the desk. He dialed quickly. "Karl Honeystein, please." He paused, covering the mouthpiece, "Honeystein heads the TV department and runs the whole New York operation of Ashley-Famous."

Betty smiled and nodded.

"Karl? It's Ed." Slight pause. "No, I'm not in the building. Listen, what are you doing right now? I need you to do something." Another pause. "I need you to come over to the offices of an agency called Action Talents at 1650 Broadway right now. I have something you absolutely have to hear." Garland paused, listening. "Karl, think about it. I am just a lowly agent and you are the top dog at one of the biggest and most important talent agencies in the world."

And Garland was right. Ashley-Famous had everybody. Movie and TV stars. Major music stars. They were, as Garland had said, one of the biggest and most important talent agencies in the world. It was led by eventual Warner Bros. studio head Ted Ashley.

"Would I call you up and ask you to come over, through crosstown traffic, to an agency you've never heard of, in the middle of the day, if I didn't have an unbelievably good reason?" He listened again and then he said, "Action Talents, 1650 Broadway, 4th floor. End of the hall."

Garland hung up and smiled at Betty. "He's on his way."

Karl Honeystein showed up about 40 minutes later and after introductions Betty once again dropped the needle.

Honeystein also waved it off about halfway through and I wondered to myself if anybody was ever going to listen to the entire song.

"What in the world?"

So Betty went through the entire history of Kasenetz and Katz. "I'm not sure I can get Sullivan," she said.

"I can get Sullivan," Honeystein said.

"Really? How?"

"We represent him," Honeystein said, smiling.

"Cool." Betty smiled back.

Honeystein stared at his feet for a moment, obviously thinking hard. "I've got an idea. I need a phone."

And so, once again, Betty pushed the visitors' desk phone across. Honeystein dialed quickly.

"David Merrick, please. It's Karl Honeystein."

Holy Broadway, Batman! David Merrick was a super-famous Broadway producer with more than 25 Tony Awards to his credit, including one for his current production of *Hello, Dolly*. (How big? That play would close after winning ten Tony Awards and doing 2,844 performances.)

"David? Karl Honeystein. Listen, what are you doing right now? I need you to do something for me." A slight pause. "I need you to come over to the offices of an agency called Action Talents at 1650 Broadway. I have something here you absolutely have to hear." Honeystein listened for a minute. "Action Talents, 1650 Broadway, 4th floor. End of the hall." Another pause. "That'll be fine David. Thank you. We'll be

here. See you then." He hung up the phone and smiled up at Betty. "Tomorrow morning, 6 AM, right here."

Betty, Karl Honeystein, and David Merrick *(left)* all met the next morning at 6 AM as scheduled. Ed Garland and I stepped back. The situation was that Merrick was closing *Hello, Dolly* and sending it on the road, thus the Broadway theater where it had been playing would be dark.

But Merrick would still have to pay the union workers whether there was anything playing or not. Apparently, as stupid as it sounded to me, those were the union rules. So the idea was to maybe put The Kasenetz-Katz Singing Orchestral Circus into the darkened theater.

A 46-piece Rock orchestra rockin' it on Broadway. A very ambitious idea. It was decided to call in Jeff and Jerry and see what could be worked out.

Right about this time, Gene & Debbe surfaced again.

I don't remember the exact circumstances but somehow, for some reason, I had booked them into a supper club in Columbus, Ohio, through my good friend Jeff Franklin. Everything was just fine with the booking.

Until it wasn't.

At the last minute Debbe, terrified of flying, would not get on the plane. Even Mr. Gnarly Houston couldn't talk her into it. She would not do it. This was just two days before the gig. So, after scrambling a bit, Jeff and I came up with a comedian named Stanley Myron Handleman to cover the date and the club owner went along with the last-minute substitution. Handleman was a fixture on programs such as *The Merv Griffin Show, Dean Martin Presents the Golddiggers, The Ed Sullivan Show,* and *The Tonight Show Starring Johnny Carson.* He was a strange, weird-looking little guy with a goofy little hat, but he was funny: "Hey, I just got up from a sick bed. I don't know what's wrong with it. It just lies there."

Betty decided I should fly out to Columbus, supervise the booking and finally meet Jeff Franklin in person. He'd been a phone friend since my Washington days. We met at the club he was running and together picked up Handleman at his hotel and ferried him to the gig.

To our surprise he was fall-down funny, drew a nice crowd who loved him, and the club owner was a very happy camper. I don't remember exactly when it hit me, but at some point I came up with a big idea.

Since, particularly with The Kasenetz-Katz Singing Orchestral Circus concept being worked on, we were growing, and because, honestly, I was getting antsy again and considering moving on, why not bring Jeff Franklin, who was a sharp as they come, back to New York to meet Betty and see if I could get him hired?

I had known Franklin for years, and he was as sharp and hardnosed a businessman as anyone I knew. He had a lot of experience as a promoter, club owner/manager, booking agent, and general music business hustler.

Plus I liked the guy.

I liked being an agent well enough, and I was very good at it, but the job was more about money than it was about artists and music and, at the end of the day, I was about the music and the artists who made the music. So the idea of bringing Jeff to New York to see if I could get him hired as my potential replacement seemed timely.

I knew of no one sharper than Franklin. He was excited about the opportunity and ready to go, so we jumped on a TWA flight to New York, and Betty, as I suspected she would, hired him on the spot. Jeff instantly became interested in The Kasenetz-Katz Singing Orchestral Circus and almost immediately threw himself headlong into that project.

I had my reservations.

Neil Bogart had locked up Carnegie Hall for Friday night, June 7th. And, remarkably, even though union scale meant the largest payout Ed Sullivan had ever paid to anyone, including Elvis and The Beatles, either Betty or Honeystein, or a combination of the two, had booked *The Ed Sullivan Show* for June 9, the following Sunday.

Jeff Franklin stayed busy booking the Circus on an extended tour of Top 40 radio stations set for later that summer, but I still had my reservations.

We needed Sullivan to happen, not only to cement the tour, but also to get top price for the act. I'd have been a lot more comfortable if Jeff had waited until after Carnegie Hall and the Sullivan show before booking a tour. But Jeff was aggressive and, although I did express my reservations, I wasn't going to do anything to discourage him. Betty was impressed with his efforts and even hired him a secretary, a beautiful young gal named Susan.

I was still worried, but I did my thing and Jeff did his.

And then, all of a sudden, it all went south.

On the night of Wednesday, June 5th, Jeff and Chris Bang came home after a night on the town (we all roomed together) to wake me and tell me Bobby Kennedy had been shot and severely wounded at the Ambassador Hotel in Los Angeles.

Neither of them were particularly interested in politics, it was very late, and they headed to bed.

But I stayed up and watched the coverage through the night, partly because I had once met Bobby when he came to WHVW to do an interview while running for the U.S. Senate in New York. His magic was real, and I was genuinely heartbroken. Also, because I suspected that if Bobby Kennedy died, the planned Sullivan show with The Kasenetz-Katz Singing Orchestral Circus the following Sunday was sure to be canceled or, at a minimum, altered from the acts that had already been scheduled.

And that is exactly what happened.

Robert Kennedy died at 1:44 AM on June 6, 1968.

The Circus played Carnegie Hall the following night, Friday, June 7, and it was truly an extravagant display with the addition of an array of non-musical acts, fire eaters, and a slew of attractive young women.

Barbara Alston
Bookings: Alan White, Pamount Artists Corporation,
1203 28th Street N.W., Washington, DC - 202-337-7015

I walked onstage before the show to congratulate and get a hug from a very excited Barbara Alston, my beautiful friend and former lead singer for The Crystals, who I had booked into the Circus aggregation.

Neil Bogart was in top form, and the show itself was truly amazing. But, just as I had guessed, *The Ed Sullivan Show* Kasenetz-Katz Singing Orchestral Circus appearance was canceled in favor of "A Tribute Show: A National Day of Mourning for Robert F. Kennedy".

It featured Dionne Warwick singing "The Battle Hymn of the Republic", Duke Ellington playing "David, Dance Before the Lord", Richard Harris doing "Camelot", Ed Ames singing "Who Will Answer?", Kate Smith with "The Lord's Prayer", Robert Goulet singing "The Impossible Dream", and a host of others all paying tribute to Bobby.

It was the last live show of the season, and The Kasenetz-Katz Singing Orchestral Circus was never re-booked. Jeff was forced to cancel the tour he had booked; I helped him where I was able to.

Jerry Kasenetz, who was always a bit of a hothead, apparently held out for more money than David Merrick was willing to consider. The way I heard it, at some point Merrick became annoyed by Jerry's stubbornness over one-half of a percentage point, simply donned his little round hat and walked out of the room, forever ending the Broadway hopes of The Kasenetz-Katz Singing Orchestral Circus.

Although Jerry and Jeff caught one small hit called "Quick Joey Small" the following November of 1968, the record only reached #25 on the Billboard Hot 100 and what was left of The Kasenetz-Katz Singing Orchestral Circus soon disbanded.

The album was eventually released, but without Ed Sullivan or a big hit single, it did nothing. For Kasenetz-Katz it was effectively the end of their run of hits.

They had only one small additional hit almost 10 years later in 1977 when they produced "Black Betty" with a couple of our old friends from The Lemon Pipers under a new name, Ram Jam. But the record stalled at #18 on the Billboard Hot 100. Ram Jam and The Kasenetz-Katz Singing Orchestral Circus soon faded into musical and cultural obscurity.

When I left Action Talents at the end of 1968, Jeff Franklin took over. When Betty got a big chunk of money from the settlement with the Hendrix estate, she moved to the U.S. Virgin Islands and bought a hotel.

Franklin bought Action Talents from her and changed the name to ATI, American Talent International Ltd., which he quickly built into one of the nation's top concert booking agencies. He followed Neil Bogart to Hollywood, where Bogart opened Casablanca Records and Film Works. I heard that for a while Jeff had identical offices on both coasts.

Working with Neil, Jeff developed many of Bogart's most famous artists, including KISS, as well as acting as agent for some of the world's most popular recording artists, including Bob Seger, Rod Stewart, Neil Young, The Eagles, John "Cougar" Mellencamp, Rush, Yes, and Dire Straits.

Later in his career Jeff produced or executive-produced both films and TV. Theatrical releases include *Casper*, *Kull the Conqueror*, *Cold Around The Heart*, *Stuart Little*, *The Black Stallion* with Mickey Rooney, *Air America*, *Mowgli*, and *Stuart Little 2*.

His TV productions (U.S. and Canadian) include *High Tide* with Rick Springfield, *Mike Hammer* with Stacy Keach, *African Skies* with Robert Mitchum, *Boogies Diner*, *Stunt Dawgs*, and *Mutant League*, among others.

As CEO of ATI Video Enterprises Inc., Jeff produced television series and specials, including *Radio 1990*, *Heart Light City*, *Love Songs*, *FM TV*, *The Beach Boys Endless Summer*, and *Fall from Grace*.

Jeff's production of USA Network's cult classic *Night Flight*, which ran 9 years, successfully combined his musical talent pool with television and film.

Films which Jeff either produced or executive-produced have grossed over a billion dollars.

To make a long story short, Jeff Franklin became one of the most successful Hollywood agents and producers ever. There was never a doubt in my mind.

Can I pick 'em or what?

The Five Stairsteps & Cubie, circa 1968

40 O-o-h Child

While I was working at Action Talents we mostly booked psychedelic bubblegum rock acts like The Lemon Pipers, 1910 Fruitgum Company, The Ohio Express, The Kazenetz-Katz Singing Orchestral Circus, and The Music Explosion. We booked other artists too, such as Len Barry, Joey Dee & The Starliters, The Crests, The Del-Satins, and most of Buddah Records' roster, including The Brooklyn Bridge.

The Five Stairsteps & Cubie were a family act from Chicago, made up of Betty and Clarence Burke Sr.'s six children: Alohe Jean, Clarence Jr., James, Dennis, Kenneth (Keni), and the youngest, Cubie. They were similar in some ways to The Jackson Five. Clarence Sr. was a former detective for the Chicago Police Department and backed the group on bass guitar, served as manager, and co-wrote songs with Clarence Jr.

They were signed to Buddah, so naturally we booked them, too. This was before their big hit "O-o-h Child", which didn't hit until a couple of years later. It was during their development period when Cubie was only about 5 years old.

Betty booked them on Merv Griffin's afternoon talk show. Our whole office went to the theater to see the show live. Merv had a sidekick, his version of Ed McMahon, a thoroughly disagreeable British actor named Arthur Treacher, who reminded most people of a mean old English butler.

So The Five Stairsteps sang and then Merv brought little Cubie over to the desk. Treacher thought it would be cute to pick Cubie up and put him on his lap, and so he did. Cubie promptly peed all over him. Merv lost it. Merv could not stop laughing. Cubie kept peeing and the crowd went nuts. Treacher was mortified and, if it was possible, even more disagreeable than normal. When he was done, Cubie gave Treacher a big hug. Merv lost it again and went to commercial.

Betty was also mortified, but we were all on the floor laughing. I said to her, "What do we care? Arthur Treacher is not our problem, and Merv thought it was hysterical."

So then she lost it, too.

As a result, though I didn't know them well, I always had a special fondness for The Five Stairsteps and particularly for little Cubie, so I was delighted when they caught their super-sized Top 40 hit "O-o-h Child" in 1970.

The Steps, as we called them, were a cool and very talented act. And although a lot of people through the years have pissed off talk show hosts, to my knowledge, The Five Stairsteps' little Cubie was the only artist ever to piss *on* a talk show host.

Clarence Burke, Jr., lead singer of The Five Stairsteps and a resident of Marietta, Georgia, died May 29th, 2013.

He was 64.

O-o-h, o-o-h child.

Jeff Franklin arriving in Atlanta for a Rod Stewart
show he booked, circa 1977

Mickey Rooney

41 "The Mick"

It was the beginning of the summer of 1968 and I was one of the two or three hot agents on the street that year. David Geffen at the William Morris Agency was another. I was 27.

So here come The Classics IV, an Atlanta soft rock band with a huge hit. Their managers — Cotton Carrier, general manager of the Bill Lowery booking agency, and their former guitar player, now turned songwriter and record producer, Buddy Bowie — flew into New York to meet with Betty and me to see about booking the band.

The Classics IV's first hit, 'Spooky" — "Stormy" and "Traces" would come the following year — was very much soft and middle of the road. Their management was looking for a way to get them booked onto the adult nightclub circuit, particularly into Las Vegas.

Betty wanted to sign the band, but the adult club circuit wasn't exactly our bailiwick, so I reached out to an old friend, King Broder, owner of Entertainment Unlimited in Town of Hempstead on Long Island in New York.

Broder had been a writer for the TV star and comedian Phil Silvers (and even looked and sounded a good deal like him). He was a classy gent famous for exclusively booking nearly all of the comics who went into the resorts in the Catskill Mountains. Broder was an expert on booking comics.

His agency also booked most of the nightclubs on Long Island and his longtime assistant, Helen Gershon, booked virtually every prom dance out that way, too.

King and I were friends long before I made it to New York. When I got there, I made sure all Action Talents artists were available to him and his agency, and that he was allowed to list them in his publicity.

So, for that one small favor, he felt like he owed me one. Plus, we were friends.

It turned out prom week wasn't too far away and the famous Long Island nightclub, The San Souci San, which normally booked only artists like Vic Damone and Jerry Vale, would always book something during the height of the prom season as an opening act for the youngsters.

The San Souci San was a Broder exclusive so, as a favor to me, he booked the Classics IV for one week as an opening act for the headliner, the gigantic movie star Mickey Rooney.

I booked a zillion gigs I didn't go to in my life, but I went to that one. Are you kidding me? Mickey Rooney was a movie star forever. He once famously said, "I've been in the movies all my life, but it seems longer."

I was neatly ensconced in a front row table with an adorable little blonde I had met at the bar and was working my way nicely through a bottle of Chivas Regal when The Classics IV opened with a short set.

Then Mickey came on. He was only 5'2" but this guy owned the entire room, and it was not a small room.

The first part of his nightclub act was a funny standup monologue, after which he perched on a stool and opened it up for questions. He said you could ask him anything at all and he meant it. And they did. They asked about all the famous movie stars he had worked with through the many years. He would ad lib sometimes funny, sometimes informative answers. Mickey Rooney was married 8 times. He was asked about that; in particular about wife #1, the movie star Ava Gardner, who many people still believe was the most beautiful woman ever to grace the silver screen.

I don't remember his exact, fairly explicit answer about her, but suffice it to say my takeaway was that both Rooney and Frank Sinatra (who also married Gardner) must have had a real good time.

As his show went on, for some unknown reason people were looking up, way up over his head. He turned and looked up, too. And there they were.

The Classics IV. Sitting in the balcony orchestra pit, feet up on the railing, dressed in t-shirts and crappy jeans and passing around a big ol' fat doobie.

Mickey Rooney did not like the 1960s. He didn't like the music. He didn't like the way movies and television were going. In particular, he didn't like the hippies. He didn't like the counter-culture generally. He had torn them up pretty good in his opening monologue. So he did what movie stars do — he walked off.

Broder wasn't there that night, so it was on me.

"Mr. Rooney, I am sooo sorry. I'm sad to say that I'm the idiot who booked those guys in here."

"Really? Well, do me a favor kid and book 'em the hell out of here."

"Yes, sir."

I canceled them immediately. King was always such a mensch and he was very cool about it. "So how would you know?" he asked. "Don't worry about it." But I heard later he almost lost the room over it.

Almost 40 years later, Dennis Yost, lead singer of The Classics IV, was touring with my artist Len ("1-2-3") Barry and apparently still yearning for a booking in Las Vegas. So Len told him to call me.

"Alan White can do anything," Len said, not knowing, or possibly not remembering, the Rooney story, and he gave Yost my number. And so Dennis called me with a whole long story about how he had been mistreated by agents though the many years and how he had never gotten his due to be booked into Las Vegas. I waited until he was finished.

"Dennis, we've had this conversation before."

"Huh?"

"Do you happen to remember Mickey Rooney and The San Souci San? I'm the guy who booked you in there."

Long pause, and then, *Click.*

In 2008 Dennis Yost *(below)* died at 65 of respiratory failure following a brain injury he suffered in a fall.

Ava Gardner died of cancer in 1990 at 67. Sinatra paid for her funeral.

Mickey Rooney died in 2014 at 93.

King Broder was the agent who put Eddie Murphy on *Saturday Night Live.* It took a lawsuit, but he told me later that it made him a millionaire. He retired soon after.

He died at 93 in 2015.

Paraphrasing Mickey: You know, I've been in the entertainment business all of my life. But, honest to God, sometimes it seems longer.

The Classics IV, circa 1968

The Lemon Pipers

42 The Lemon Pipers — Lost in New York

Even though "Green Tambourine" was a huge #1 record and I booked The Lemon Pipers *(previous page)* regularly, I never did get to know them very well. They were not guys I hung out with.

At one point they had a very important record hop to do in Brooklyn and, as I was not particularly involved with them personally, and the hop was fairly critical, Betty rented them a limo and assigned her assistant and security blanket Chris Bang to go along as their watchdog and keeper.

It was a Friday night. I had other things on my mind and never gave it a thought. Chris and I were roommates living in a nicely priced third-floor walkup in the Bronx. When I got home later that night, I noticed Chris wasn't home yet.

I wondered if he had decided to stay in town, but again, I thought nothing of it. The phone rang early Saturday morning. It was Chris. The conversation went something like this.

"Um, hey man," said Chris, slurring slightly.

"Hey. What's up?"

"Well, um, I'm not sure."

"Huh? Where are you?"

"Well, that's the thing. I don't really know."

"You don't know where you are?"

"Um, right."

"What the hell?"

"Well, you see what happened is we did a couple of tabs and we got pretty messed up."

"Tabs? Like acid? LSD?"

"Yeah."

"Did you make the record hop?"

"Oh man. Record hop. I knew there was something we were supposed to do."

"You never made it?"

"No. No record hop."

"Jesus. And you don't know where you are?"

"Right."

"Do you still have the limo? Are the boys still with you?"

"Yep. Got the limo. Got The Lemon Pipers too, yep."

"Alright. Do you know our address?"

He correctly repeated our home address.

"Alright. Give our address to the limo driver and have him bring you all here."

"Well, that's another thing. We gave the driver a tab and he's really pretty well strung out, too. He doesn't know where we are either."

I took a deep breath.

"Alright. Let me ask you this. Do you see any cabs?"

"Cabs? Yeah, lots of cabs."

"Alright. Flag down a cab, give him our address, and have the limo driver follow him here."

"Okay, that's good. I'll do that."

And that's what we did, but I was not a happy camper. This proved to be the beginning of Janis Joplin's prophecy about drugs being the end of Rock & Roll.

The Lemon Pipers' music was known as psychedelic bubblegum. As Hank Williams Jr. wrote years later in his song "Family Tradition": "Why must you live out the songs that you wrote?"

The Lemon Pipers never got another hit, although several of them surfaced some years later under the name Ram Jam *(below)* and caught a Top 20 hit with a cover of "Black Betty", an African-American work song often credited to Huddie William "Lead Belly" Ledbetter.

"Black Betty" was produced by our old friends, Jerry Kasenetz and Jeff Katz. It was their final hit as well.

Gary Puckett & The Union Gap

43

"Puck it!"

His name was Gary Puckett and he called his band The Union Gap. They were on fire with "Young Girl" and followed that with "Woman, Woman", "Lady Willpower", and "Over You", similar sounding million-sellers all in a row.

Betty Sperber, understandably, wanted us to sign them. "Puckett wants three things," Betty said. "Sullivan show, a booking in Las Vegas, and a $5000 one-nighter." The latter was about three times what similarly situated artists were getting.

"I can get Sullivan," Betty continued. She was very tight with Vince Calandra, the show's talent coordinator. "Who do we know in Vegas?"

"I don't know a soul," I said. "I've never even been there. I might know some Mob guys who could hook us up."

"No, no, let's stay away from them," she said. "I'll figure Vegas out. You go get me a $5000 one-nighter."

"I don't know, Betty. Five grand? For this kid? That's way outta line."

"What's our deal? If I can do it, you can do it, right?" She smiled. "I've got Sullivan and I'll figure out Vegas."

"Okay, let me see what I can do."

So I went back to my desk and put on my thinking cap. It was an empty cap. Nothing. The phone rang and I answered it, preoccupied and glum. "Action Talents."

"Alan White, please." A loud voice I didn't recognize.

"Speaking."

"Hey, boy! Watcha doin'? This is ol' Sam Caldwell down here in Dallas. Took me a minute to track your ass down."

Sam Caldwell. Jesus. Sam was a guy who would call me from time to time, completely out of the blue, at all hours of day and night, mostly at 3 AM. He'd ask questions about various artists and just want to bullshit. He never booked anything, but I talked to him anyway because he was interesting, bursting with energy, fun to talk to, a wild and crazy guy. I figured one never knows when a guy like him might buy something.

I could never quite figure what Sam did to make all this money he seemed to have but, since he was at his sharpest between midnight and 6 AM, I figured he might be in the hooker business. Or maybe card games. I could never figure how he got my home phone either, but I never asked.

"Hey, Sam."

"Man, you sound like your dog died. You alright, son?"

"Yeah, I'm fine." But I told him about the Gary Puckett situation anyway.

"Five grand a night for that guy? Man, your dog really did die." He laughed. "When is this idiot open?"

"For five grand? Anytime you can book it."

"Let me see what I can do. I'll call you back."

"That'd be great. Thanks, Sam." And he was gone. Yeah, right. Nothing was gonna happen with this.

But, an hour or so later, Sam called back. "Hey, boy, it's Caldwell in Dallas again. I got your $5000 one-nighter."

"What?" I jumped to my feet.

"Yep. One show each in two different clubs though. One in North Dallas and one in South Dallas. $2500 each."

"I don't care if he sings in a phone booth as long as he gets $5000 for the night. Is this real? Sam, you're a genius. When?"

I was on my feet, ripping open the routing book.

He gave me a date which, thankfully, Puckett happened to have open, and guaranteed the $2500 deposit would hit my office before the close of business that day. I sauntered into Betty's office and sat down in the chair in front of her desk. Big grin.

"You look like the cat who ate the canary," she said.

"I did. It was tasty. One show for $2500 in North Dallas, one show for $2500 in South Dallas. Same night. Five grand. Deposit by 5. Boom."

Bigger grin. The deposit arrived right on time for Caldwell's $5000 one-nighter in Dallas. Betty locked down Sullivan that same day. The Vegas booking came a couple of days later.

All three dates played and then Gary Puckett *(below)* signed with the William Morris Agency. He wasn't so popular around our office after that.

When his name came up at all, we referred to him as Gary [Something That Rhymes Nicely With Puckett].

Bobby Lewis

44 We Didn't Sleep At All That Night

While an agent at both Paramount
Artists and Action Talents, I booked 1960s
recording star Bobby Lewis a fair amount. He only had one
big hit ("Tossin' & Turnin'"), but boy what a hit it was.
Billboard magazine ranked it as the 27th-biggest song of all
time that charted on the Billboard Hot 100. It is one of only six
songs from the 1960s to spend at least seven weeks in the #1
position on the Hot 100.

Still, Bobby was a solo artist who did not carry a band, so
he was priced reasonably, was thoroughly professional, and
always showed up and showed out.

He was a particular favorite at my own club, The Rumpus
Room in upstate New York, 90 minutes from Manhattan.
When Bobby was booked there, my dad would bring the
mayor of our town, Torrington, Connecticut, only about 40
miles or so of mountain driving away.

One weekend in the summer of '68, when I had Bobby
booked, I picked him up at his small, dark hotel in Harlem on
Friday night after work and we drove up together to The
Rumpus Room for the two-night gig and got rooms at a mid-
line motel not too far from the club.

Bobby opened the shows with one of the most memorable
opening lines in Rock & Roll history —

"I couldn't sleep at all last night!"

It was a great couple of shows, and both were very good nights. Dad loved it, the mayor was happy, the club made some money and, when it was all over Saturday night, I grabbed a couple of bottles from the liquor closet. Bobby and I went back the motel to drink. Already pretty good friends, we gabbed and laughed and drank the long night away. The next thing we knew there was a knock at the door.

Check-out time! What? We hadn't even gone to bed yet. Bobby looked at his watch.

"Damn, man," he said. "I'm supposed to be picking my boys up in Jersey and taking them to a Mets doubleheader."

I laughed. "We're pretty drunk."

"Yeah, we are."

"So we better get going."

We set a little bar up in the back seat of my 1967 Chevrolet Camaro convertible, fire engine red with a white top and interior, tapered off the booze a bit without stopping completely, and off we went, hellbent toward New Jersey.

When we got to the Holland Tunnel to cross over into Jersey, there was lot of traffic, and since we were late as hell and I was pretty trashed, I was driving like a crazy man, speeding and swerving in and out to get around the traffic. When I passed one of the tunnel police, standing in the little booths along the side of the tunnel, I realized I'd better slow the hell down.

And I did. But not in time.

They were set up and waiting at the end of the tunnel, lights flashing. Bobby turned and covered up the little bar with his jacket when he saw them.

I said, "Well, this is the great Bobby Lewis and I'm his agent and he just did a really long, late show and we are supposed to pick up his kids and take them to a Mets doubleheader and we are late as hell and so I guess I was driving a little faster than I should have been and I'm really, really, really sorry officer."

"That ain't Bobby Lewis," said the cop.

"No, it really is."

"No, it's not."

"Yes, officer, it really is."

So now Bobby, who has no jacket and is wearing a wrinkled white shirt opened two buttons down, and is pretty trashed himself, climbs into the back seat, crawls out onto the trunk of the car, stands up, throws back his head and screams:

"I couldn't sleep at all last night, 'cause I was thinking of you," and then he proceeds to sing the entire song, dancing around on the trunk of my car.

I figured we were both going to jail. But I was wrong.

There was no more talk of speeding or reckless driving or tickets, just autographs, same banter about the Mets, and shaking hands with the police fanboys.

"What exit those boys live at?" asked one of the cops.

Bobby told them and they said to follow them. They got into their patrol car, hit the lights and took off about 80 miles an hour all the way to the exit, where they waved us past the toll booth and on our way.

It's good to have a hit record.

We got to Shea Stadium about halfway through the first game, switched to beer and stayed until the last out. I took it that Bobby had missed a lot of other promises to the boys, as entertainers often do, but he didn't miss this one. The boys, about 8 and 10, had a blast. We took them back to their mom in Jersey and slogged slowly back into the city.

We were exhausted.

When we got to his hotel, he took a deep breath and slowly got out of the top-down convertible. Then he turned to me, threw back his head and shouted, "We didn't sleep at all last night."

We both laughed the laugh of the stupid, exhausted, and drunk, with Bobby doubling up with laughter and hanging onto the car fender. Then he stood up, took another deep breath, gave me a big, long, tired grin and a wave, and disappeared into the dark Harlem night.

I never saw him again.

As of this writing in 2019, Bobby is 86 years old.

45 The Man Who Sold The Brooklyn Bridge

Once every month while I was at Action Talents, on a Monday, Betty Sperber would host a band showcase at Cloud Nine, a nightclub on Long Island near where she lived. On each occasion she would promise the club owner that she would bring in one of her "name" recording artists to make a brief appearance.

One particular Monday night, recording star Johnny Maestro *(left)* of The Crests, who lived nearby, was the scheduled guest performer.

All the bands, save one, played guitar-driven Rock. Johnny asked which band he should rehearse with.

"Can any of these bands even play 'Sixteen Candles?'" he asked suspiciously.

"Well," I replied, "none of these hard Rock bands can. But there is this one, a big 7-piece horn band called The Rhythm Method, which has a leader, a keyboard player named Tom Sullivan, who has written charts for West Point. He and they are very musical. And the band is large, not guitar-driven, and has horns. They are all very young, but I think they'd be okay."

So Johnny went off to rehearse with the very, very young Rhythm Method. The rehearsal in the kitchen went so well that, although he was just supposed to sing "Sixteen Candles", Johnny decided to do all of the other Crests hits as well —

[275]

"The Angels Listened In", "Trouble In Paradise", and "Step By Step".

Johnny and The Rhythm Method absolutely killed it.

The result was so cool that the next afternoon Sperber announced in a staff meeting she had decided to merge Johnny and The Del-Satins (who Johnny had been singing lead with and who also worked as his Crests) with the big band The Rhythm Method.

"Man," I said, "that's 12 people."

"Eleven," Betty said. "One of the Del-Satins is leaving."

"Still," I said, "It would be easier to sell The Brooklyn Bridge than 11 people."

Betty loved the name. "That's it! I love that. That's going to be their name. The Brooklyn Bridge."

"Too much coffee, Betty," I said wearily. "I'm going home. We can talk about it more tomorrow."

Johnny Maestro & The Brooklyn Bridge

The next morning, when I came into the office, nobody was there except the receptionist, Andrea.

"Where is everybody?" I asked.

"Um," Andrea replied, somewhat frazzled with about four phone lines all ringing at once.

"Betty, Maestro, three of the Del-Satins, Neil Bogart from Buddah, that band from Monday night, The Rhythm Method, everybody else from our office, the Mayor of Brooklyn, and some photographer are all on the Brooklyn Bridge."

Wes Farrell

Lordy, this woman is going to make me sell The Brooklyn Bridge for real. Betty signed the group to Buddah Records, which was oriented toward hit singles.

At some point, I was called upstairs into an A&R meeting with Betty, the 26-year-old Bogart (head of Buddah), red hot

Neil Bogart

producer Wes Farrell (The Cowsills and The Partridge Family), also 26, and Johnny Maestro.

Farrell had produced three songs on The Brooklyn Bridge. Neil hated all three. They were screaming at each other when I arrived. I sat down on the couch next to Johnny and he leaned over to me and said in a soft voice, "Alan, there is this Jimmy Webb song I found on a Fifth Dimension album and I think I could really sing the heck out of it."

"Hey!" I screamed over them. "Johnny is the guy who has to sing the songs. Listen to him?"

The room went quiet and Johnny went on to describe "The Worst That Could Happen".

"Fine!" shouted Neil Bogart.

"Fine!" shouted Wes Farrell.

"The Worst That Could Happen", produced by Farrell, released by Buddah, became the best that could happen for everybody involved. I didn't know Johnny well. We didn't hang out or anything. But from time to time he'd call me on my hotline and ask me to intervene with Betty on some deal he didn't want to do. I think he thought of me as his hammer, and I was happy to do it.

That was the way it was during the summer of '68, when The Best That Could Happen to Johnny, The Del-Satins, and The Rhythm Method actually did.

They are all gone now — from cancer.
Neil Bogart. 1982. Age 39.
Wes Farrell. 1996. Age 56.
Betty Sperber. 1993. Age 63.
Johnny Maestro. 2010. Age 70.

46 The Pig That Squealed

By the end of the summer of 1968 I was looking around for something else to do. My time at Action Talents had been great, and we had done a lot of cool, meaningful things, but it was all becoming routine and repetitively predictable.

I was getting antsy again. I was always pushing Len Barry. Buddah promo genius Marty Thau was always pushing Tony Orlando. With Al Schwartz it was Billy Vera.

From left: Billy Vera, Jerry Wexler of Atlantic Records, and Al Schwartz (Photo courtesy of Billy Vera)

In 1967, Vera, a songwriting and production genius, had a groundbreaking hit record, "Storybook Children", an interracial duet with former Gospel singer Judy Clay, and their follow-up "Country Girl, City Man" also charted. Vera also had another hit later that same year, this time a solo with Bobby Goldsboro's "With Pen in Hand", a great song.

Al Schwartz and I were running buddies. At night, after work, we'd run the streets of Manhattan going from club to club. He was tight with Jilly Rizzo, so Jilly's was a stop. I liked the cool acoustical joints in the upper 70s, where hipsters like Turley Richards *(left)* held forth.

There were 3 people considered to be breakthrough artists in New York during that summer of 1968. One was Jerry Jeff Walker, who had a great record with song he had written, "Mr. Bojangles". Everybody, including me, thought that on the strength of that record alone, Jerry Jeff Walker would become a huge star.

Another was Kenny Rogers who, with his group The First Edition, had a big hit record titled "Just Dropped In (To See What Condition Your Condition Was In)".

The third was the guitar-playing, acoustic, Folk, R&B, and Soul singer Turley Richards, who had been knocking on the door of big-time recording success for several years. Richards was already blind in his right eye from a childhood accident and slowing losing sight in his other eye.

He had a nice 6-night gig at Malachy's II, located at 72nd & Lexington in the now-historic Upper East Side. It was cool, laid back, and off the normal rush-rush pace of New York. Al and I would stop in there a lot. The drinks were good and priced right.

And Turley Richards was magical.

Al Schwartz knew some very cool people.

One night we dropped into the office of Claus Ogerman *(left)*, the brilliant German arranger who had written the charts for some of my favorite records, like "Cry To Me" by Solomon Burke and all of the Lesley Gore smash hit classics such as "It's My Party", "Judy's Turn to Cry", "She's a Fool", and "Maybe I Know".

They had hired Quincy Jones to produce Lesley Gore *(left)*, but they hired Claus Ogerman to write the charts. We had an interesting conversation about race and music production in America.

Knowing I was getting restless, Al set me up with an interview for a job as a record promoter with RCA Records.

The guy at RCA was well dressed in a corporate-approved white shirt and tie and sat behind a small desk in an even smaller, windowless office. While he was nice enough, he got right down to business. He played me three records.

The first one was terrible, just awful. And I told him so.

The second was "Nicole", the follow-up to Four Jacks & a Jill's big hit single "Master Jack". It was a pleasant enough record, but not special enough to be a hit, and I predicted it would get to #70 and crash.

The third record was a masterpiece.

"That's a Top 5 million-seller right there," I told him. "You're going to the Grammys with that record."

He thanked me for coming in and told me he'd let me know. I found out from Al the next day that I didn't get an offer because RCA thought all three records were pigs.

"What the hell, Al? Pigs? They've got a big hit record over there. I'll grant you that the other two records he played for me were pigs, but that last *pig* he played me...that one is a stone smash."

"Record executives are not generally known for their great ears," Al said, philosophically and correctly.

"Jesus." And that was the end of that.

Until it wasn't.

I was in Winston-Salem, North Carolina, visiting my great friend The Flying Dutchman, known to his friends as simply Dutch. Dutch was the morning man and Music Director for WTOB radio, the #1 Top 40 station in Winston-Salem, and his morning show dominated the ratings.

Top 40
Radio legend
The Flying
Dutchman,
on-air at WTOB

We were very drunk.

It was a party thrown by some local record distributor in a Holiday Inn suite for all the Top 40 radio DJ's in Winston-Salem. "Daddio" from competitor WAIR was there. All the top radio guys in Winston-Salem were there.

It was late, maybe 3 AM, and everybody was pretty trashed. I got to talking with a very nice, college-looking couple in their mid-twenties. He was dressed in the college-issue paisley shirt and khaki pants, and she had on honest-to-God polka dots.

He was handsome and she was pretty. But he was depressed because he felt he was about to lose his job and that made Wifey sad, too. It turned out he was a record promoter for RCA and had "gone out on" (an industry term meaning committed himself to) a record that wasn't going to make it.

I asked what the record was. Yep, you guessed it. It was record #3 RCA played me, the *pig* that was a masterpiece.

"You have any of those records with you?" I asked.

"Yeah, I've got 10 boxes in the trunk of the car."

"Go get me one."

The Dutchman was a highly intelligent, super Type A personality who had been a radio star forever. He was my best friend. But you couldn't tell Dutch anything. However, Dutch could tell you things. And so, that's the way I played it.

"Hey, Dutchie."

"Yeah? What?"

"This fellow here works for RCA and he and I and Wifey all think this record he went out on is a smash, but he can't get it going and he thinks RCA is about to fire him. Wondering if you'd listen to the record and give us your opinion on why we're wrong."

"Shore," he said, finishing off his drink. "Play me the record." So we did and two verses in, he got serious. "Jesus, that's a smash." He turned to the kids and said, "Don't worry about a thing. Alan and I will break this record for you. Done deal. Don't worry about a thing. We got this."

And then he made himself another drink. It was a Saturday morning and he had to be on the air in three hours, but somehow he drank himself sober and went in and did the morning show like he'd never had a drink in his life.

I went home and crashed with my girlfriend, Connie Moore *(left)*, who wasn't so thrilled I came in at 6 AM.

At 10 the phone rang. It was Dutch.

"Where the hell are you?"

"Um, I'm in bed with sweet Miss Connie, right here where I'm supposed to be on a Saturday morning at 10 AM."

"You lied to those kids?"

"Huh?"

"You told them we'd break their record."

"It's Saturday."

"What? There's a law I don't know about? You can't break a record on Saturday?"

"Well, no. But…"

"Then get your ass in here."

I sat up slowly, my hangover protesting loudly. "Alright. On the way."

"Hurry up. We've got work to do."

"Yeah, okay."

"What the hell?" asked Connie.

"Long story. Gotta go. Make it up to you tonight."

"You better."

So I packed up my hangover, got dressed, gussied up as best I could, and drove to the station. By the time I got there Dutch had already sewed up the big, #1 Top 40 station in Charlotte, North Carolina, and WTOB's sister station, Big WAYS. The program director there already had the record in his junk pile, pulled it out while he was on the phone with Dutch, loved it, and immediately, as Dutch had also done, made it his pick hit of the week.

Not bad, WTOB in Winston and Big WAYS in Charlotte. Two big pick hits. Nice start.

"Let's go to Greensboro," Dutch said.

"It's Saturday."

"What is it with you and Saturday? Is it some kind of religious holiday for you?"

So off we went to Greensboro. When we got to the big Top 40 station there, it turned out to be located in a house on the outskirts of town. Dutch knocked on the basement door, which had a small sign with the station call letters.

The fellow who answered the door had headphones hanging around his neck, so it was clear he was not only the only one there, he was also the DJ on the air.

"Hi, sorry to bother you." Dutch said. "I'm The Flying Dutchman, and…"

"You're The Flying Dutchman? Wow!" He held out his hand. "Come on in, man!"

Dutch and I shook his outstretched hand and into the station we went. Sometimes it's nice to be famous. It turned out he was the Program Director and was only working the Saturday mid-day shift because someone had called in sick. Ten minutes later the record was his pick hit of the week.

"Let's go to Raleigh and see Charlie Brown at WKIX," said Dutch.

"It's Saturday."

Dutch let out a very long sigh. I just laughed. "No, I mean I don't think Charlie Brown works on Saturday."

"What do you know? You've never even been to Raleigh."

"He's a big star."

"I'm a big star. I work on Saturday."

So we went to Raleigh. And damned if Charlie Brown wasn't on the air, glad to meet Dutch, and more than willing to make the record his pick hit of the week, too.

WTOB, Winston-Salem. Big WAYS in Charlotte. The Top 40 station in Greensboro. Charlie Brown and WKIX in Raleigh.

That first record RCA played for me was never heard from again. "Nicole" reached exactly where I said it would: #70, and the next week it dropped off the charts altogether. The third record — the *pig* that was a masterpiece — was "Light My Fire" by José Feliciano.

Dutch and I broke it out of the Carolinas. It went Top 5, reaching #3 on the U.S. Pop charts, with over one million copies sold in the U.S. market alone. José Feliciano won Grammy awards in 1968; one for Best New Artist and another for Best Pop Song of the Year.

It may have been a pig. But if it was, that was one pig that really squealed. Can I pick 'em or can I pick 'em?

Kenny Rogers went on to become a major force in American music.

Jerry Jeff Walker's version of "Mr. Bojangles" failed. It took The Nitty Gritty Dirt Band to make it a hit several years later. Walker never became a star.

Turley Richards lost his eyesight completely after a few more years. He continues to struggle along in the music business to this day.

Although Al was no longer his manager, Billy Vera and his band The Beaters had a huge #1 hit record, "At This Moment". Billy lives in L.A., where he continues to perform and has a book called *Harlem To Hollywood*.

I never called RCA back.

Vince Montana playing the vibraphones for "Keem-O-Sabe"

47 "It's Time For Indians."

It was November 4, 1968, the day Nixon was elected president, when I got to Philly. I needed a job and, with the exception of the Norman Joyce Agency, the booking agency business in Philadelphia was totally Mob-controlled.

Best not to get too deeply involved with the Mob and Norman didn't need an agent, so I took a job at a small employment agency, Edison Personnel. It was pretty much the same job as being a booking agent — phone sales — but I was selling accountants and computer programmers instead of singers and musicians.

It took me about 6 weeks to catch on, and then I began to make placements hand over fist and cash began rolling in. It was a small agency, just three or four of us, and we all answered the phone.

"Edison Personnel," I said, answering the ringing phone in the middle of a weekday afternoon.

"It's time for Indians," said Len Barry.

"I beg your pardon."

"It's time for Indians," he repeated.

"Okay," I responded, hesitatingly.

"Yep, we got civil rights pretty much done. So now it is time to draw attention to what is happening to Indians. Let me ask you a question. I can't sing on a record unless it goes through Johnny Madera, right?"

"As you know, I haven't seen the contract, but as I understand it, yeah, that's right."

"Can I produce a record?" he asked.

"Again, I haven't read the contract, but as far as I know you can."

"Okay, good. That's what I'm gonna do."

"But you can't sing on it," I reminded him.

"No problem, it's an instrumental."

Now I was really scratching my head. "Um, no offense, but all the success you've had, first with The Dovells, and later with your solo career, has always been due to the amazingly unique sound of your voice. An instrumental? I don't know about that."

"It's gonna be great. I'm going over to Vince Montana's house this afternoon and we're gonna write it together. I'm gonna call it 'Keem-O-Sabe', and I'm gonna call the band The Electric Indian."

Len Barry and Vince Montana wrote it. Tommy Sellers from Gulliver arranged it. Len produced it. Daryl Hall and Tim Moore, also from Gulliver, played on it.

It cost $2500 to produce.

A number of the investors were key DJ's at Philadelphia's #1 R&B station, WDAS. Hy Lit, Butterball, Jimmy Bishop, and WDAS General Manager Bob Kline all put up money.

Even Bernie Bennick from SWAN Records had a piece.

When it was finished, all the investors hated it. No one wanted to pay for it. Every record label turned it down.

"No problem," Len said. "I'm going to put it out on my own label."

"I don't know, Len."

"It'll be fine. You'll see."

Boy, did I ever.

WDAS was the number one black station in Philadelphia and with three of their DJ's and their General Manager involved as investors, you can bet they played it like a station jingle. That broke the record wide open.

It sold 16,000 copies in like 10 days on a local imprint Len named Marmaduke Records, created just for the "Keem-O-Sabe" release.

U.A. paid $50,000 for the master, with an album to follow. It was re-released on United Artists Records. Instrumentals could become big hits back then because they could be faded down to create perfect timing going into the network and local newscasts. Beginning its run in August of 1969, "Keem-O-Sabe" eventually reached #16 on the Billboard Hot 100.

Len Barry had plans to create a large 9- or 10-piece all-girl band of Native American and black musicians. He wanted me to put it together, manage the daily, and book the band.

Johnny Madera *(left)*, the hit songwriter (Danny & The Juniors, Lesley Gore) who had co-written and co-produced Len's solo hits and had a valid production contract on Len, had pushed his way into the project, apparently by way of a songwriting clause in the contract I had never seen.

A meeting of all the partners was called at John's office to discuss the future of the project.

Everyone was there — Len, John Madera, all three WDAS DJ's (Butterball, Jimmy Bishop, Hy Lit), and a few others.

Len and I sat there for over an hour and no one said a word to Len. He looked over at me and made a fist with his left hand and moved his right hand in a circular motion alongside the fist. Then he got up and left the room.

Another half an hour or so went by and then someone asked, "Where's Len?"

They looked at me. "He went to the movies," I answered.

"What do you mean he went to the movies? What does that even mean?" someone asked.

"It means he's out," I said. "No one bothered to even speak to him in this meeting and that tells him everybody is going to try to have a say in everything going forward. He created this out of whole cloth and isn't going to waste his time making this production by committee. So, he's out."

I got up and left the room.

Vince Montana finished the album brilliantly, but without Len's creative input the follow-up single and album did nothing. It was, indeed, Time For Indians.

It just wasn't Time For Partners.

48 Peak Performance

My great friend Clarence Peaks —
Michigan State, Philadelphia Eagles, and
Pittsburgh Steelers running back — was a
Heisman runner-up and the #7 pick in the first round of the
1957 NFL draft. Although he was injured and did not play in
the final game, Clarence was on the Philadelphia Eagles' 1960

Championship team. From the moment I first met him, about 1970, until 1973 when I left Philadelphia, Clarence (*left*) and I were great running buddies.

He was funny, handsome, smart, well-spoken, smooth, and well-dressed. With his gigantic personality and fabulous smile, he was selling life insurance and making money right and left and hand over fist in his full-time retirement job for a major insurance agency.

Night after night we haunted the singles bars and chased the pretty ladies of Philadelphia. Our favorite was hot spot The Grog Shop, located in the Suburban (Train) Station building, where thousands of office workers worked and tens of thousands more had to pass each night on their way to the train and home. The band, Terry Briggs and Company, started at 5 PM.

In 1972, I produced a record for Terry Briggs under the name The Electric Cowboy. Daryl Hall and John Oates both played on that session. So did the great Vince Montana and rhythm guitar genius Bobby Ely.

The record was a cover of the "Theme From M*A*S*H" coming out on Hickory Records the first year the TV show went on the air. Unfortunately for me, the show wasn't a hit until year two, long after my record had come and gone.

Clarence and I were deeply committed to our pursuit of damsels fair, and we did some outrageous stuff. For instance, Clarence and I would sit at a table next to the bar playing an imaginary game of chess with salt shakers, cigarette packs, lighters, coins — any small objects that could act as chess pieces. We acted it out in full dramatic fashion, moving pieces around on the table, taking each other's pieces, and gushing fake anguish and despair as one of us took a piece from the other.

It was all imaginary, but the people who gathered around to watch thought we were playing a real game. Often they would ask to play the winner.

It was hysterical.

We had bets going on as to who could catch the prettiest gal. Often, on Friday nights, Clarence would rent an upscale hotel suite and throw a party, inviting all the gals we had met in the most recent few weeks. Various NFL football buddies often turned up.

One time my office manager, Eddy Rahn, and I got there early to help Clarence set up the suite. There was only one other person there at that early hour. He was a handsome black man dressed in turquoise and white and carrying a purse. I thought he was a pimp. The fellow sat motionless as Clarence, Eddy, and I worked and talked football. On this occasion, I was once again banging on with my favorite steadfast opinion about Tom Landry, the Dallas Cowboys' coach: He was a racist prick.

"I can't believe Herb Adderly and Bob Hayes can play for that guy."

Clarence burst out laughing hysterically. "Alan," he says, pointing in the direction of Mr. Turquoise, "I'd like you to meet my good friend, Herb Adderly."

I just met my all-time favorite Dallas Cowboy, Herb Adderly, and very likely totally insulted him. I was crushed and got busy apologizing. "Oh man, I'm really sorry."

But Herb was the smoothest of the smooth. "No need, brother. You got it right. Tom Landry is a complete and total racist pig. Bob and I play there for the money."

Clarence and Eddy and Mr. Turquoise and I had a glorious time that night.

When I left Philly and went on the road in 1974, Clarence and I lost touch. I looked him up in 2006 but found only Clarence Jr., his son. Clarence was in the hospital with heart trouble. His son told him I was looking for him, but he suffered from some dementia as well, and could only sort of remember me.

He was such a super friend and, believe me when I tell you, a man could have no finer running buddy than the great Clarence Peaks. Only my friend "Notepad" can compare.

Shortly after I had tried to reestablish contact, Clarence died of congestive heart failure in 2007. I think of him often, especially when I see Michigan State or the Philadelphia Eagles play football.

He must have been in heaven for real when he saw the Eagles win it all in 2018.

RIP, old friend. I'll be along soon enough. We'll chase us some angels and play that game again.

49 The End of the World

When the money was right, I went on the road. The money got right in upstate New York, and I spent 6 months in early 1976 DJ'ing at The Pump House Tavern in Watertown, where summer occurs every year approximately on July 11th.

We had 17 inches of snow on opening night and were sold out. The Watertown experience was weird. The Pump House *(previous page: Alan at The Pump House Tavern, 1976)* was packed every night because I went to the one and only local radio station and recorded a banging, professional 30-second spot for the club. I was a much more experienced radio DJ than the local fellows; the other DJ's were mesmerized as they watched me produce and voice the spot. I used KC and The Sunshine Band's "That's The Way I Like It" under the spot. It has a 24-second walkup before it sings the title. So you can say your club is hot, or whatever, and the record will answer you with the title, "That's The Way, Uh Huh, I Like It." Cute, but professional.

I did it in one take and the guys just stood there, watching and learning. It ran every ten minutes and I became Pump House Watertown famous.

It was pretty weird.

McDonald's didn't charge me for food. The manager was a Pump House customer. I don't remember his name, but I remember his record, "Green-Eyed Lady" by Jerry Corbetta and Sugarloaf. I met Corbetta a few years later when he was playing keyboards and rehearsing for a Frankie Valli tour.

The cleaners didn't charge me either. The gas station charged me for gas, but not to put the snow chains on the tires of my van. When I went into a local restaurant for a solitary dinner, you could see them shyly looking my way and nodding for their friends to take a look: *That's him over there.*

It was pretty strange.

There was, however, a parallel universe of long-haired hard rockers who held forth at a dive bar right up the street from The Pump House. Since all the girls were dancing at our place and buzzing about the big-time radio DJ from the big city, these dudes hated my guts.

We had a bouncer, Charlie, who was supposedly the toughest guy in Watertown. During the winter he liked to cross into Canada and go up into the mountains all by himself and hunt wolves. Clearly this fellow had a different pain threshold from normal people.

The club had Charlie wearing a ruffled tuxedo shirt, which he complained about because he figured the first few weeks there'd be guys wanting to challenge him and the shirts would be ripped right off.

"Every year there are some new boys who figure to take me out and build a reputation for themselves," he explained.

And sure enough there were. Over the first month or two there were probably four or five, but Charlie quickly dispatched them. A couple of times it didn't even rumple his shirt. The hard rockers did not love me, and occasionally I would find threatening notes on my car windshield. I told Charlie I sure was glad he was around.

On one occasion, at the end of the night walking to my car parked in the back of the club, three longhairs were waiting for me. I was judging the distance from where I was standing and evaluating my ability to get to the trunk of my car to get a tire iron to maybe even the odds a little when I heard a voice from behind me.

"Good evening, gentlemen," Charlie said. He looked at me. "I'll take care of this, Alan."

I backed away. It was over quickly.

Charlie knocked one of them cold as a cucumber, had one holding his broken nose and crying for his mama, while the third one took off running with a singular dedication to speed. That was the end of threatening notes on my windshield.

Because there was virtually nothing to do in Watertown, when I wasn't at the club I mostly I stayed in the motel room, which the club graciously paid for in addition to my considerable salary. I had to drive all the way to Syracuse to even buy records.

I did, however, have a lovely girlfriend, one of the prettiest gals I ever spent time with. But other than seeing her, all you could do there was save money. Watertown lives in its own frozen, isolated little world.

It's not the end of the world, but if you stand real tall on the bumper of your car, you can probably see it from there.

Ted Turner at Atlanta-Fulton County Stadium

50 The Power Of Power

I was booked to emcee an event at Atlanta-Fulton County Stadium on the night of Friday, the 20th of May 1977, that was considered by some to be so lascivious that the authorities would eventually step in and stop it before it ever happened.

Only they didn't.

It was College Night for the Atlanta Braves, featuring a wet t-shirt contest after the game. Some contestants were sponsored by fraternities, so that brought the college crowd out in force. All of that was followed by 15-cent draft beer in centerfield after the game.

Lots of nightclubs were having wet t-shirt contests around Atlanta in the spring of '77, none more visibly than our own regular Thursday night contest at the Roswell Road hot spot, Second Sun, where I was the resident DJ and nightly promotion emcee.

My girlfriend at the time, the super-hot and totally lovely Miss Nanette Fernandez (*left*), was going around town from club to club winning one wet t-shirt contest after another as a way of making a fine living. She won nearly every contest she entered: $100 here, $200 there.

I guess the Braves figured they needed a real, big-time, professional wet t-shirt emcee for their promotion, and because our Thursday night contest at Second Sun was advertised on radio, thus highly visible, they called owner Greg Decker. Being a sharp businessman and promoter, he jumped on the idea and booked me for the gig.

No money, there never is with these kinds of deals, but the event was great promotion for Second Sun.

It came out many years later that the Braves' Promotion Director, a man with the unfortunate name of Bob Hope, was quite the Puritan and thought the contest was a terrible idea — one so lewd, so perverse, and so offensive that public officials would obviously step in and stop it.

Only none ever did.

The Metro Atlanta Christian Council summoned both Hope and Ted Turner to a meeting to discuss the promotion. Hope thought for sure they would demand an end to this foolishness once and for all.

But they didn't.

Instead all they wanted was for it to be moved to after the game so families and children could leave the stadium without having to be exposed to the almost pornographic spectacle of pretty females with actual water on their t-shirts.

Oh, and just one other little request: The Metro Atlanta Christian Council wanted their own judge.

I didn't know any of this when I arrived to do the gig.

There had been a two-hour rain delay, so it was a hot and muggy Georgia pre-summer night. There was a huge crowd which, depending on who you listened to after the event, ranged from 27,000 to 49,000.

It looked more like the 49,000 to me.

Whatever it was, it was lot more than the 10,000 or less the Braves had been averaging. The place was absolutely packed, the crowd was raucous, and just about everybody was having themselves some fun.

Ted Turner was in the dugout; it was his first night back after being suspended for — reportedly — getting drunk at a party and "tampering with" pending free-agent superstar outfielder Gary Matthews.

The Braves got killed 11-0.

The Braves' brain trust had assembled a group of about 25 local sort-of-famous celebrities to be judges. They were lined up from home plate to first base, roughly halfway between the dugout and the baseline.

The Cubbies were setting up chairs in front of their dugout to watch the contest even before the game ended. To hootin' and hollerin' from the crowd, forty-three lovely contestants sashayed out to the baseline and lined up from home plate to first base.

I was led out to the field and handed a microphone. When I said "check, check," three things became apparent. Number one, you could not hear the microphone on the field. Number two, you could sure hear it in the stands because even "check, check" had the crowd cheering louder. Number three, this crowd was R.E.A.D.Y.

A uniformed police officer walked out onto the field, came right up to me and said, "My name is Captain Whalen and if any of these girls take their top off, you're going to jail."

"Hey man, it's got nothing to do with me if some chick takes her top off. I'm just the emcee," I replied.

"Yeah, well I'm just saying."

"Really?"

"Yeah, really. If any of them take their top off, you're gonna go to jail."

"We'll see," I muttered.

Then Bob Hope comes up to me and says, "Tell those judges to kneel down. They're blocking everyone's view."

"You can't hear the microphone on the field," I explained, amazed he didn't already know that.

"Just do what I tell you," he barked.

There was a distinct lack of politeness going on here. Alright man, I can play. This was not my first rodeo.

"Are you ready?" I asked Hope. Captain Whalen looked on suspiciously as he kept a sharp eye out for anybody trying to show naughty parts.

"Yeah, do it."

So I did. Since I wasn't getting paid, I was for sure going to promote my own club gig first.

"Good evening, ladies and gentlemen. Welcome to Atlanta-Fulton County Stadium."

The crowd cheered.

"My name is Alan White and I am the emcee for tonight's wet t-shirt contest as well as our Thursday night wet t-shirt contest at the Second Sun nightclub located on Roswell Road at Wieuca."

They were screaming now. I paused to let the noise subside. "I'd like you to meet this gentleman right here."

I pointed to Captain Whalen. There was a scattering of polite applause. "His name is Captain Whalen and he says that if any of these gals takes her top off, I'm going to jail."

The crowd booed louder than I ever heard a crowd boo before or since. Whalen flushed and, rattled, turned quickly and rapidly jogged off the field. I never saw him again. Bob Hope did not look pleased, but I was having fun.

"Tell 'em to move," Hope said.

I spoke slowly and distinctly to give the judges the best chance of hearing me. "Okay, now what I need you judges to do is to please kneel down so people can see the girls."

The crowd screamed in anticipation, but the PA system could not be heard on the field, so none of the judges moved. Ted Turner, standing on the steps of the dugout, was close enough to the stands that he could hear clearly.

Ted caught on real quick that the judges couldn't hear and charged out to the field, waving his hands to get attention and pushing his palms down. "Get down, get down," he yelled and gestured frantically. The crowd cheered him on. "Get down, get down," he continued.

And so, as the judges turned, they saw it was Ted Turner personally screaming at them and, almost as if they had been choreographed, knelt in unison.

Seeing that, the crowd went wild, and I said, "That, ladies and gentlemen, is power."

Seeing Turner and hearing me, the fired-up crowd went crazy. But Turner, who by that time was too far away from the stands, did not hear my witticism. Terry Tingle, Turner's secretary at the time — wonderful gal and a good friend of mine — later told Ted what I said about power.

It cracked him up.

I was told that Playboy magazine had a photographer at the event and, in one their subsequent editions, they published pictures of all the gals getting splashed with water, but even with all my thorough and deep Internet searching, I have not yet been able to find that issue.

Captain Whalen was eventually fired from the Atlanta police force. Allegedly he was involved and implicated in a major police force cheating scandal. Bob Hope was transferred to the Hawks as vice-president. Urban legend has it that Bob Hope was told to lose every game so the team could nab the #1 draft pick.

That night my gal Nannette came in second, won a nice TV, and together we went right back to Second Sun to finish the always-fun Friday night party.

The winner of the wet t-shirt contest and $500 first prize was the 24-year-old daughter of a Methodist minister.

Karma is a bitch.
And Power is really powerful.

Tim Monig, Polydor Records promotion head in the South,
presents Alan White with a Gold record for breaking
Alicia Bridges' "I Love the Nightlife".
At back, DJ Barbara Woods — BJ The DJ.

51

I Love The Nightlife

My good friend Tim Monig was head of promotion for Polydor Records in the South. He walked into the sound booth at Jeryl's where I was doing a happy hour show one Monday afternoon in the late summer, early autumn of 1978.

Polydor Records' offices were in the same office complex as Jeryl's, so there was a group from Polydor in there pretty much every evening after work. Tim was the man at Polydor, he ran the place. Don Studley was their super promo man who could sell anything to anybody. But the official head honcho, the General Manager, was a real nice guy named Herb Heldt.

"Herb is drunk," Tim said, smiling. "He wants to know why his Alicia Bridges record isn't a hit. If you get a minute come over. Say something smart. Calm him down."

I picked up my copy of Billboard and checked the chart. The Alicia Bridges record, "I Love The Nightlife", was still stuck on the Hot 100 at about #60, where it had been for weeks. I put on Donna Summer's "Four Seasons of Love" concept album, which contained extremely long tracks named "Spring Affair", "Summer Fever", "Autumn Changes", and "Winter Melody". Each side was 16 or 17 minutes.

I walked over and sat down at the Polydor table. Herb was trashed, so I spoke very slowly. "The problem, Herb, is that the song is called 'I Love The Nightlife', and, parenthetically, 'Disco Round'. It's a Disco record. But it's only a 45. Radio doesn't play Disco records which aren't hits in clubs. And we don't play 45s."

Herb looked confused. Tim was grinning. Studley was laughing out loud.

"So, what I gotta do?" Herb asked, with a nice slur.

"You need a 12-inch version. A club remix."

"You do that?"

"No. But I know a terrific guy who does."

A year or so earlier I had spent the goodly part of a night visiting in the sound booth with the amazing DJ Jim Burgess. We got along famously. He was DJ'ing at The Casbah, a super hip, alternative music Disco down in the back of a small strip shopping center right off Peachtree Street downtown. The Casbah didn't even open until midnight.

Because Jim and I spent a lot of time talking about the subject of remixing, much of it relevant to a record I had just finished co-producing in New York for the all-girl band Isis, it was clear to me the man knew his stuff.

I was new in Atlanta and Jim was nice enough to steer me toward Jeryl's, a mainstream Disco which played hits and had a DJ who sometimes talked. Playing hits and talking is exactly what I do, and it worked out nicely. I became the resident DJ and Music Director at Jeryl's for the rest of the Disco era.

In turn, I promised to check with United Artists to see if they'd go for a remix on one of the dance-oriented Isis tracks, "Give It Up" .

They wouldn't.

We exchanged phone numbers that night, and I still had his number in my wallet as I sat with Polydor discussing the "I Love The Nightlife" issue. So I passed his number on to Tim.

"I'll give it to Herb in the morning." Tim grinned. "This guy is good?"

"He is. And he is in Atlanta. Or was."

"Cool."

That was a Monday.

Friday night a gal came up to the booth and asked if I was Mr. White. "Mr. White is my father," I smiled. "Whatcha got there, Kiddo?"

And she handed me a 12" version of "I Love The Nightlife", remixed by Jim Burgess. Holy cow. Four days? When Herbie Boy sobers up he can get things done. Either that or Tim took the lead. I played it next. It was wonderful. The sax solo was mixed too loud, but other than that it was terrific.

So now I had skin in the game. The next Monday I raced to get my copy of Billboard. Still stuck at #60. But I knew radio was on it now.

The number one radio DJ in Atlanta history, Gary McKee, worked at Jeryl's every Wednesday night, and I knew him well. At Jeryl's, we were very associated with his radio station, the oddly named 94Q, and I knew for sure they were now playing the record. Still stuck at around #60.

But I was playing it too and knew what most radio stations didn't. "I Love The Nightlife" was an instant dance floor hit. So, to me, it was just matter of time.

The following week I was stunned to see the record still stuck in the 60s on the Hot 100.

What the heck? I checked the Dance chart. Nothing. But the record was packing my dance floor and generating so many requests I had to play it twice, sometimes three times a night. It was a huge hit. The following week I went straight to the Dance chart, but I still didn't see it.

Then I checked to see what the #1 record was.

Boom!

#1 on the Dance chart — first week on the chart! Since a #1 debut is very rare, I rushed to see the Hot 100 chart.

Boom! Racing up the Hot 100 into the Top 10.

In total, "I Love The Nightlife" spent 31 weeks in the Billboard Hot 100, peaking at #5 on December 23, 1978.

The 1979 Grammys opened with nothing but a black screen. Then a deep-voiced announcer said only this, "Ladies and Gentlemen, Miss Alicia Bridges." *(Below)*

And there she was, opening the Grammy show and loving the hell out of the nightlife. Tim Monig arranged for me to get a Gold record for helping break the record.

Tim eventually left Polydor and went on to open the Justin Records distributorship in Atlanta. He died suddenly, heart attack, leaving behind his only son, Justin.

Tragic.

Don Studley went on to many adventures in and out of music. He died in early 2019.

Jim Burgess went on to remix many Disco records, including "Do Ya Think I'm Sexy" for Rod Stewart.

To my knowledge, he never knew who passed his number to Polydor. The many remixes made him a lot of money and garnered him a lot of fame. He eventually made the move to Philadelphia to pursue his first ambition, opera singing.

Although he was never diagnosed with AIDS, Jim Burgess took ill soon after Labor Day in 1992. He died of an AIDS-related opportunistic infection four months after taking ill, January of 1993 at his home in Philadelphia.

Alicia Bridges had a rebirth of sorts in 1994, when "I Love The Nightlife" was re-released as a featured part of the movie *The Adventures of Priscilla, Queen of the Desert.*

She asked me to help her promote the record and manage her comeback. I accompanied her to the Atlanta premiere of the movie. At her request, I arranged a brand new record deal with Island Records, but oddly she turned it down and, without warning nor explanation, requested all efforts on her behalf be halted.

She lives in North Carolina.

As far as I know, she never sought a record deal again.

Gary U.S. Bonds

Len Barry

Gunthers Bus

52

Who Do You Think I Am?

Not only was Jeryl's located between
what Penthouse magazine said were two
of the hottest singles complexes in America, it was also located
in the Shadowood Office Park containing three huge office
buildings totaling almost 200,000 square feet. Jeryl's was the
primary ground-floor tenant in one of those buildings.

In those days stopping for drinks after work at happy hour
was popular and, given where we were located, we had a
huge potential for after-work partying. Jeryl's offered the same
two-for-one drinks as everyone else around us did, but our
competitive advantage was me running my mouth and, more
importantly, playing great music. I did a radio-style show in a
club, introing songs and providing interesting and
entertaining patter between them. The first year I DJ'd for
Jeryl's, I began promptly at 5 PM and went straight through
until the night DJ began at 9. It was an interesting format.

The first two hours I alternated between a current Top 40
hit and an oldie. The third hour I played the biggest Disco hits
of the moment in order to get the dance floor going. The last
hour, with the dance floor already rocking, I backed away
from hits so the night DJ could repeat them and only played
new music on its way to hitdom.

I always left a full dance floor for the night guy, a very
handsome black guy and former radio DJ who, oddly I
thought, didn't talk very much. His name was Dave "Brown
Sugar" Smith.

When I got off work my first night there I saw a
cameraman seemingly interviewing a bartender. The club was
packed and the music was deafening. I went over and

watched as he did this and, given the ear-splitting volume at which Dave was running the music, I stepped forward and asked, "Excuse me, but what's the deal here?"

"I'm from Channel 17. It's a spot for a bartending school."

"May I ask who is producing this?" I pressed.

"I am," the cameraman said. "Nobody else showed up."

"You know the music is drowning out any conversation?"

"Yep, but what can I do? They ain't gonna turn it down."

"No, you're right, they aren't. Good luck." I smiled and went home.

The next day when I arrived at the club, in what would become a daily ritual, I stopped into the boss's office to let him know I was there and see if there was anything I should know, such as food or drink specials or maybe an upcoming promotion.

The General Manager was just a kid, Jim Sissine, who was maybe 25 — if that. He came from a gig at McDonald's and was one of the sharpest, most aggressive people I ever met.

"What happened with that bartending school?" I asked.

He was pissed. "Ah, it was a mess. The sound was all screwed up. That's over. Too bad, there was going to be an overlay at the bottom of the screen saying Jeryl's Discotheque, Restaurant and Backgammon Club. Would've been great promotion."

"You are done with it?"

"Yeah. Guy at the school doesn't want to pay to re-cut it."

"You mind if I fool with it?"

"Nope. Not at all. Have at it." He gave me the contact information for the guy at the school, Marcus Katz.

First words out of Marcus' mouth were, "I'm not spending another goddamned dime."

"You got 15 bucks?" I asked.

"15 bucks? For what?"

"To re-cut the spot. I just got off the phone with Channel 17. Sixty minutes of audio booth time is $30. I only need 30 minutes. So $15."

"What do you want to do?"

"I want to wipe the audio off the track completely and cut a radio-style 30-second audio commercial to insert under the video footage of the packed club."

He thought for a second. "That's not a bad idea."

So he met me at Channel 17, put up the $15, and I recorded a banging 30-second commercial, which gave the school's phone number like 4 times. Once again I used KC and The Sunshine Band's "That's The Way I Like It" and its perfect 24-second walkup.

The video footage was already cool, my spot was banging, and I got them to constantly flash the phone number all the way through. We added the overlay at the bottom of the screen that Jim wanted, "Jeryl's Discotheque, Restaurant and Backgammon Club."

Now here is a little historical context:

WTCG, Channel 17, was a lowly UHF station nobody much watched until Ted Turner bought it. During the day, Turner ran reruns of popular shows from years gone by and from midnight until 6 AM he ran movies all night, hosted by a clever off-the-wall young comedian — and news reader — by the name of Bill Tush.

Tush caught fire. It seemed like every TV in Atlanta was tuned to Channel 17 after midnight and whatever nonsense Tush came up with was water-cooler fodder the next day.

Commercials were not expensive, particularly after midnight, so Marcus Katz bought an aggressive late-night schedule for very little money. The phone rang off the hook right away. Katz had to bring in more people just to answer the phones. Almost immediately he wanted to re-shoot the video with me on camera doing the spiel.

I never had much interest in acting because, for one thing, I'm lousy at memorization. But I had done many short TV commercials in my career and 30 seconds, or even 60, is not exactly *Gone With The Wind*. But I prepared like it was.

I wrote the copy and memorized it until I had it backwards. Then I pre-planned every physical move I would make on-camera and chose to dress all in black.

On the day of the shoot, once again Channel 17 sent a solitary cameraman. No one from the bartending school showed up either. It was just me and the camera guy, who had his truck parked at the front door and ran his cables into the club. We set up on the dance floor so he could shoot me in the sound booth. He stood on a chair so he'd be the same height as I was in the raised booth.

He said, "Let's do it once and see where we are for time."

I began by picking up a record from a turntable and sliding it into its jacket, all while looking at the camera. This establishes that I'm a DJ without me having to waste the time to say so.

"Hi. This is Alan White from the Disco here at Jeryl's."

That was both my personal plug and, along with the overlay that would be added at the bottom of the screen, the plug for the club itself.

"I know who makes all the money in the bar business, and it's men and women just like you. Now I don't know if you could make big money in the bar business, but I know who does know. It's the Georgia School of Bartending."

Here is where the phone number would start flashing on the screen for the rest of the spot.

"Call them now at..."

Then I gave the phone number again.

And again.

"Nothing will happen unless you call, so call right now."

I gave the phone number. And we were out.

"Let me go out in the van and check the time," the cameraman said. When he came back he was laughing.

"It's 29:59."

One-sixtieth of a second short of a perfect 30 seconds.

"You want to do it again?"

"Hell, no. What are you? Nuts? That's perfect. I've never even seen that before. I'm outta here."

"Can I see it?"

"Sure."

So we went out to the van and watched the spot. I hit all the moves, the video was clean and sharp, and the vocal was spotless. We both went home.

The commercial ran something like 16 times every night after midnight on Channel 17 for many, many years and the Georgia School of Bartending was gigantically successful.

Bartenders everywhere recognized me and made fun of the commercial. But they did it in good fun, and most of them bought all my drinks.

Years later, long after Jeryl's had stupidly gone Urban Cowboy and closed, I was in Houston, Texas, on business when one night having dinner with a lovely young lady, a gal came up to our table and asked for my autograph. This was not completely uncommon as I was around a lot of music events and occasionally someone would think I was an artist.

"Sure. Who do you think I am?" I asked, smiling.

"I think you're Alan White from the Georgia School of Bartending," she smiled back.

"Oh, you're from Atlanta?" I asked.

"No, I'm from here," she said. "We get Channel 17 here and I see you all the time."

So I signed the autograph, my date was very impressed, and that's how I found out about Ted Turner and his idea for nationwide cable TV in quite an interesting way.

The Memphis Belle

53

Backed up against the PDK Airport in Chamblee, just outside of Atlanta, is the popular 57th Fighter Group Restaurant *(previous page: entrance and Alan DJ'ing in the club area)* on Clairmont Road. Its entrance is built with sandbags like a WWII bunker. Its bathrooms feature recordings of inspiring speeches of famous folks from that time.

Lots of pilots frequent the joint, and that is where, in 2008 as I was DJ'ing in the lounge/dance side of 57th, I met the pilot of The Memphis Belle, one of the first United States Army Air Forces B-17 heavy bombers to complete 25 combat missions and about which movies were made. The pilot was now in his mid-80s, drinking Scotch on the rocks, surrounded by a crowd of admirers, still as sharp as they come.

I walked over, introduced myself, and offered to play his favorite tunes, but he said, "No, I'm afraid my favorites were way before your time, young man."

"Really? Well, I'll tell you what I'll do for you. I'll play your two favorite songs, back to back, and you don't even have to tell me what they are."

"Well, now, that'd be a good trick if you can do it."

So, I figured if he'd been on the dance floors of America, his favorite song would have been "Sing, Sing, Sing". But he wasn't on the dance floors of America, he was serving overseas, which meant Armed Forces Radio, which meant Glenn Miller. So, back to back like I promised, I played "In The Mood" and "String Of Pearls". Yep, sure enough, they were his two favorite tunes. He walked around all night saying, "That DJ played the damnedest trick on me and I still don't know how he did it."

I love doing stuff like that. I must have put him In The Mood: He tipped me $20.

54 I Can Go For That

A little over 45 years ago in Philadelphia I hired a couple of guys from the band Gulliver *(previous page)* to play on a session I was producing at Sigma Sound on the theme from the soon-to-debut TV show *M*A*S*H*. They were John Oates, guitar, and Daryl Hall, Hammond B3 organ.

Daryl *(left)* was a great player; great singer too even then. I didn't know about his songwriting; the world found that out later. Guitarist Tim Moore was the primary songwriter for Gulliver.

I had never met John Oates *(below in 2016, with permission of mattchristine.com)*, but he came by my office on Chestnut Street in Center City one day and we worked out what I was looking for with the record. Nice of John to take the time. Nice guy, another great studio musician. And I didn't know about his songwriting then either. All the members of Gulliver became successful.

Tommy Sellers, the genius bass player who had arranged "Keem-O-Sabe", went on to arrange the Top 40

Disco smash "Rock The Boat" by The Hues Corporation. He also arranged and produced "Wham Bang Shang A-Lang", a big Top 40 hit by Silver. Under his own studio name, The Assembled Multitude, he had a Top 40 hit with "Overture" from The Who's rock opera "Tommy", reaching #16 on the Billboard Hot 100.

Intellectual songwriter and musician Tim Moore, who wrote many important songs including "Charmer" (which won a significant national songwriting contest) and "Second Avenue" (Art Garfunkel's biggest solo hit), played guitar for Gulliver and wrote most of the songs on the album "Gulliver" released in 1969 on Elektra Records.

Moore currently lives in Woodstock, New York. We're Facebook friends and occasionally chat and revisit the heydays of Philadelphia.

Gulliver drummer Jim Helmer went on to play for Patti LaBelle. John Oates joined Gulliver only briefly, recording several demos shortly before they disbanded.

Tragically, Tommy Sellers died in March of 1988 in a famous Philadelphia house fire that killed his entire family.

We all know what happened with Daryl and John. But...

John and Daryl never took anybody with them. Not that I ever heard of anyway. Nobody from Philly ever got a call. Daryl didn't return any calls. They recorded in New York and seemingly forgot about everybody and anybody Philly.

I once reached out to Daryl on behalf of Len Barry. Nothing. Crickets. And so, massively talented as they both were, and as much as I loved their music, Daryl Hall sort of pissed me off. It didn't feel right, given all the help they had gotten from the Philadelphia music community at large, that on the way up they never reached out to anybody back home.

As it happened, in 2014 I was watching HBO when Daryl and John were — deservedly! — inducted into the Rock & Roll Hall of Fame. John spoke at considerable length about Philly. About how and when he moved to Philadelphia from New York, and how the town influenced his thinking, music, and such. It was very nice.

Leaning down into the microphone without bothering to adjust it for his tall height, Daryl said the following I quote here word for word:

"And speaking of Philadelphia, I did some research. Do you know we are the only homegrown Philadelphia band that has been put into the Rock & Roll Hall of Fame? You guys know that? Now I'm not saying that because I'm proud of that. I'm saying it because that's fucked up.

"What happened to Todd Rundgren, The Stylistics, The Delfonics, Harold Melvin & The Blue Notes, [John grins, claps, and says "Bring it!"], Lenny Barry, Chubby Checker? How about the biggest hit single in the history of the world, Chubby Checker, 'The Twist'? Why isn't he in here? Huh? Huh?

"You guys tell me. Alright? So I'm calling everybody out. There better be more Philadelphia artists in this place. Okay? That's all I got to say. And I now wanna go play."

And he did.

A legendary 40-year Hall of Fame career and that's what he had to say about what he thought was important. Daryl Hall had just erased 40-odd years of my pissed-offed-ness.

John Oates grinned and clapped along, every bit of the way. All is forgiven. Now I can go back to digging their music and watching *Live From Daryl's House* on the Internet. Because that shit Daryl said on the show was Righteous.

Daryl sent me a nice, very short email after he saw what I had written about him and his Hall of Fame speech.

"Amen, Brother" is all it said.

In a post-induction interview Daryl said something else I liked almost as well. Speaking about his surprise at being inducted into the Rock & Roll Hall of Fame at all because the Hall of Fame crowd represented music business people and he wasn't friends with people in the music business, he said: "The music business is organized crime."
To that I say: Amen, Brother.

Damn Daryl, you're on a roll here, son.
Because, once again, that shit was Righteous.
And I can go for that.

55 Take Me Home Tonight

Eddie Money and I got really drunk. Here's how that happened.

It was during the 1986 Bobby Poe Pop Music Survey Convention, held at an Atlanta airport hotel. My old friend Bobby Poe had comped admission so my then-wife, Miriam, and my late foster son, P.R. Grim (who signed on as my driver so I could drink), decided we'd go check it out and see what we could see.

The entire floor was dedicated to the convention. Every record company had a room. Many with suites all to themselves. Directly across from the elevator was the Universal/MCA suite. It was gigantic and lavish. Atlanta Falcons cheerleaders pranced around everywhere. It was packed when we arrived. Naturally Miriam and P.R. headed for the MCA party.

I wandered the area looking at what else was happening. All of a sudden there was a scrum of people pushing its way across the floor, headed for who knows where.

When the scrum halted for a moment, I found myself face to face with ex-Van Halen frontman David Lee Roth (*left*), who at the time was red hot with a hit record cover of "Just a Gigolo", the Louis Prima classic.

"Congratulations on Gigolo," I said to David Lee. "I'm a DJ at an oldies club here in Atlanta. They like your version as well as they do the Prima version."

"Really?" he said as the scrum began to move a bit. "Hold on a minute, guys," he said to the scrum generally. "I need to talk to this guy."

He turned back to me. "If you were me, what song would you do next?" The scrum was inching forward.

I knew the perfect song, but I just couldn't come up with the title. "Ah," I stumbled as the scrum began to move forward once again, even as David Lee was trying to hold it back. "Ah…"

It just wasn't there. I was brain dead on the song I knew would be perfect, and with time running out as the scrum had a mind of its own, I had to come up with something else.

"I guess I'd jack some old Sinatra song like 'That's Life' or something."

"Cool. Thanks." And the scrum took him away and pushed him into a relatively small room, which turned out to be the Warner Bros. suite not far up the hall.

I let the scrum pass and followed it into the suite. But I never really got much past the doorway and found myself standing next to the open door to the bathroom. As much as I would have liked a free drink, I wasn't about to push my way through that crowd to get to the bar at the far end of the room, so I stood where I was, people-watching. All of a sudden, a fellow came into the room who looked familiar.

"I know you," I said.

"I'm Eddie Money."

"Of course you are," I said, laughing. "I'm Alan White, a local DJ." We shook hands. "I used to work for Bobby back in the day."

"Bobby?"

"Poe. It's his convention. The Pop Music Survey."

"Oh yeah, right. You got enough influence around here to get us a drink?"

Eddie Money

I laughed. "Not at all. Even if I did, I'm not about to fight my way through that mess."

"I hear ya. Come on man, follow me. I know where we can get all the drinks we want."

Boy did he ever.

It was the Columbia Records suite. Twice the size of Universal/MCA, five times the size of Warner Bros. — and, with the exception of about half a dozen black, all-male servers dressed in tuxedos — the room was totally empty.

There was an unbelievably long couch upon which a dozen people could have perched. Eddie and I landed on it while servers rushed to get us drinks.

Scotch and ice for me. Jack and ice for him.

Sometimes you just click with a guy, and that was the case with me and Eddie Money. We sat there drinking, talking, and laughing, totally oblivious to the convention going on outside.

"What do you think the greatest oldie of all time is?" Eddie asked.

"I think it's whichever one is your favorite."

"Which in your case is…" he pressed.

"Me? 'Be My Baby', The Ronettes."

"Oh, that's perfect." I knew where he was going. He was looking to cover it.

"No," I said. "It won't work. That record, as great as the song is, and as cool as the production is, it's all about Veronica's voice. You can't cover it. Andy Kim tried it in, like, 1974 and he had small hit with it, but it was nothing to write home about. It is all about Veronica Spector."

We drank, laughed, and talked for hours, ignoring the convention. But Eddie kept coming back to the idea of covering "Be My Baby".

"No, I'm telling you, man. It means nothing without Veronica. Her voice, with all that magnificent vibrato, is maybe the greatest female vocal sound in all of Rock & Roll. Great song. In fact, it might be the best song Jeff Barry, Ellie Greenwich, and Phil Spector ever wrote, but it is not a hit without her. Not a big hit anyway."

And so it went. The free drinks kept coming. And coming. We were getting trashed. We drank the convention away and had a really great time. And every so often Eddie would come back to "Be My Baby".

But I wouldn't budge. "Nope. Not without Veronica."

Finally the night was over and we shook hands and said our goodbyes. I never saw Eddie Money again.

But several months later Eddie's new record came out. It was "Take Me Home Tonight" and right in the middle of the record it breaks down into "Be My Baby" with none other than

Veronica Spector *(below)* herself singing the title line. The
rascal went out and got her. I love it when they listen.

"Take Me Home Tonight" by Eddie Money reached #4 on
the Billboard Hot 100 in 1986.

David Lee Roth did "That's Life". It wasn't much of a
radio hit, though the video dominated the MTV playlist for
months. The song I was reaching out for that night to
recommend to David Lee — but could not remember the title
of for the life of me — was "Closer To The Bone", a classic
Jump Blues song by Louis Prima's singing saxophone player,
Sam Butera.

Too bad. Would've been a smash.

I wonder if it's too late.

Hey, David Lee.

Call me.

56 Be-Bop-A-Leap

It was very early on a Saturday night in 1994 and, as there is no happy hour to set up for a Saturday night crowd, Johnny's Hideaway was virtually empty.

The manager, "Waxie" Gordon, was there, stationed at his usual spot at the front door. A solitary couple was sitting at Joey's back bar. But that was pretty much it.

These were the days of CDs and I was busy setting up my CD list and the sound booth for what promised to be a very busy night when Waxie came up to me, nodded toward Joey's back bar and the couple, and said:

"That's Steve Martin *(previous page, bottom)* back there. And Catherine O'Hara from *Home Alone.*"

So I looked and, yep, although I couldn't recognize the gal, the fellow was sure enough Steve Martin.

"Oh, cool. Joey must be digging that."

I went back to my setup, getting the sound booth just the way I wanted it before I opened the night with some jazzy Big Band music, as we always did in the early evening. A little Sinatra here, some cool Basie there, a little laid-back chill thrown in the mix upping the "atmospheric pressure" if you get my drift. I began to wonder what would it take to get the Wild & Crazy Guy out on a very early and quite empty dance floor. I guessed he was around my age. (Actually he is three-and-a-half years younger.) People from that era could partner dance. I wanted to play something Steve probably hadn't heard in many years. After considerable thought I settled "Be-Bop-A-Lula", the 1957 one-hit wonder Rock & Roll classic by Gene Vincent and His Blue Caps *(previous page, top).*

Boom. Martin and O'Hara hit the dance floor.

The Wild & Crazy guy must have had a few drinks because he was wild and crazy. O'Hara, to her credit, struggled but kept up. Again, after considerable study of the situation, still trying to keep him dancing, I went with 1958's "Queen of the Hop" by Bobby Darin. Boom. That worked, too. I lost him on the third song, whatever that was, and as he walked by the booth he said, "Thanks for the tunes, man."

"Thanks for *Leap of Faith*," I replied.

(Leap of Faith is a movie with Debra Winger where Martin's character is a tent revival preacher and the movie exposes all the tricks they use to con and deceive their flock.)

Martin stopped in his tracks, turned to me and said, "Of all the movies I've made, you are thanking me for *Leap of Faith*?"

"Somebody had to do it," I said.

He threw back his head into a big ol' hearty laugh and gave me big thumbs up. He went back to the bar, O'Hara, and his drink. Soon the place began to fill up, and he and Catherine left before the crowd began to bug them.

Be-Bop-A-Lula.

And I don't mean maybe.

57 The Most Beautiful Girl, Part 2

It was always the two of them.

Around 2004 they started coming to our Swing dances in Reunions Lounge at The Perimeter Marriott, and later at the 57th Fighter Group Restaurant.

Kemp looked the part of the runway model. Tall, slender, absolutely gorgeous; stunning, really. Big brown eyes, full lips with a gleaming white smile and dark, reddish hair. She was all of 17. I hadn't seen anything like her since 18-year-old Paulette back in the old Action Talents days. Eden was shorter, cute as she could be, with reddish blonde hair, a ready smile and a gigantic, super-friendly personality.

They said they were sisters, but later I learned they were inseparable friends since toddlerhood.

Eden took her Swing dancing seriously, learned quickly and mostly danced with the better leads. Kemp less so. She had a Holly Golightly free spirit way about her, sometimes twirling around barefoot. All the boys wanted to dance with her. The girls would sometimes come to the Waffle House

Kemp and Alan's son Zach at a Georgia Tech Swing Kids Dance.

with "Notepad" and me for breakfast after the dance, where we learned that both girls played guitar and wrote Folk songs with surprisingly strong melodies that both sang beautifully. If that wasn't enough, Kemp and Eden both are smart, smart, smart. Big IQs.

One night, when my then-ten-year-old son Zachary was with us at the Waffle House, he and Kemp went out into the parking lot to rollerblade. There must have been half a dozen guys just standing outside, leaning on the restaurant wall, watching in awe.

Kemp ignored them.

That Kemp was a perfect runway model was obvious. "Eden, the way she looks, Kemp should be doing some modeling."

Hmmmm was her non-response.

So I tried again. "I mean, she just has that look."

"She does a little of that." Eden didn't seem interested in talking about it, so I let it go.

Each week at eleven o'clock at our Wednesday night Marriott dances, I shut down the music, read any announcements for the upcoming week and, if there was a birthday or two, we did our birthday dance. Given that it was a weekday, and the fact the dance ended at midnight, people began to file out after that.

One night Kemp came in about five minutes before eleven. "Oh wow," I said by way of greeting, "I didn't think you were gonna make it tonight."

"That airplane sat on the damn tarmac in Paris for four freaking hours," she said. "It was unbelievable."

"Glad you made it."

Later that night, sitting at the computer in my home office, working through the night as I often do, all of a sudden I wasn't buying it.

What is a 17-year-old girl doing on the tarmac in Paris flying to Atlanta for a Swing dance? Or for any other reason? So I did an Internet search on Kemp, getting Kemp Technologies and The Kemp Instructional Design Model, which was apparently some kind of technology. Finally, on a whim, I typed in Kemp Supermodel.

Boom! She was everywhere. Vogue, Cosmopolitan, Allure. You name it and she had the cover. New York, Paris, London, Rome. Her name was actually Kemp Muhl and she was a real-life, big-time Supermodel.

The next week when Kemp showed up at the window of my sound booth I said, "Well, good evening, Miss Muhl."

"Aw no, how'd you find out?" she said glumly.

"New thing called the Internet," I grinned.

She was not happy. "Please don't say anything or I'll have to stop coming."

So, other than "Notepad", I told no one.

It turned out that after winning a modeling contest at an Atlanta-area mall, Kemp had been modeling since the age of 13. She was the youngest model to appear on the covers of Harper's and Queen, two British magazines, when she was just 16. She'd been on the cover of virtually every significant fashion magazine in every corner of the world and featured in campaigns for Tommy Hilfiger, Sisley, D&G, Donna Karan and, most recently, as a Maybelline girl.

Even back then, young as she was, as she traveled all over the world, we heard that she earned an amazing $10,000 an hour. One night Kemp came with Zachary and me to a Georgia Tech Swing dance.

After the dance a large group of Swing Kids decided to go Steak 'n Shake for breakfast. Kemp wanted Zach and me to go with her. We went. She ordered a big cheeseburger and we split a Coke.

"Don't you have to watch your weight?"

"Not really," she laughed. "I'm lucky that way."

She was lucky in a whole lot of ways. When it was time to pay she wanted me to walk her to the cash register, which of course I did.

She handed the cashier an American Express Black card, the one with no spending limit.

The guy looked at me like I was her father.

"Don't look at me, pal. It's her card."

"Okay. Who are you paying for?" he asked.

"Everybody."

"Everybody?"

"Everybody we came with," she motioned to where everyone was seated. "All those guys over there."

Cashier Boy looked at me again. I shrugged and said, "Quit looking at me. It's her card and it's good. Trust me." To Kemp I said, "That was very nice of you."

"My pleasure."

Eden, quite the artist, went off to art college in Savannah. When Kemp turned 18 and her stockpiled money came through, she moved to New York.

Through Eden, who occasionally came back to Atlanta and showed up at dances I was doing, we learned Kemp had moved in with Sean Lennon, John Lennon's son, and together they formed an alternative Folk music band, The Ghost Of A Saber Tooth Tiger, titled after a children's book Kemp wrote as a child.

A few years ago Kemp and Sean Lennon blew through Atlanta on a tour to promote their latest CD, and I went to their show. There was Kemp playing recorder, keyboard, guitar, and doing vocals, with Sean on guitar and vocals, too. They had a trumpet player from Julliard and a sound man who doubled as the van driver. Eden ran the merch table.

At the end of the night Sean was walking out the front door of the small club, pulling his little cart. Kemp called out, "Sean. Hometown, honey. I have people to see here."

Kemp, friend, and Sean (Photo by Nicolas Genin)

And even though they had to drive to Houston that night, Sean said, "Oh, okay." He pulled his little cart to the bar and ordered a beer.

I joined him there and we talked for 20 minutes or so. "I hope you are enjoying all of this," I said. "As hard as the road seems sometimes, the real fun's the journey. Once you get wherever it is you are going, it all becomes kind of routine."

"Oh yeah, I get that," he replied. "I'm having fun enough. I like these small venues. I can't play the big ones. If I do, all they want me to play are Beatle songs."

"I'll bet."

"I wasn't in The Beatles," he said.

Overall, I found Sean to be impressive. He was quiet, a bit reserved, polite, and respectful. And smart. John would be very proud. I left that night feeling that my friend Kemp had found the perfect fellow for her. They have so much in common: Brains, fame, talent, and music.

And they both have a whole lot of Nice.

Alan and Kemp
at Eden's
engagement party

A few years ago I got a call from a fellow who said he was Eden's boyfriend. He was planning a party where he was going to propose to Eden in front of all of her close friends. It was going to be a complete surprise, and he wanted to hire "Notepad" and me to DJ this party. The night of the party there was a CD signing in New York for "The Ghost Of A Saber Tooth Tiger" but, ever the loyal friend, Kemp flew to Atlanta, leaving Sean to tend to the CD signing.

This young man of Eden's, a fellow named Justin, turned out to be quite the guy. He had this thing planned down to the most minute detail. He thought of everything. Music, where everybody should be standing when she came in, the whole bit. In a quick dry run, he even knelt down and practiced the proposal to a hassock.

As part of the plan, Eden had been pulled away from the house and was somewhere shopping with a friend who was, of course, in on the surprise.

It went off without a hitch, Eden said yes, everybody was tearful, and I can't tell you how good it felt to see them all this way. Kemp up there in New York with Sean. Eden agreeing to spend forever with this handsome young man who clearly adored her.

As of this writing, Kemp is still with Sean and remains one of Maybelline's hottest models.

"The Ghost Of A Saber Tooth Tiger" continues to get positive reviews.

Eden *(below with Alan at the 57 Fighter Group in 2005)* and Justin have two beautiful daughters.

I'm a sucker for a happy ending.

The original *Swingjugend,* or Swing Youth, in 1930s Germany
used dance to stand up for freedom

The Swing Kids

58

In 1993, my then-wife and I went to see *Swing Kids*, a movie based on true events, directed by Thomas Carter and starring a young Christian Bale, among others.

It is the true story of the *Swingjugend,* or Swing Youth, in 1930s Germany. They were a group of young Jazz and Swing lovers, boys and girls between 14 and 21, who admired the British and American way of life.

At the time, young supporters of Adolf Hitler were successfully recruiting young people with, as we now know, false promises of success. Defining themselves — and their quest for true freedom — through music and dance, the Swing Youth opposed National Socialism, especially the Hitler Youth Movement.

The dancing in the movie is authentic, very fast, Big Band, Lindy-style dancing to bands like Count Basie, Benny Goodman, The Andrews Sisters, and more.

As I sat watching the film, I got to thinking. I always knew partner dancing would come back with a vengeance. This movie might be the catalyst.

"You really think kids will go out and learn how to do all this fancy Swing dancing?" Wifey asked as we left the theater.

"Um, yeah," I ventured. "Maybe."

"So, even if they do, how will you get in front of them? You're older than dirt."

I had to admit she had a point. I was 52. Old dirt.

"I'll figure it out," I replied cheerfully, with my normal, if not feigned, optimism.

By 1996, it was clear to me if the nightclub industry was going to survive the DUI checks at all, they needed to develop a customer base that would go out to dance. Since dancers don't drink much, they'd have to be willing to pay a cover charge. It was clear that alcohol alone would no longer be a sufficient revenue stream to operate a nightclub.

After looking around a bit for a club with dancer potential, I chose startup restaurant and nightclub Carey's Corner, operated by Carey Dunn, a very sharp fellow with a long and successful history as a nightclub and restaurant operator. Clearly, revenue from food sales would have to supplement decreasing alcohol sales, and Carey had a reputation for great food, so that looked like it would work.

Carey's Corner also had a gigantic wooden dance floor.

His problem was that he had set aside $30,000 to advertise his new club, but the local building inspectors required he rebuild the grease trap to the tune of almost exactly $30,000, so he had no money with which to advertise.

The club struggled.

One night a bunch of dancers came in wanting to dance West Coast Swing. I didn't know much about West Coast Swing and sure didn't know their music. The leader of the bunch, a beautiful and aggressive gal named Kerry Frost, brought in her West Coast Swing CD collection, demanding I play from that.

So, just to placate her, I tried few songs. They were absolute masterpieces. Once I heard the music, which was primarily Blues, and I understood what they were doing, I began to program exclusively for them and before long they started a club around my Carey's Corner gig.

They called it the Atlanta Swing Dancers Club, or ASDC.

When Carey's Corner eventually folded, I moved the ASDC to Bella's, a smaller place. When Bella's was sold, we moved to a once-a-week Sunday night dance in Reunions Lounge located in The Perimeter Marriott Hotel, which had a fabulous sunken dance floor.

The club continued to grow, and the Sunday ASDC West Coast Swing night was well attended. I DJ'd every Sunday for many years and, now that I had learned their tastes, I always kept them in the latest and greatest West Coast Swing music from around the world.

At about the same time in 1996, Masquerade, the downtown Atlanta alternative music club, began running what turned out to be a highly successful Sunday night promotion for an alternative crowd of mostly college-age kids interested in Swing dancing.

It was based on the 1993 *Swing Kids* movie and also the 1996 movie *Swingers*, which introduced alternative music audiences to two new Neo-Swing bands — The Big Bad Voodoo Daddies and The Royal Crown Revue.

These kids were actually learning those same fancy Swing dancing moves I'd seen in *Swing Kids*. They were dancing East Coast Swing, which featured a lot of high-flying aerials. By the spring of 1998, worldwide clothing retailer The Gap used Louis Prima's "Jump Jive & Wail", featuring solid Swing dancing professionals, in a widely shown commercial they titled *Khakis Swing*.

The alternative Swing dancing kids had become nationally known as The Swing Kids. In the spring of 1998, in the heart of what was the then-entertainment district known as Buckhead, a club opened called Swingers, dedicated to attracting the new Neo-Swing movement Swing Kids. At the time I was happily ensconced DJ'ing Thursday, Friday, and Saturday nights for the lovely Sue Abel at Flamingo Joe's, a terrific Beach Music and Shag dancing club in East Cobb County.

I liked Sue, the crowd, and the club, which had a lot of Carolina Shag and Beach Music Swing dancers for whom I had been DJ'ing for years, and I was not looking to move. Out of the blue, I got a call from Jim Killeen, a longtime professional nightclub entrepreneur and consultant.

He had an investor who had $25,000 and they were opening Oscar's, a club in the Center Stage building in Midtown Atlanta.

While Killeen was a wildly successful nightclub guy who I both liked and respected, he had given up on the nightclub industry because of the DUIs and was now in chiropractic school. I also knew that $25,000 wasn't enough to do much with and, since I was happy where I was, I was just about to pass on the deal when just out of curiosity I asked, "What kind of music did you have I mind?"

"We want to go after those Swing Kids," Jim said.

Boom! "How much money?" I asked.

He hit me with a decent number. "I'll take it."

The first night at Oscar's, a Friday, about half a dozen couples stopped in. I had acquired every Neo-Swing CD out there and, using a combination of vinyl and CDs, had just about every Swing tune that was popular.

I killed it. *(Alan above with The Atlanta Swing Kids.)*

Word spread, and the next night we were packed.

Not long thereafter I decided that since Elvis-era Rock & Roll was Swing music (Barry Manilow even put Lindy hoppin' in his lyrics for the Les Elgart instrumental theme of *American Bandstand*), I'd give the genre a try. So I took a shot and played "Rip It Up" by Little Richard.

"Rip It Up" jammed the dance floor, and soon I was adding the entirety of Jitterbug Rock & Roll into the mix of classic Big Bands and Neo-Swing, something none of the other Swing Kid DJ's were doing.

Musically, we were killing it, making Oscar's a great success from an attendance standpoint from the very beginning. We were busy virtually every night.

Top-rated local radio station Power 99, and their top DJ and Music Director, the late great Sean Demery, came down and did a special Saturday night appearance. The club was packed to the rafters; a standing line out front all night long.

What I was doing as a DJ was very complicated and very much not for beginners. I had two turntables, two CD players, a cassette deck and an open microphone. I alternated between CD and vinyl, LPs and 45s, and an occasional cassette. Plus I was running my mouth, introing and outroing every two-minute song while a packed club full of hundreds of blissfully elated Swing dancers hit the floor.

It was crazy hectic, but I'd been doing it for decades so, for someone watching me do it, other than appearing busy, it probably looked easy enough. But Sean Demery knew better. I still remember the look on Sean's face.

"Damn," he said, watching me work it. "I don't know if we are going to do a Swing show on Power 99 or not, but if we do, you are absolutely the DJ."

As it turned out, they never did a Swing show, but I was very flattered by his comment. I've always been proud of the fact that radio guys treat me as one of their own, which they do not normally do for club DJ's.

Top Atlanta DJ's like Gary McKee, J.J. Jackson, Brian Wilson, Jeff McCartney, Craig Ashwood, and most especially the late Skinny Bobby Harper, along with Sean Demery himself and so many others, have all treated me with such kindness and professional respect. Interestingly, most of the top Atlanta club DJ's — like Aron Siegel, the late Randy

"Spike" Dethman, Randy Easterling, Yvonne Monet, and so many more — have done the same thing.

It's pretty unusual for a DJ to be accepted by both groups, and I remain flattered by their across-the-board acceptance.

As a business venture, Oscar's was a disaster. They had a number of huge problems. One, they were dramatically underfinanced. Two, they didn't understand how to monetize dancers. They comped the door charge for virtually every Swing dancer every night. They were trying to operate as a pre-DUI venue, and it was no longer possible. Even then, cover charges were essential. They didn't offer a solid food menu, and they didn't offer special, solidly priced non-alcoholic drinks. They were angry when the Kids asked for water, thinking that water was a substitute for drinking alcohol.

But it wasn't. Dancing is an athletic event. Dancers get hot and overheated. They need water. It has nothing to do with alcohol. But the club management refused to understand that and remained angry at the requests for water.

The investor kept pumping small amounts of money into the club just to keep it going, but I could see the writing on the wall. Even as I DJ'd to packed audiences, I could see the end was near. They were losing money in a very busy venue.

A lot of the Swing Kids would come into my sound booth and, since I was literally there *back in the day* and had met many of the original artists, I could tell them stories about what it was really like back then.

It was fun.

They were a bunch of great kids and I loved interacting with them. Many of them are still close friends today.

One night a giant young black fellow named Kevin Stanley stepped into my booth. He informed me he was a writer and as a result he had long been called "Notepad". He had lots of questions. We got along really well.

He spent a lot of time in the booth. As I am fond of saying these days, he was 6'3" and 300 pounds, so who was going to move him?

As the summer wore on and "Notepad" and I became closer, I decided to see what he was capable of. One night R&B singer Will Downing was appearing at the Center Stage venue next door. I thought it was the Don Downing of Little Willie & The Hand Jives from my Paramount Artists days but who had changed his stage name from Little Willie to Will Downing.

I was wrong.

In any case, I had a press shot of Little Willie from back in the day and tasked "Notepad" with getting past security and getting the photo directly to Downing for an autograph.

I already knew that "Notepad" *(below with Alex Trebek)* was an intellectual and wicked smart.

So smart, in fact, he not only passed the *Jeopardy* pre-show test, he appeared on the show, coming in second to long-running champion Ken Jennings.

"Notepad" did the Downing chore with such ease that, although we didn't find out for quite a while it was a different Downing, his competence and effectiveness was well-proven. One day Oscar's management announced everybody was going to have to take a pay cut.

"Oh, that is awful," I said. "I'm so sorry for y'all."

"You too," the manager said.

"Not me. My contract was just for the summer and it is up in a week."

And so, a week later I left. I had explained to "Notepad" my belief the club would close soon and suggested we throw in together, wait it out, and, when it did close, we could promote dances ourselves, with him taking the money at the door and being the event manager and me being the DJ.

My prediction was that they would close by New Year's Eve, when the new and very expensive liquor license would be due the following day.

So I booked myself into The Blue Moon Supper Club, which wanted Carolina Shag Beach Music, just to kill some time, and "Notepad" and I did one-nighters throughout the fall, Christmas parties and such.

I contacted my friend Jack Galardi, who owned the after-hours place Club Anytime, to see if we could use his venue up until midnight, when they opened for their regular late-night business. The idea was we'd get the door and he'd get any beverage sales. He thought that was a pretty good idea, OK'd it, and so we were just waiting for Oscar's to close.

When The Blue Moon Supper Club was sold to new owners, a friend of mine was DJ'ing there. He called to say he had a wedding to do and asked if would be able I fill in for him on a Saturday night. Sure. I could do it.

As it happened I was out by the Blue Moon that Saturday afternoon, so I stopped by and ducked my head into the sound booth to see if the equipment was still the same as it had been when I had DJ'd there before.

The two new owners, who were from Peru, came up asking who I was, so I explained I was filling in for their regular DJ. They seemed okay with that.

"What kind of music do you want me to play?" I asked. They didn't know. "Um, I see. Well, let me ask you this. Who comes here?"

"Not anybody really. It's been really slow."

"Do you want me to bring a crowd?"

"You can do that?"

"Sure."

"Boy, that'd be great," they said in unison.

We had an Internet e-group by the name of Swingtown, which most of the Swing Kids were on. When I got home I posted that night's Blue Moon gig on Swingtown. One hundred and fifty Swing Kids showed up.

One of my friends said, "Man, you're like the Pied Piper."

I laughed. "Yeah. But remember one thing. The children of Hamelin weren't following the Pied Piper. They were following the music he was playing."

We had a great night, and when it was over we all left and nobody ever went back again. The poor newbie owners had to be like, "What just happened?"

Oscar's final night was indeed New Year's Eve, and the following Friday and Saturday we opened at Club Anytime.

Club Anytime was a real dive, but it had a huge wood dance floor and a glorious sound system. The Swing Kids quickly named it Club AnySlime. We were there for a long time. When they closed down and remodeled it into The Riviera, we waited until they reopened and returned to the venue. But Jack now had his idiot nephew running the place and he was a huge pain in our ass, one time actually grabbing our door money.

"You want me to get that money back?" "Notepad" asked, thoroughly capable of doing so.

"No, I'll get it from Jack on Monday," I smiled back.

And I did. But the idiot nephew was the straw that broke our back. We moved the whole thing to Reunions Lounge in The Perimeter Marriott on Wednesday nights.

The Wednesday night Swing Kid Marriott dances were successful right away, and we soon added a strictly Lindy night on Thursday. Eventually the Lindy kids started their own Monday night dance, Hot Jam, where the music was strictly Lindy-oriented Big Bands and Jazz, and we dropped the Thursday night Lindy dance.

At the Marriott I played a solid mix of classic Big Bands, Groove Jazz and Blues, with plenty of Neo-Swing, and we kept the wonderful Wednesday night Marriott Swing dance going for many, many years until 2007, when Reunions Lounge was torn out in favor of meeting rooms.

I was admitted to two Swing DJ halls of fame, and a Georgia Tech computer genius named Jason Brotherton and I put up one of the first Internet radio stations, based on the music of Neo-Swing: SwingTop40Radio.com. It became the station of record for Neo-Swing music worldwide.

But that is, as they say, a whole 'nother story.

Big Mike Ammons and the lovely Jennifer Elise
leading the way at the Marriott, circa 2005

59 Zoot Suit Grapefruit

"Hi, I'm Weird Al," he said.

I smiled. "You certainly are."

I was spinning for the Swing Kids one night at Club Anytime, the gigantic 24-hour-a-day after-hours club owned by my friend, the late Jack Galardi, when "Weird Al" Yankovic *(previous page)* popped into the sound booth, unannounced. Jack had given us permission to promote Swing dances at Club Anytime any night of the week we wanted to, right up until 12 midnight, when his regular door people came in and began charging for the late-night crowd.

But it was still a bit unusual to see any non-Swing dancer just drop in during the shank of the evening. When we weren't there, Club Anytime never even seemed open until after midnight. Weird Al told me he had just stopped in for a drink with this gal, but please not to tell the crowd he was there or he'd never get any peace. I took that to also mean not get to make out with the gal.

"You can announce me just when I'm leaving if you want," he said. Sure. Right. Of course. Anyway...

It was interesting because, while Weird Al was a big music star, the girl was a very ordinary-looking person. She might have been the smartest, loveliest gal in the entire world but, by any standards, she just didn't have that Rock Star Groupie heat. Weird Al hung out with me in the booth for a few minutes more, watching me work the Swing Kid dancers.

"So, this is that Swing Kid thing," he said.

"Yep. We do this a couple of nights a week at a minimum. The music is great."

"Let me ask you this," he said. "Is there a song in this thing I could mess with?"

"You bet."

So I played him "Zoot Suit Riot" by The Cherry Poppin' Daddies, the only one of the big Swing Kid records to have hit the mainstream music charts.

"Man, that is a cool record," he said. "I can definitely do something with that."

We chatted for a while longer, he listened to more Swing Kid Neo-Swing songs, and off he went to work his lady friend.

It was a good night at the club, and we rocked the place for a few more hours. Toward the end of the evening I saw Weird Al, who had still not been recognized, get up with his lady friend and prepare to leave.

I introduced him to the crowd on his way out. There wasn't much audience reaction. A few people looked up, and one gal waved at him. Weird Al waved back, and then he and his gal were gone.

Soon thereafter he went into the recording studio and turned "Zoot Suit Riot" into "Grapefruit Diet" and, in doing so, he caught another one of his novelty record and novelty video hits.

I don't know how he did with the gal, but on that night, he sure made out with the music.

60

SwingTop40.com

As a kid who grew up with the Big Bands in the background and now immersed in Neo-Swing, I knew Swing music forwards and backwards.

Jason Brotherton was in the final stages of his computer science PhD at Georgia Tech, with an IQ that was off any known chart. UGA journalism major and another off-the-chart IQ wordsmith, Amy Winn, was our literary expert.

So we had the smarts.

The issue at the meeting of the three of us at my house was this: Did we want to put out an online magazine to replace the Neo-Swing printed magazine Swingtime?

Swingtime had been a professionally produced, full-color, glossy magazine with interesting stories covering most of the top Neo-Swing bands of the Swing revival of summer '98. But, feeling they were not making enough money, they had ceased publication. Our simple issue: Was it a good idea to replace the hard copy Swingtime with an online version?

In terms of Swing music becoming the next big thing, Amy was mindful that "Prodigy" (meaning EDM) was still out there, and I was pretty sure Hip Hop had not come anywhere near running its course. Jason was enthusiastic.

"We could even play music and people could request songs," he said.

"Play music?" I asked. "That sounds more like a radio station than a magazine."

"Sure, a radio station. Be easy, right?"

"Then why are we talking about a magazine? I don't know jack about magazines, but I can program a radio station in my sleep. A radio station where we could make a weekly chart that makes some sense out of all this new music would be fantastic. A Top 40 station: Swing Top 40. We could do a weekly countdown show *à la* Casey Kasem. We could actually call it SwingTop40.com."

"Yeah, we could do that. Easy," Jason said.

And so we left it like that. Maybe not a magazine, but perhaps an Internet radio station based on Neo-Swing.

Jason called two weeks later.

"Does your wife still have that computer in the living room with AOL dial-up?"

"Yeah."

"Write this down – https://www.SwingTop40.com."

"Alright. Got it."

"Get on your wife's computer and enter that URL."

And there it was. SwingTop40.com. A full-blown, complete radio station. Beautifully designed with everything covered. A chart. Bios. A way to vote. A music player. It was visually, and operationally, absolutely stunning.

My little Toshiba laptop only did DOS, and I kept the record and CD collection on FilePro, a DOS database. I called him back. "I'm gonna need a bigger computer."

Tommy Dean was a top Atlanta Jazz and Swing singer, songwriter, music producer, and musician who led a fabulous Swing band, The League of Decency.

To promote Neo-Swing he had a new studio band he called Mondo Heptet. He was anxious for me to play their music, so we talked about SwingTop40.com. He thought it was a great idea.

"As soon as I get a computer," I said. "My credit cards are maxed."

"How much is a computer"?

Boom! He put on his credit card a top-of-the-line Compaq. $2000. I paid it off in monthly installments. And I signed up for high-speed Internet cable.

The late Jim Boling — my friend as well as a musician, music producer, and top-flight recording engineer — and I created a great, professional SwingTop40.com station jingle at his home studio, a sophisticated setup.

Jason and I thought it would be good idea to create a placeholder Top 40 show until we were ready to launch a weekly, so I came up with a list of the Top 40 Swing songs of the past and we produced a Top 40 show counting them down 40 to 1. That streamed from our station 24/7. Just for the record, "In The Mood" was #1 and "Sing, Sing, Sing" was #2.

I am a professional Top 40 radio DJ and when Jason heard me DJ'ing the show, with the jingle and all, I remember him saying, "We're gonna need a bigger server."

We signed on the Internet at one minute past midnight, January 1st, 2001. On September 11, 2001, in a diner having breakfast, Jason and I sat and discussed the possibility of the monetization of SwingTop40.com.

We watched in horror as events unfolded in New York. Like everybody else in America, we were trying to think of some small way we could help.

The wildly talented L.A. movie soundtrack producer Bill Elliott (*Dick Tracy*) put together a monster Big Band and they had several big hit Neo-Swing CDs. One of them had a swingin' version of the patriotic tune "Stars & Stripes", literally titled "Swingin' Stars & Stripes". We decided to call Bill and see if he would greenlight us to offer it to our listeners as a free download.

Bill couldn't have been nicer, he loved the idea, and he immediately gave us the go-ahead. We weren't expecting much since we were a new station but, to our astonishment, we had over 1600 downloads of Bill Elliott's Swing tune.

Since pretty much every Swing artist in the world was hoping the Neo-Swing revival would be the next big thing, virtually all of them had a new Swing CD. Once word got out about SwingTop40.com, I was getting as many as 10 CDs a day in the mail from all over the world. England, France, Germany, Australia, Sweden, Denmark, Canada, Central and South America, and more countries all checked in with Swing bands, proving that the Swing was still loved worldwide.

One day I went to my mailbox and found a CD from The
Mr. Lucky Syndicate. It had a full-blown, big-horn band
production of an absolutely amazing radio theme song for
SwingTop40.com.

Rock & Rollers had their king
and everybody roared.
Classic crooners called their king the
Chairman of the Board.
Old Tito Puente played o' plenty,
rode the Latin wave.
But who have we to lead the way when
Swing is what we crave?
SwingTop40, SwingTop40 –
the dance-wax for your modem.
SwingTop40, SwingTop40, SwingTop40.
The worldwide Swingin' website,
say the words and say no more.
The dance floor for your desktop,
SwingTop40.com.

After receiving that amazing theme, I opened each and every Countdown Show with it thereafter.

Monday was music day.

I made a commitment to myself to program at least one track from every CD we got. Most were terrific. Occasionally I'd get a CD that was hard to find a decent track on. I listened to at least part of every track and managed to program something from every CD but, admittedly, a few were logged in at only #40 and dropped off the chart the following week.

Tuesday I did the chart for the week.

I based the chart on a number of different factors, such as requests, dance floor success, quality of recording (song,

 performance, production), popularity of artist, and my gut instincts developed by decades of Top 40 experience.

Wednesday I recorded.

Each show was recorded in approximately eight 15-minute segments. Computers were slow back then and saving a recorded segment was essentially in real time, i.e. a 15-minute segment took 15 minutes to save.

Thursday was dedicated to converting the files to the proper file format for the station player and uploading the show to the server. Once again, the conversions and uploads to the station were in real time.

There was a terrific gal in California named Diana Gosliga *(above)* who had created SwingAwards.com.

She had Swing fans vote online and then she gave out little awards to the each of the winners. She didn't just give out a CD of the Year award. She gave out awards for each instrument — best drummer, bass, saxophone, trumpet, guitar, piano, and so on.

I contacted her. We decided to work together.

"We need an awards show," I said.

"We can't do that," she said. "There isn't enough money in this to get all these artists in the same place at the same time."

"Of course not," I said. "But this is radio and I can create the show in the studio and make it sound almost live."

"Really? Wow!"

And that's what we did, adding Grammy-like categories for Best Male Vocal, Best Female Vocal, Best Band, Best New Artist, and Single of the Year. My friend Jim Boling created an instrumental opening theme song. The show's opening voiceover was done by a professional voice guy friend of mine named Rick Dovi, so it would sound different from my own voice, being the master of ceremonies. The opening of the show said, "Live, from the Fantasy Ballroom, high atop Atlanta's Tower Of Imagination, it's the First Annual Swing Awards!"

For the first show we had all the presenters and winners call and leave their speech on my message machine. Those were transferred to my computer. They didn't sound great but, surrounded by the sound effects of a live audience (applause, laughter, crowd background noise), they were passable. I ad libbed a monologue and off we went.

Since we were on the Internet and not on a terrestrial station, there were no time constraints. Following their acceptance speech, we played a track by each winner, making the show long but extremely musical. There were three Swing Awards presentations, but only two were produced as radio shows. Our first year was pretty good, but because of the presentations and acceptance speeches being pulled from my message machine, it was far from perfect. For the second year that we were involved, we had all the presenters and acceptors send MP3s. The quality was so much better that it sounded pretty close to being live.

All in all, over a period of two years, we recorded and streamed 108 weekly Top 40 Countdown shows and two Swing Awards shows. All the Countdown segments can be heard in random sequence, along with the second Swing Awards show, archived at SwingTop40Radio.com.

In the end, we are proud we became the historical location of record for the Neo-Swing revival worldwide. The dance floor for your desktop.

Indeed.

Ruby Lair, sensational Hall of Fame West Coast Swing DJ living in Texas, who built my Swing Internet radio stations mentioned in this book and designed the JiveBop logo

Photos of Virginia Wicks courtesy of Brien Engel

61

"Everybody's talkin' 'bout Miss Thing."

In 2001 I had a non-commercial Internet radio station (now in archive as SwingTop40Radio.com) documenting the music of the late '90s worldwide Neo-Swing explosion into a weekly Top 40 Countdown show, *à la* Casey Kasem, as a way of sort of organizing all the new Swing music suddenly being released worldwide. I did 108 of these weekly countdown shows.

By the time we signed off in 2003, we had proudly become the worldwide location of record for all of the music of the late '90s and early 2000s Neo-Swing movement. In other words, in the world of Neo-Swing, we were a pretty big deal.

During that time I was often in contact with the famous longtime Los Angeles publicist Virginia Wicks, who was then representing the estates and children of Big Band leader Les Brown and Jazz singer Mel Torme, among many others living and dead.

David Berger was one. Famous for being the conductor and arranger for the Jazz at Lincoln Center orchestra from its inception in 1988 through 1994, Berger had a great Neo-Swing orchestra, The Sultans Of Swing. They were hot during the Neo-Swing revival.

Berger co-wrote the big hit song "Everybody's Talkin' 'Bout Miss Thing" with Neo-Swing superstar singer Lavay Smith, who recorded it as the title track on her bestselling CD of the same name.

Virginia was nearly 80 years old when we were in touch, but back in the day she had represented Swing-era Big Band leaders Benny Goodman and Tommy Dorsey, as well as Dizzy Gillespie, Artie Shaw, Ella Fitzgerald, Charlie Parker, Art Tatum, Oscar Peterson, Ray Brown, Josh White, the Modern

Jazz Quartet, Norman Granz and his Jazz at the Philharmonic concerts, Verve Records, and many, many others, including a huge slew of major Hollywood movie stars.

She started her career as a model and actress, then wrote a song that legendary singer/pianist Nat King Cole wanted to record for a 1944 movie. She so impressed Cole on the publicity tour for the song, he insisted she be his publicist.

And a superstar PR gal was born.

Virginia often called to try to interest me in one or the other of her artists' new Swing records.

Once she sent me Mel Torme's final recording, a version of "Straighten Up & Fly Right", which he recorded with his son, Steve March Torme. Father and son engage in a battle of scat singing, which the elder Torme easily wins. Almost no one else in the world has this track, so I delight in playing it at Swing events.

Now, Michael Jackson was considered to be the best dancer in the world. He was so good he was the only Pop/Rock star ever inducted into the Mr. & Mrs. Cornelius Vanderbilt Hall of Fame at the National Museum of Dance.

As Dani Van Buskirk, a professional dancer, explained: "Astaire called him an 'angry' dancer. Gene Kelly called him amazing. Baryshnikov said he would pay to just watch MJ bouncy walk across the stage…[but] he did not do technical dance. What made him stand out was the sharpness of movement, the fully extended limbs, the speed combined with smoothness, the fingers and feet always in perfect position. His plastique and smooth transitions …to each position were always on point."

Jackson, Dani went on to say, "was not 'ballet man'…but his timing was out of this world. He was…a natural talent… [practicing] 4 hours in the mirror with no break or water to get one finger or hand movement correct.

"Quick-cut camera work always makes [Chris Brown] seem like a better dancer than he really is. MJ usually had long cuts with the camera just like Astaire, so you can see his entire body the whole time; that is a ton more difficult to do than just quick cuts of film...Jackson's execution was much more smooth and graceful...He was very much an innovator," Dani said. She also said Jackson never freestyled anything, repeating the same moves for twenty-plus years.

Knowing all that about Michael, I told Virginia that if Michael Jackson — who was struggling at that time for various reasons — did a Swing/Lindy-oriented album, with Quincy Jones arranging and producing, it would blow up Neo-Swing bigger than Elvis. Kiddingly, I said, "But Michael Jackson doesn't exactly take my calls."

She loved the idea, but said, "I can't reach Michael either. However, I can reach Quincy."

Seems she represented him. Wow.

About a week later I got the following message on my answering machine. I still have it on tape somewhere:

"Alan, this is Virginia Wicks in Los Angeles. I spoke with Quincy, and I wrote down his response so I would get it exactly right, word for word. And I quote:

"#1 — That is one of the best ideas I have ever heard.

"#2 — Michael Jackson is crazy.

"#3 — I'm retired."

Model, songwriter, actress, and eventually publicist. She was a lovely, brilliant, funny, and ever-so-engaged human being. I miss my conversations with her. And sometimes I wonder if David Berger might have written "Everybody's Talkin' 'Bout Miss Thing" with Virginia Wicks in mind.

Virginia Wicks died in 2013 at age 92.

62 Joan, My Beautiful Friend

Her name was Joan Meltzer and she was my beautiful friend for almost 40 years. I first met Joan *(previous page)* when she came into my combination HR consulting/music management company, Creative Management Associates in Philadelphia, sometime in early 1971, looking for work.

She had a huge background.

Born in Philadelphia, she graduated from Girls' High before attending Wheaton College in Massachusetts and earning a degree in English. From there she moved to New York City to affiliate herself with Ayn Rand at the Ayn Rand Institute, where she worked with Alan Greenspan and reviewed books for The Objectivist Newsletter.

Politically Joan was an unusual combination of a strong free-market Capitalist and a heartfelt hippie Socialist.

Like Frank Zappa and me, Joan felt free-market capitalism was the way to make enough money flow to fund all the social programs she felt any country should have.

She held jobs as a lyricist for BMI records and as a book reader for Universal Studios, going through volumes of books looking for those suitable to be made into movies. In all her time as a book reader she recommended only one book be made into a movie, and that was *Midnight Cowboy*.

Although *Midnight Cowboy* was eventually made into an Oscar-winning film, Universal Studios ignored her, and eventually Joan moved back to Philadelphia.

She had been married twice by the time I met her, but never spoke about her first husband. However, her second husband was Ed Kleban, the Tony Award and Pulitzer Prize winning lyricist for the legendary Broadway musical *A Chorus Line*. Even after they divorced, Joan talked about him often.

Apparently Joan and Ed shared a mental illness — some version of what is now called bipolar disorder — which spun them from bursts of high energy to occasions of deep depression, seemingly without warning. There is no question in my mind that Kleban's writing genius rubbed off on the already talented and experienced Meltzer, making her an even better and more literate lyricist.

She and Kleban divorced long before he died from mouth cancer complications on December 28, 1987, at age 48.

Her daddy was rich — the marquee head of a top Philadelphia law firm — and Mama was good-looking. Joan didn't have to work, but she briefly took a job as a writer with The Jewish Times in Philadelphia before leaving to devote her time solely to the profession of writing song lyrics.

We both lived in the same apartment building in Center City Philadelphia and instantly became fast friends. It wasn't a romantic thing. We were just 24/7 pals. She lived on 6; I lived on 4. She had a key to my apartment. Most mornings she'd let herself in, clean the dishes in the sink, make coffee, wake me up cheerfully, and help me kick-start the day.

She was one of the smartest people I ever met and by far the most literate. Joan read everything. She turned me on to things as diverse as *Stranger In A Strange Land*, a 1961 science fiction novel by American author Robert A. Heinlein; to John D. McDonald generally; and to Travis McGee specifically.

When we first met she had just finished writing the lyrics for producer Richard Landis' first album as primary artist.

Joan's favorite track was 1972's "Natural Causes" and my favorite was "A Man Who Sings"; but no Top 40 hits.

The album was greeted with generally mixed reviews and had only limited success. But it got Landis on *The Tonight Show Starring Johnny Carson* on November 2, 1972.

That same year Landis produced and played piano on the now-legendary second Peter Allen album "Tenterfield Saddler", which Joan and both I deeply loved. I still think "Tenterfield Saddler" is one of the most beautiful and literate songs I've ever heard. It quickly became the signature song for Peter Allen.

When Richard Nixon's attention was distracted from the economy by Watergate, the government made a bunch of economic moves unfavorable to my consulting business. In 1972 a nice offer was made and I sold the company.

Tied up in litigation with my first wife's lawyer, I pretty much hung out with Joan for most of the year. She drank a lot of wine. I never drank at home, but we both smoked a ton of weed. It was during this time that Joan began to write songs with melody writer and piano-playing singer Bonnie Molluso.

It was the very definition of a perfect combination.

Molluso wrote some of the most hauntingly beautiful, totally commercial melodies I'd ever heard, and Joan wrote some of the coolest and most literate lyrics I'd ever read.

Joan wrote no melodies, and in this particular songwriting partnership, Bonnie wrote no lyrics. Most people who heard these songs relate them to Carole King, primarily because the demo tapes are just Bonnie singing and banging out the melodies on piano, just as King herself did on her classic "Tapestry" album, which was #1 for a lot of the time period during which the Meltzer/Molluso songs were written.

Neither I nor Joan held that opinion; I thought it a limited comparison. But we both related her and Bonnie's working relationship to Elton John and Bernie Taupin.

The main reason was the process. Elton John described the Elton John/Bernie Taupin writing process in one of his extensive interviews with British TV journalist David Frost.

It goes like this: Bernie writes a lyric and then sends the edited and totally finished version to Elton. Elton then sets the lyric up on the piano and begins by gently playing around with some old church chords. If Elton doesn't have the melody in 20 minutes or so, the lyric goes in the trash and Bernie doesn't get to rewrite nor resubmit it.

As tough as it might have been for Bernie to lose a great lyric that way, the sum of the ones that worked is the stuff of legend. Only The Beatles did it better, and more often.

The process was the same with the Meltzer/Molluso songs. Joan wrote the lyrics first. I'd sit in her apartment for hours while she worked on them, sometimes struggling for a week or more with a single word or phrase.

But when she got it, she got it. There was no question, no hesitation. It was finished. Then the lyric would go off to Bonnie who, I believe, is some kind of crazy, talented-from-birth melodic genius because you just can't teach that kind of melody writing. Either these haunting — and in this case commercial — melodies come flowing forth or they don't.

It never took Bonnie long to set the lyrics into song. The finished songs always came back to us pretty quickly. In total there were 16 songs. That is all. Sixteen songs, eleven of which would be terrific singles. And that was it for them.

Through the many years of my wanderings, Joan and I always stayed in touch. Often by phone, but just as often she would travel to wherever I was.

In 1976, I went out to Denver to do a nightclub show with The Flying Dutchman, who was working afternoon drive at a Top 40 station there. Joan came with us and we — along with my then-girlfriend Cindy — shared an apartment.

Up until that time Joan's musical tastes ran from Broadway to the singer/songwriters of the late 1960s and early 1970s. She also loved R&B music and always said Marvin Gaye's "What's Going On" had changed her life. However, even though she loved Dutch and me personally, she was no fan of Disco, Top 40 radio, or DJ'd music generally.

Until Boz Scaggs.

"Lowdown" was a Boz Scaggs Top 40 single which was never really intended as a Disco record. But the groove was right and, at that time, there were few pure Disco records being released. So club DJ's selected groove records they thought would be suitable from the general record promo pool. "Lowdown" was one of those.

Joan didn't come to our nightclub show very often, but somehow "Lowdown" fell into her hands anyway. Cindy and I would hear it play endlessly through Joan's closed bedroom door. Constantly. For hours. Days.

Weeks.

One day in early September of 1976, Denver got 20 inches of snow, and I quickly moved to Atlanta. Six months later I became the resident DJ and Music Director at Jeryl's, Atlanta's top Disco throughout the *Saturday Night Fever*-inspired Disco era. Joan was busy with a project to turn the book *Saloon Society* — which had become the bar scene bible for Greenwich Village — into a play. She came to Atlanta and checked into a motel close to Jeryl's while she worked on it.

She came to the club fairly often, drank wine, and listened to the music. And then, when she moved back to New York, she called me with the most astonishing request. She wanted me to teach her to be a DJ.

"What?" I asked, in total disbelief. "Like radio?"

"No, clubs, like you. But I don't want to talk like you do. I want to learn to beat mix the records together."

"Alright. That's wild. 'Lowdown', huh? Fair enough, but I can't be the one to teach you that, it's not what I do. In fact,

I'm no big fan of beat mixing one record across to the next record so seamlessly that no one notices anyway. It has always seemed to me that only stresses what is maybe Disco's only valid criticism, which is its sameness.

"However, that said, when it's done right, which means not just mixing across on the fly, but with lots of creative work put in beforehand, it can be amazing.

"So here's what I want you to do," I advised. "You're not broke, you have money. Go to all the best clubs in New York and when you find a DJ you think is the very best, hire him to teach you."

I remember her excitement to this day.

"Yes, yes, yes. That's perfect. Yes! That is exactly what I'll do." She was excited. "You're a genius."

"I know."

She found and hired a club DJ named Shep Pettibone
(*previous page*). Pettibone was a top club DJ and one of the only
DJ's in the country at that time to have his own radio show. In
Shep's case, his show was on the top-rated New York Disco
station WRKS 98.7 Kiss-FM.

Pettibone turned out to be a truly stellar human, and he
and Joan became great friends. Shep was gay so it was a
plutonic relationship, but she loved Shep and he loved her
back. They talked often for many, many years.

When Shep began to write with and produce Madonna, he
sent her a song he wrote and produced. Joan told him he
would never have to work again. And she was right. "Vogue"
was a monster hit in 1990. People still like to dance to it today.

Between his astronomical number of remixes, record
production, and songwriting with Madonna on her "I'm
Breathless" album — which contained "Vogue" and "Deeper
and Deeper" — and on "Erotica", Pettibone became a
millionaire and eventually purchased and now operates the
Empress Hotel, a popular gay resort in Asbury Park, New
Jersey. The hotel features a restaurant, gift shop, lounge, The
Paradise Nightclub, and an outdoor pool. The nightclub lured
crowds of gay travelers away from Fire Island to the beaches
of Asbury Park.

When Joan and I talked, she spoke a lot about Shep. Shep
said when he talked with Joan she spoke all the time about me.
We really were her soulmates.

Shep Pettibone is a true genius, and he taught Joan well.
She adopted the stage name "Jenny Fields" (Garp's mother in
The World According to Garp) and, with Shep's help, began to
work in Discos in and around New York City, eventually
creating long rope lines outside clubs where she appeared. She
was very proud that she was the only straight white woman
doing so.

She traveled to and DJ'd in South America and in the red-
hot club at Merv Griffin's casino on Paradise Island in the

Bahamas. Jenny Fields had become one of the top club DJ's in the world.

Around 1981 or so my then-girlfriend, Miriam, and I traveled to New York to hear Joan play at a legendary gay club in Greenwich Village, The Cock Ring. It was the week of the Gay Pride Parade. The Village was packed wall-to-wall with many streets closed off. It was over 90°, the club was not air conditioned, and Miriam and I couldn't stand the heat for very long, but we stayed long enough to hear Joan's (now DJ Jenny Fields) opening set.

Here is how it went.

First, on turntable #1, she played a foul-mouthed spoken word rant from Maryanne Faithful.

Then, after about a minute of that, on a second turntable, she started Bette Midler's opening monologue from "The Rose" and, for a short time, the two women actually spoke back and forth to one another.

Then on a third turntable she dropped out Faithful and started a bass line under the now-solitary Midler.

Next she added drum under the bass and dropped out Midler. Then she added a keyboard to the bass and drum and let that trio play for a minute before mixing across into a fully mixed record.

And the night had begun.

God, I was so proud of her. That was such top-notch mixing that only the best DJs in the world would even attempt it. And to think a non-Disco record by Boz Scaggs started it.

We returned to the club just as it closed. The place had been so hot that the walls were literally dripping. There were a handful of exhausted couples sort of leaning on each other and moving slowly to the down-tempo groove. She closed the night with Gene Kelly's "Singin' In The Rain."

It was perfect.

In 1980, Ronald Reagan became president and, true to his word, followed through on his promise of the forced national drinking age and the strict national DUI standard. Nightclubs all across America began to fold.

When it became The Cock Ring's turn to close, Joan played their final night. She promptly retired and called me.

"I want to do radio!"

"What?"

"Radio. I want to do radio. Shep's mom is a voice teacher, and she is going to teach me to talk on the radio."

"Fine. You'll be great."

And that's what she did. After DJ gigs at radio stations in Florida and Colorado, Joan (still as Jenny Fields) joined WOWI-FM, then Hot 103, in Norfolk, an Urban Contemporary format — a black music station.

I heard an aircheck of her doing middays and she was absolutely wonderful — happy, cheerful, and full of sunshine. She had a terrific, warm, smooth, upbeat voice filled to the brim with a huge smile. She closed every show with the last line of Tom Robbins' novel *Still Life With Woodpecker* — "This is Jenny Fields saying, remember, it's never too late to have a happy childhood."

Through the many years I never stopped suggesting people we should send the Meltzer/Molluso songs to, but Joan never found that one musician/voice combination she thought was right.

"How about Roberta Flack?" I asked one time.

"No. She could maybe sing a couple of them, like 'When Last I Slept Beside You' or 'Now That I Know Your Face By Heart', but 'Did You Dig My Daddy' is Rock & Roll. She could never do that. Roberta Flack. No!"

And then a few years later. "How about Sheryl Crow?"

"What? Are you crazy? She's a guitar player. These are piano songs. I don't like her voice anyway. No Sheryl Crow."

This went on for years and years, and as time wore on I suggested fewer and fewer ideas as to where I thought the magnificent Meltzer/Molluso songs might find a forever home. Finally, long before she stopped talking to me, I gave up altogether.

At some point in the early 1980s Ronald Reagan struck again and deregulated radio so that primarily one company, known at the time as Clear Channel, could own almost all the stations. It took them a while to buy up all the stations but eventually they did and, as soon as they could, they automated everything and got rid of all the DJ's.

"We don't care about music or DJ's or even ratings," the CEO of Clear Channel said in a pre-Internet interview around 2002 with Fortune magazine.

"If they aren't listening to Station A, then they are listening to Station B and we own that, too. The only thing we care about is time sales."

Joan saw that coming, and in the mid-'80s, she abruptly retired once again, this time from radio.

For many years thereafter, Joan volunteered and read books to elementary school children in the Ghent section of Norfolk, in which she resided, for the Tidewater AIDS Community Task Force. She found reading to the children to be one of the most satisfying things she had ever done, and she continued to do it throughout the 1990s.

But when she stopped doing it, she seemed lost.

I could tell from her calls that depression was getting worse. Her parents and sister had all died and Joan, for reasons she never elaborated on, stopped talking with Shep. In around 2005, during a serious bipolar event, she stopped talking to me.

On July 14, 2010, Joan Meltzer died suddenly at her home in Norfolk, Virginia. According to a distant cousin I reached in

Philadelphia, she was found at the bottom of the stairs to the second floor of her condo, a spilled tray of food next to her.

No autopsy was performed, but it's pretty clear that one of two things happened. Either she had some kind of fatal event, such as a heart attack or stroke, or she slipped and fell backwards down the stairs, and hit her head.

She was 72.

And that was the end of that. No more Joan Meltzer.

My beautiful friend was dead and gone.

That is, until she wasn't.

Daryl Hall — of whom I am now back to being a huge fan of — in a fine coincidence was carpool buddies with Bonnie Molluso when both were studying music at Temple.

I often check out his *Live From Daryl's House* Internet music show. In 2017, I happened across a 2009 YouTube episode of the show, featuring a piano-playing singer/songwriter named Diane Birch.

I knew her name, but not her music, nor her talent. She was brilliant. Stunning.

She turned out to be a magnificent singer/songwriter who plays keys, guitar, and violin. She has a terrific singing voice. For all the emphasis on video these days, music is still an audio experience and the sound of the human voice is critical to the sale of music. Everybody sings. Just go to church. But not everybody Sounds.

Diane Birch understands the sound of the human voice.

And it is not subconscious. It is purposeful. I can see her forming the sounds. She knows exactly what she is doing. Her vocal sound is just plain perfect.

In addition, she has an amazing sense of harmony, is highly educated in music, and a beautiful young woman. She has been compared to Carole King, but as a singer and musician, she's a lot better. Lots of Church. A good bit Laura Nyro. Some Daryl Hall soulfulness.

In my view, Diane Birch is one big hit single away from turning Sheryl Crow into a backup singer. And so there I am watching this wonderful video, when all of a sudden Joan Meltzer screamed at me from the heavens: "Get my songs to this girl!" I absolutely heard it in my head.

Now, Live Joan screamed at me with her overabundance of enthusiasm all the time, but this was the first time I had heard from Dead Joan.

I am not a religious person and, while I'd be delighted to find any afterlife, I'm not at all convinced there is one. Nor do I get involved with cosmic energy or any of that sort of thing. I don't disparage nor dismiss people who do believe, but it's not my thing.

But Dead Joan screamed at me.

Plain as day.

I heard her in my head just as clearly as if she had been on the phone with me.

Good heavens (no pun intended).

So I tracked down Diana Birch's management, a fellow named Ben Baldwin from Bristol, U.K., which made perfect sense to me since a little research showed that Diane was a big star in Europe, particularly in England. She was bigger overseas than in America.

So Ben Baldwin seemed like a fellow who knew what he was doing. I sent him my three favorite Meltzer/Molluso songs, along with a brief synopsis of the story behind them. I stressed that I thought they would be terrific singles, even suggesting that collectively, a dozen or so of the songs would make a great album — "Diane Birch: The Lost Songs". With the great backstory to draw attention to the songs, I suggested that the album would promote itself.

He replied that he wouldn't even listen without the permission of the publisher (read: if the publishing wasn't available for negotiation).

Le sigh.

I mean, come on, man, just listen to the damn songs and let Diane hear them if you think she would dig them. I'm trying to help you here. We are talking about six minutes. How hard is that?

Nothing doing.

Le damn.

I hadn't talked with Bonnie Molluso since the 1970s and, beyond Philadelphia, I didn't have a freaking clue. Where might she be? Still, Dead Joan was right and I knew it. Diane Birch wasn't just someone who could arrange, produce and sing these songs, she was absolutely perfect. These songs should be recorded by Diane Birch.

She was every single thing Joan had never been able to find. So I saddled up and searched the Internet. Every so often, when I had time and the mood stuck me, I'd go online and search for Bonnie Molluso. It took months. Then one day, quite by accident, I found and called a phone number that went straight to voice mail and immediately recognized Bonnie's voice. That ever-so-cool voice I had heard singing the Meltzer/Molluso song demos for almost 50 years.

I left a somewhat detailed message, she returned my call, and we were reconnected. I explained about Dead Joan screaming at me and sent her to YouTube to check out Ms. Diane Birch.

She laughed. She knew Live Joan could scream when she was excited about something. And she agreed with me — and with Dead Joan. Diane Birch *(next page)* was The One.

It turned out the songs had never been formally published, so the publishing arrangement was wide open. Bonnie immediately agreed that we could split the publishing with Ms. Birch should she do anything with the songs. I asked if adding Diane as a third writer would be appropriate since the demos were raw, basic melody and lyric, and they needed fleshing out and arranging into finished productions. Bonnie agreed that too would be fine.

So I had the lyrics transcribed by my great friend "Ann The Fan" Nowlin, so named due to her longtime relationship with Frank Zappa. A former secretary, Ann is a whiz on a keyboard, and she did the best she could to transcribe the lyrics from the almost 50-year-old cassette. When I had those in hand I sent them to Bonnie for a final listen. She corrected a few, and we had final lyric sheets for each song.

I transferred the songs into MP3s, dropped them into my editing program, and cleaned them up as best I could.

So, the Meltzer/Molluso songs were back in business.

I sent the same three songs to Ben Baldwin again, complete with an explanation as to the publishing availability and the proposed songwriting split.

Crickets.

Well, I figured, he just missed the email, so I resent it and the songs. Crickets. I was trying to do the right thing and go through her management, but he would not respond. I tried one more time.

Crickets.

Le sigh — again.

I tried all kinds of things to reach Diane directly, including becoming her Facebook friend. But her Facebook page is one of those pages whereby you can follow her, but there is no way to directly send her a message. Then one day Diane posted a link to a new song of hers with a direct link to BandCamp.com, where the song could be heard. There was a contact link on BandCamp.com.

So I sent a somewhat detailed email to Contact and, lo and behold, finally, after over a year of trying, Diane answered the email personally, "Loved the songs."

So now we wait and see if the Meltzer/Molluso songs have finally found a proper, forever home. What Diane Birch does, or does not do with them, only time will tell.

And I am fine with that.

Dear Dead Joan,
    You can stop screaming now.
    Mission accomplished.
    You're welcome.
    You can thank me when I get there.
    I'll be along soon enough.
Much love,
Alan

Who Is Not A Stranger Still

(Joan Meltzer / Bonnie Molluso) ©*1971*

Who is not a stranger still
Who is not a lonely one
Mother stranger to her daughter
Father stranger to his son

Who is not a stranger still
Who in all of human kind
Teacher stranger to the body
Doctor stranger to the mind

Which is substance
Which is shadows
Ravens in the old man's eyes
Or laughter in the children's voices
Which is truth, which is lies

Even after man to woman
Gives his love 'til seedlings spill
Who can say they know each other
Who is not a stranger still

Which is substance
Which is shadows
Ravens in the old man's eyes
Or laughter in, the children's voices
Which is truth, and which is lies

Even after man to woman
Gives his love 'til seedlings spill
Who can say they know each other
Who is not a stranger still

Afterword

I quit drinking around 1986 when I took a gig as the resident DJ and Music Director at Johnny's Hideaway here in Atlanta. It was a five-night-a-week gig and I never drink while I DJ. I also never DJ with a hangover.

To my surprise, I didn't miss the booze.

I had assumed I was an alcoholic like half of the other people I drank with through the many years. But Len Barry said no. He knew I wasn't an alcoholic all along because I never drank at home. I never kept liquor in the house. Not even beer. Never. Only drank when out and about. Never thought of it that way, but it was true.

I settled down, married, had two kids, and got divorced, not necessarily in that order.

Here I am at 78, continuing to DJ, which may make me the oldest DJ working the major market clubs.

That's pretty cool and, so far, I have been blessed with good luck and manageable health. I have COPD, which I have had since 1991. But since I quit smoking in 2005, my breathing tests continue to improve and the COPD is very manageable. Other than that, the doctors say overall my health is excellent and I'm blessed with the good fortune to be still able to work in what I love and to DJ.

Many years ago, when I was just a teenager during those great summer vacations in Ocean City, New Jersey *(pictured on the following page, circa 1958),* I was crazy about The Tilt-A-Whirl, a carnival ride.

It was a little basket thingie which, when it whirled around quickly enough, its rotational force, working against gravity, created the effect of a g-force. I was crazy about the rides. Every year Dad would treat me to a ride or two, and we'd go there when the business on the ride was slow and nobody was standing in line.

The operator had to keep it running to lure other riders so, during those slow periods, if I was the only person on it, I'd get a much longer ride.

I'd spin endlessly, but always with one eye on the operator, watching to see when he would pull the lever ending the ride.

One time Dad said he thought I was spending so much time worrying about when the operator was going to pull the lever that I wasn't enjoying my ride as much as I should.

That was a pure eureka moment and one which I have carried with me ever since. I never watched the ride operator again. And so now, moving along toward the edge of my allotted time, I spend as little time as possible thinking or worrying about when my lever might get pulled.

This book is done.

On to my new project — JiveBop!

Adventures in Adventure.

Keeping it Rockin'.

Fini.

What Goes Around Comes Around

East Coast Swing, West Coast Swing, Hustle, Salsa, Jitterbug, Lindy, Zydeco, Contra, The Swing Kids, even Ballroom. As is evidenced by the popularity of *Dancing With The Stars*, partner dancing is back everywhere.

Everywhere, that is, except with teenagers.

Team JiveBop plans to change teens' enthusiasm for dance by making everything old new again. Yes, adding new flavor and color to their social panache will give them a great way to be creative and learn the social skills they need as they separate from the nuclear family.

The big plan is to build a high-end flagship teen center and dance club here in Atlanta. We will broadcast a bright, modern, digitally interactive dance party show every day after school that kids can tune into and dance along with their TV counterparts.

Team JiveBop's trademarked name for Modern Jive is JiveBop®. We will even supply an online easy-to-learn beginning partner dance lesson.

American Bandstand was the platform for Rock & Roll.

Soul Train was the platform for Hip Hop.

The JiveBop Dance Party Show will be the platform for Modern Jive, worldwide.

(Jeff Franklin, my old friend who I brought into the high-end music business at Action Talents, is helping me with it.) What goes around, comes around.

The Bop Shop reimagined.

It's about time.

If you want to have a chat about how to be a part of it, all you got to do is email me at djalanwhite@djalanwhite.com.

Alan Ray White wishes to
express his heartfelt thanks to the
many wonderful supporters of this book.

You know who you are.

CITATION INDEX

PHOTOGRAPHY INDEX

ROCK AROUND THE BLOCK
Imprint: Blue Room Books
ISBN-13: 9780985462390
© 2019 Alan Ray White
All Rights Reserved

ROCK AROUND THE BLOCK
BLUE ROOM BOOKS
DECATUR, GA 30033

51909995R10228

Made in the USA
Columbia, SC
27 February 2019